IMAGES
of America

LEOMINSTER

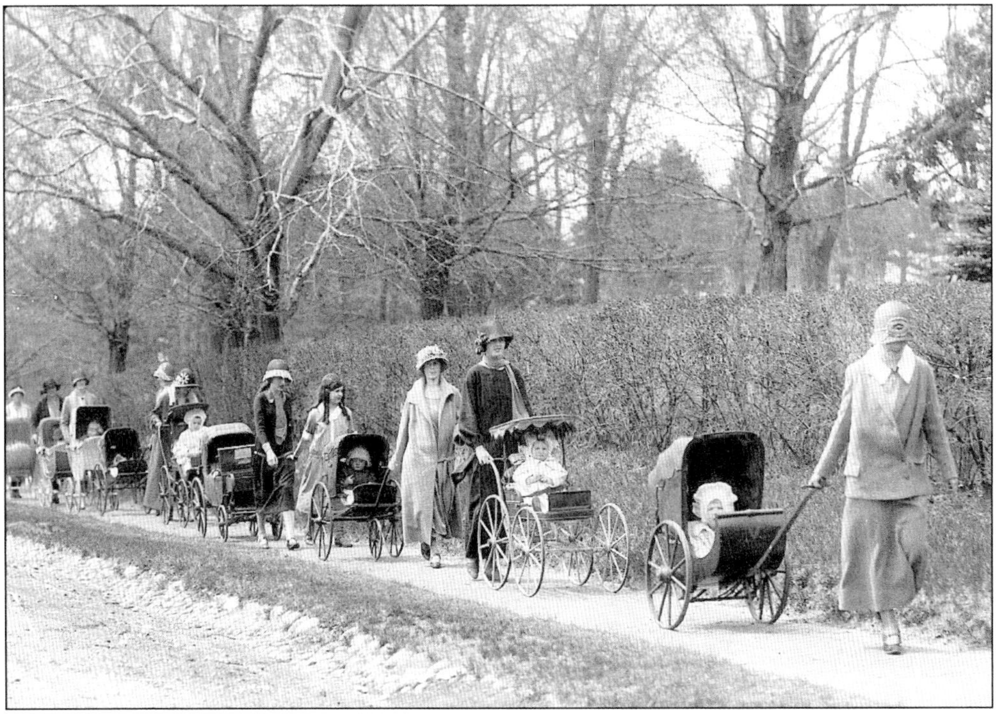

Seen on Lindell Avenue in front of the Doyle estate, the Easter baby carriage parade features Whitney carriages, *c.* 1920. Neither the road nor the sidewalk is paved at this time.

IMAGES
of America

LEOMINSTER

Thomas K. Hazzard
and Diane M. Sanabria
for the Leominster Historical Society

Introduction by Robert Cormier

ARCADIA
PUBLISHING

ISBN 978-0-7385-6338-1

Published by Arcadia Publishing
Charleston, South Carolina

Printed in the United States of America

Library of Congress Catalog Card Number: 2008927783

For all general information contact Arcadia Publishing at:
Telephone 843-853-2070
Fax 843-853-0044
E-mail sales@arcadiapublishing.com
For customer service and orders:
Toll-Free 1-888-313-2665

Visit us on the Internet at www.arcadiapublishing.com

Dedicated to my father, Donald Martin,
my first and best history teacher. D.M.S.

Dedicated in memory of my parents, Marion and Norman,
who taught me the true meaning of home. T.K.H.

Contents

Acknowledgments

A book like this is never the work of just one or two individuals. The authors wish to express their appreciation to a number of people, especially the Executive Board of the Leominster Historical Society. Their confidence, enthusiasm, and financial support enabled us to make this project a reality. We would also like to thank Paul Benoit, Kevin P. Caefer, Dr. John Cummings, Nona Ojala, and David Wilson for their assistance with writing captions.

Though most of the images in this book are from the Leominster Historical Society's collection, the authors are grateful to the following groups and individuals, who graciously allowed us access to their photographs: Evelyn B. Hachey, the Leominster Historical Commission, the Leominster Public Library, Nona Ojala, Robert Cormier, and Chris Brault.

Several people went out of their way to offer names, dates, and other particulars; our thanks go to Susan Shelton and Jeannine Levesque of the Leominster Public Library, Roger LaPointe, Richard Sarao and George Boisvert of the Leominster Fire Department, John Tata, Kelly Lanza, and Lt. Michele Pellechia of the Leominster Police Department, Dick Allen of the Highway Department, Dee North of Johnny Appleseed School, the Leominster City Clerk's Office, and Keith Lauer.

The authors made every effort to select images representing key periods, events, and personalities in Leominster's history but realize there may be gaps in their coverage. In many cases, photographs were simply not available; in some cases, what was available did not meet publishing quality standards. Ultimately, the book's length, as set by the publisher, necessitated some difficult decisions regarding what could and could not be included.

Special thanks are due to Nona Ojala for her expertise and hard work in preparing the layout and to novelist Robert Cormier for penning the perfect introduction. And, finally, the authors wish to thank their spouses, Susan and Carl, for keeping the home fires burning. They could not have done this without their patience, understanding, and support.

INTRODUCTION

Home is where the heart is. Many regard this old saying is as a cliché simply because it comes so easily to the mind when someone thinks of home. But it's become a cliché only because it is so true.

The same sentiment applies to a hometown. A hometown, particularly Leominster, is truly a place where the hearts of thousands can be found, including mine.

From the steeple of St. Cecilia's Church, which is the first sight of Leominster from Route 2 when you're coming home from somewhere, to the gentle slope of Monoosnock Hill to the west and the monuments to our heroic dead in downtown's Monument Square, the things that herald Leominster are obvious to even the casual passerby. But, for many of us, Leominster is a thousand other things as well.

I remember the three-deckers where I was raised and the old Leominster High School at the crest of West Street and the Leominster Public Library, where the whispering women of my youth presided over the treasures found in thousands of books.

Leominster is tree-bedecked streets and the shortcut I took as a kid in that narrow alley beside the Wood Block to reach Mechanic Street.

Leominster is the old Brockelman's Market, where, as children, we gazed in awe at the lobsters in the big tank.

Leominster is Doyle Field on a chilled Thanksgiving Day when the Blue and White Warriors faced the Red and Grey of Fitchburg and that mythical dog always strayed onto the field.

Leominster is the Memorial Day parade and the dying echoes of "Taps" in the air at Evergreen Cemetery and Night Before The Fourth bonfires in Whitney Field before it became Searstown.

Leominster is Barrett Park, where we took swimming lessons and Rockwell's Pond, where we skimmed rocks across the surface of the water.

Leominster is the place of factories, comb shops, tool-and-die shops, print shops, and so many other shops, where our fathers worked for the weekly paycheck that paid the bills and bought the kids two-for-a-nickel ice cream cones on paynight during a time called the Great Depression.

Leominster is the Men's Shop, where a new suit for the big dance was bought, the Boston Confectionery Store and a wonderful sundae called Buffalo Dip, and the Plymouth and Metropolitan Theaters, which became palaces of dreams on Saturday matinees and Bank Night on Wednesday nights.

Most of all, Leominster is people—not only history makers, who built and ran the city, but all the cops who walked the beats; the firemen who battled the flames (they weren't called firefighters in the old days, although they did fight the fires), store clerks, factory workers, teachers, and most of all, our fathers and mothers, aunts and uncles, who helped us across the threshold that took us from childhood to maturity when we, in turn, became mothers, fathers, uncles, aunts, and yes, grandfathers and grandmothers.

Leominster may look like a thousand other towns and cities on the surface, but it's unique to so many of us who'll be turning the pages of this illustrated history, filling the empty spaces between photographs with our memories of the city we cherish and the people we love.

That's Leominster—truly where our hearts can be found.

—*Robert Cormier*

One

Business and Industry

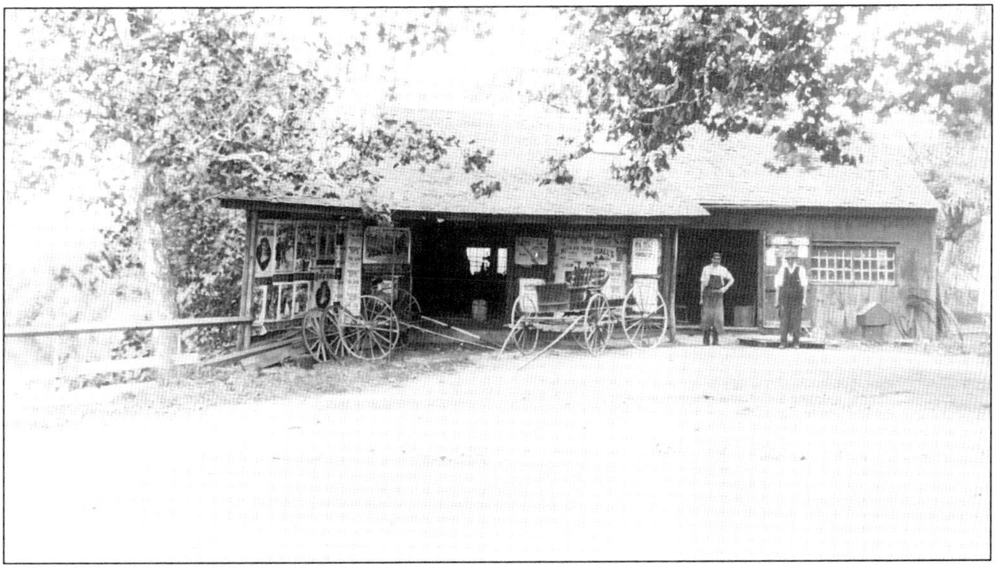

The Leander Archibald Blacksmith Shop was located on Main Street on the left as you cross the bridge over the Nashua River heading towards North Leominster. Mr. Archibald bought the shop from Emery Stearns in 1836. The left side of his shop slopes down the bank of the Nashua. In addition to shoeing horses, a blacksmith would shoe oxen using a large leather sling as a hoist.

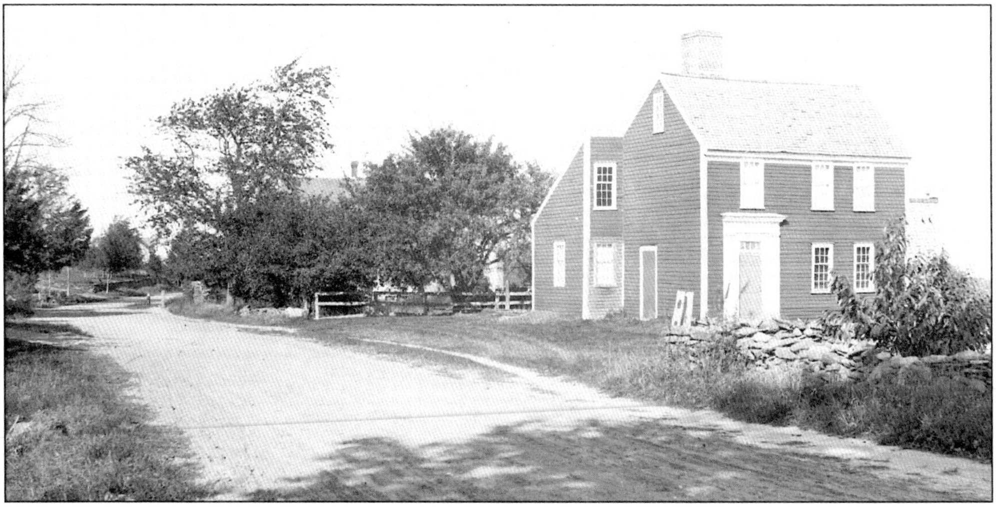

The Old Hills House on Pleasant Street is the birthplace of the comb industry in Leominster. Built in 1759 by Elias Carter, it was sold to Obadiah Hills in 1774. Soon after, Hills began making combs from horns to sell in Boston. The kitchen was the first comb shop, with all work done by hand. The house is currently owned by Mr. and Mrs. L.E. Ojala.

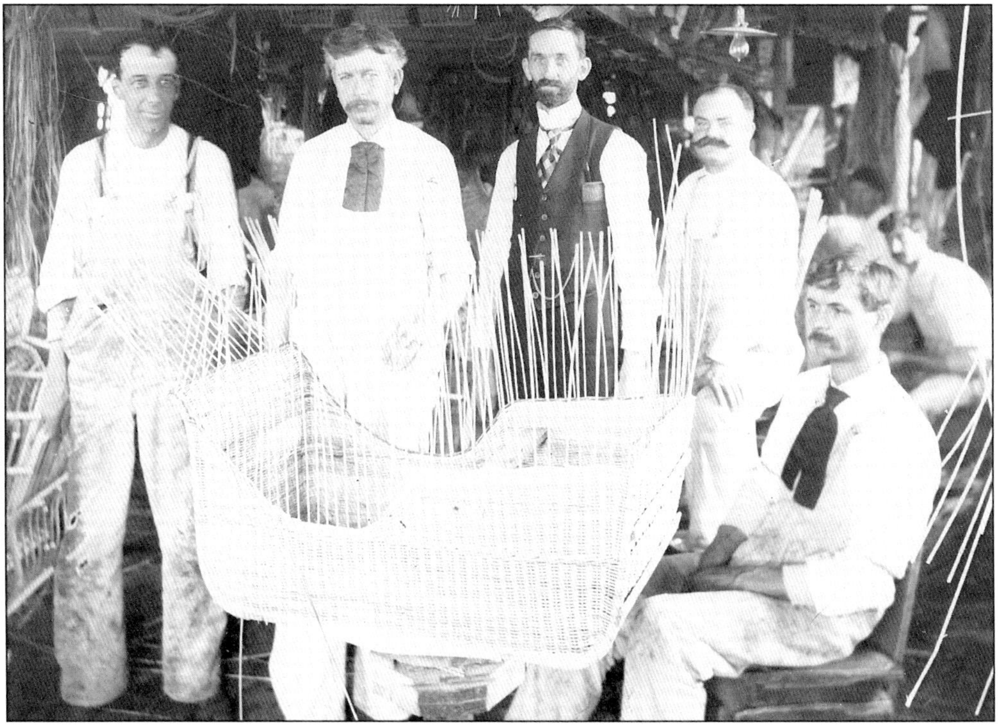

Employees of the F.A. Whitney Carriage Company weave a baby carriage. The firm began in 1858 and was once the largest manufacturer of baby carriages in the world. In the center, wearing a vest, is Frank J. Shaw. Associated with the plant since boyhood, Shaw was made general superintendent of the lower factory containing the iron work and reed departments. He was also admitted as a stock holder and director. Whitney Carriage closed its doors between 1952 and 1953 after nearly a century in Leominster.

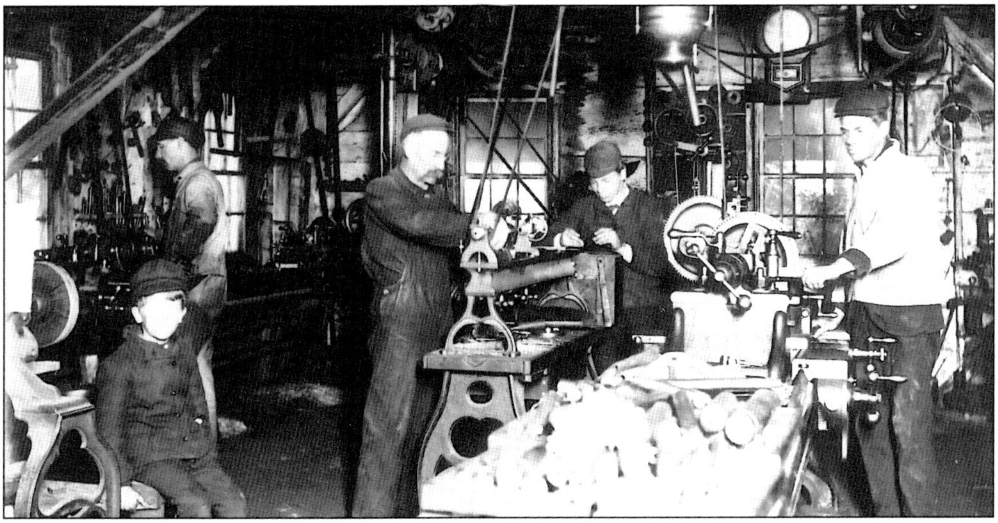

Smith's Machine Shop on Lindell Avenue was opened in 1870 by Austin Smith. The Smiths were machinists, mechanics, and inventors. It was said that you didn't want a Smith visiting your shop because after one look at your machinery, they could go back to their shop and build it from memory. Used regularly until 1978, the shop was disassembled and donated to the American Precision Museum in Windsor, Vermont, by Durwood Smith, the founder's grandson.

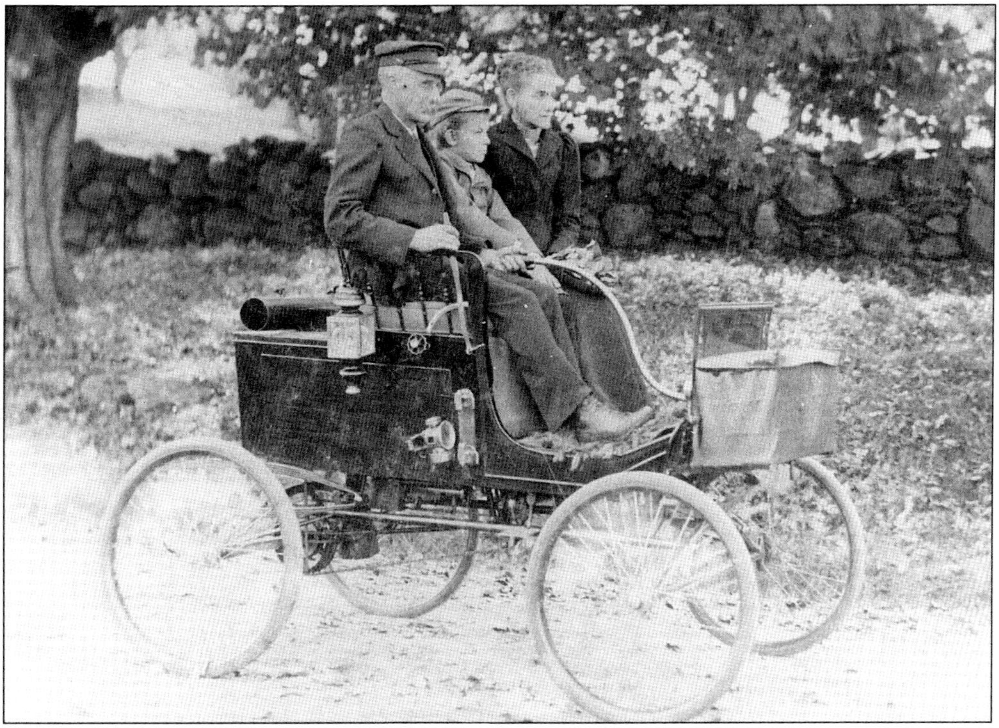

Members of the Smith family enjoy a ride in their "Stanley Steamer." This automobile is believed to be the first one to make the drive to the Summit House on Mount Wachusett, a trip previously made only by horse-drawn carriage. Seen here, from left to right, are Austin, George, and Ella Smith.

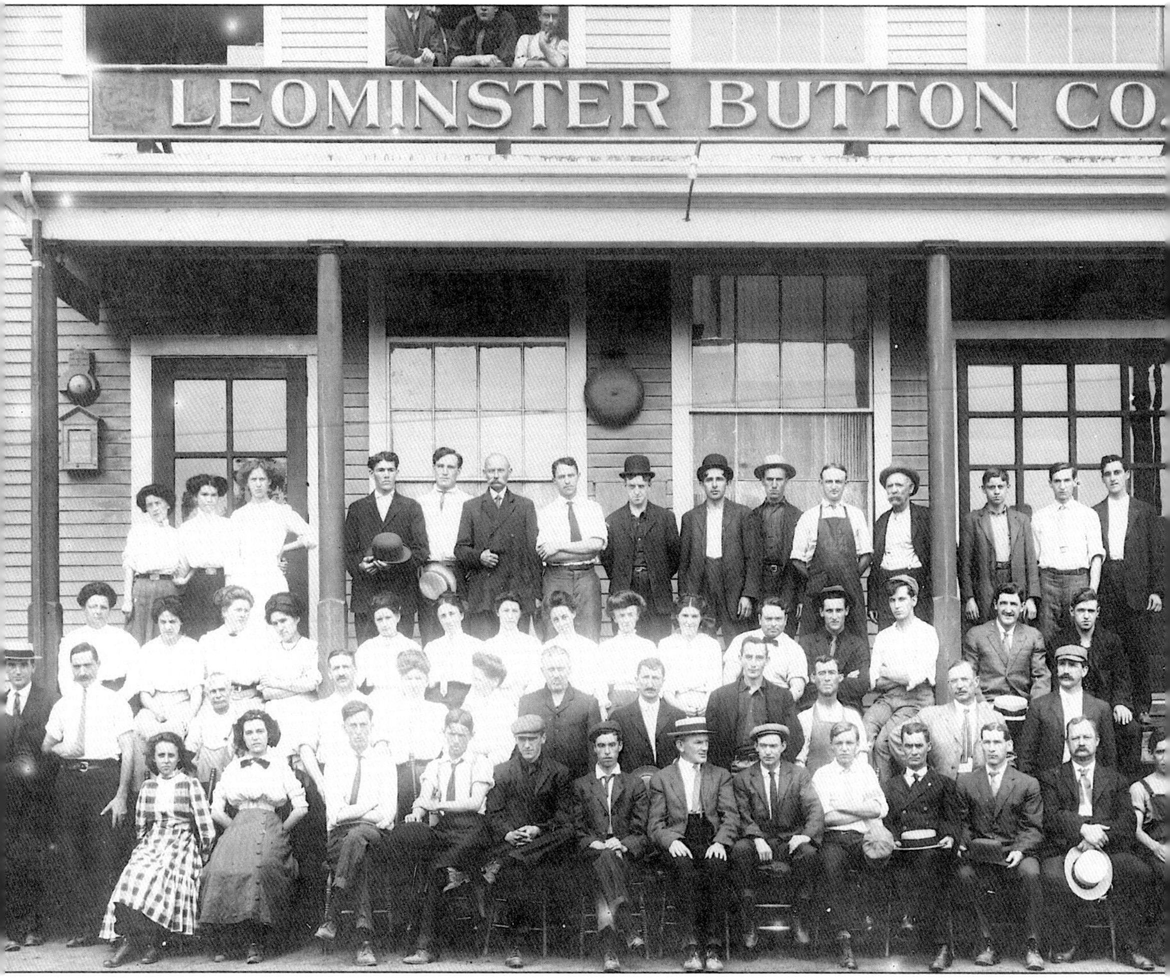

The Leominster Button Company, manufacturers of fine horn buttons, was located at the corner of Whitney and Williams Streets. The proprietor was Herbert Prevear, who bought the shop from W.D. Earl. Mr. Prevear had been a salesman with the Earl Company. Pictured here are the employees, *c.* 1895.

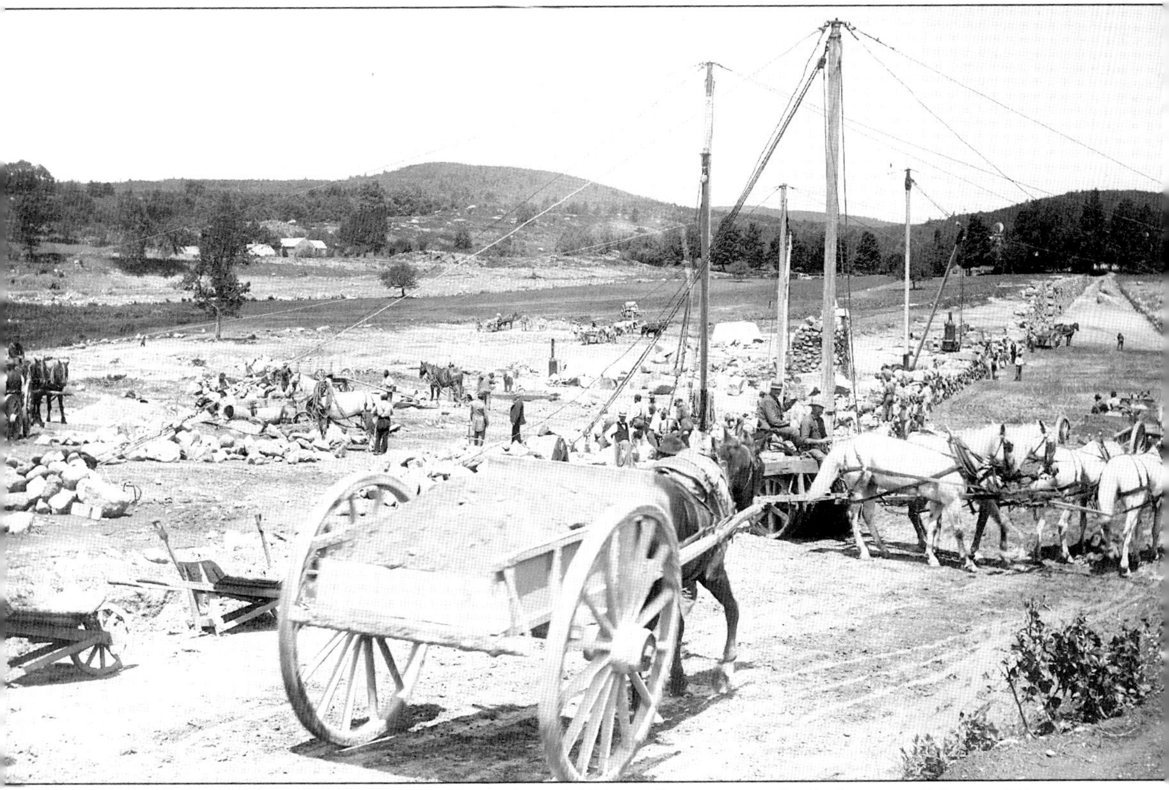

The Fallbrook Reservoir was constructed in 1891 with a primarily Italian workforce. Many descendants of these hard workers still live in Leominster today. The laborers in this picture came directly from Italy to work on many projects in the New England area. Note the horse in the center who seems to be his own supervisor! The completion of this reservoir nearly doubled the city's water capacity.

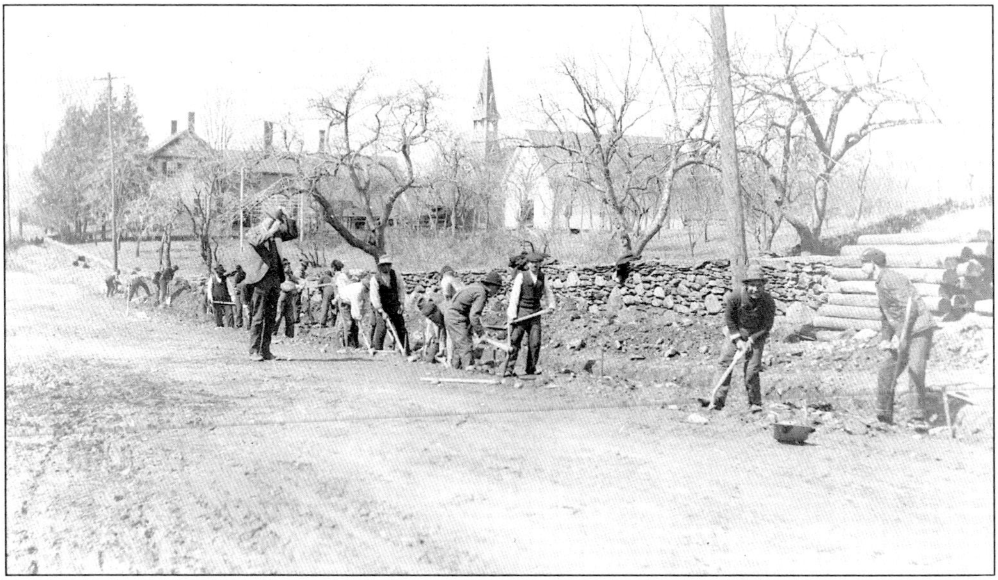

The railbed of the Leominster, Shirley, and Ayer Railway is being prepared on Prospect Street in this 1906 photograph. There is a stack of railroad ties behind the first man with a pick on the right. The steeple of the Congregational church can be seen in the background.

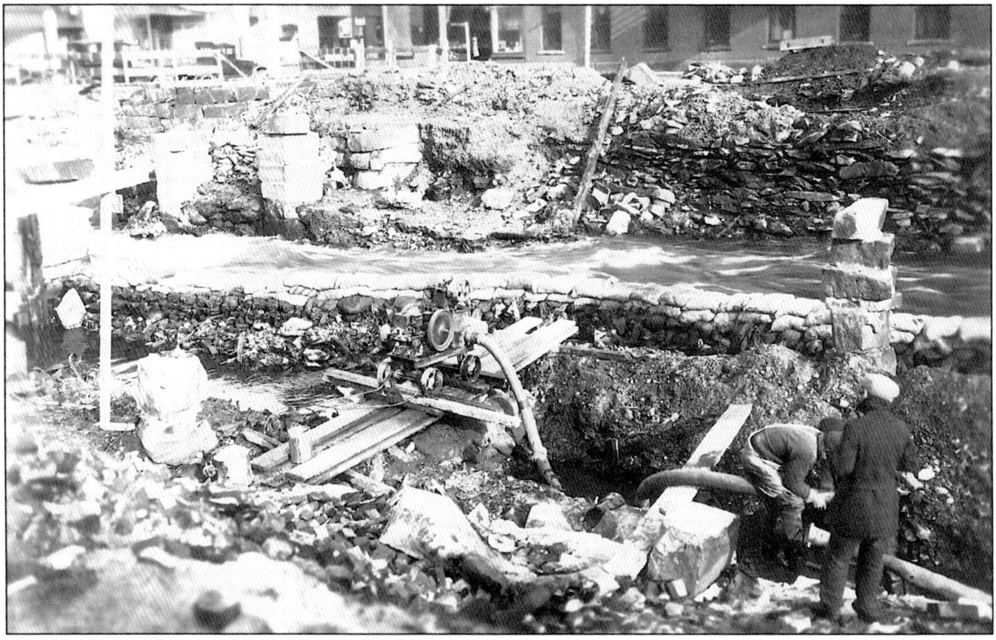

The copper dam on the Monoosnock Brook was one of many dams and bridges destroyed during the worst flood in the city's history in March of 1936. Monument Square was filled with over a foot of water from the corner of Park and Pleasant Streets to below the Metropolitan Theater; Pleasant Street to Cottage Street was under two feet of water. Fortunately, the dam at Rockwell's Pond held, averting a catastrophe.

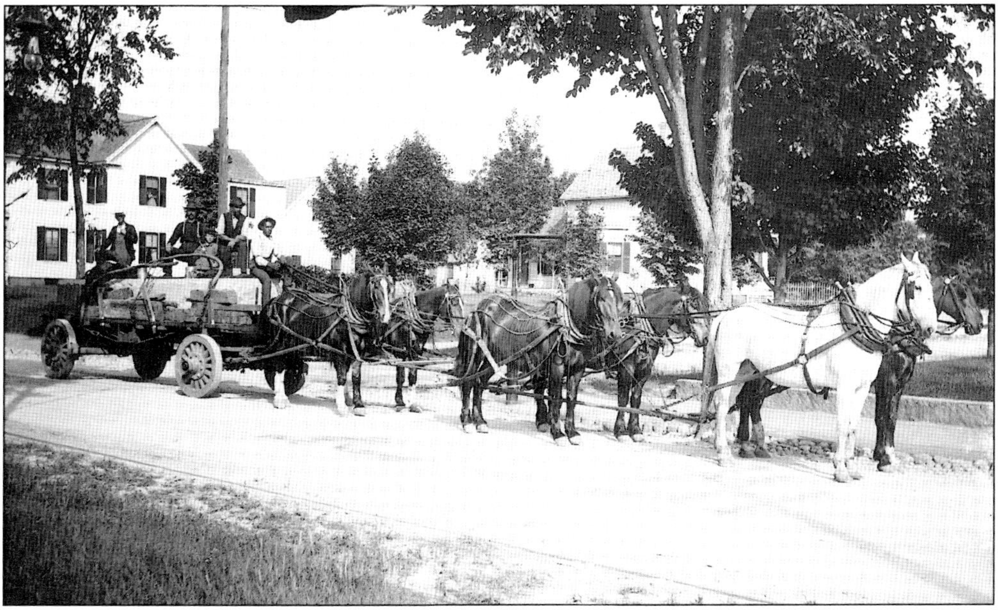

A wagon belonging to the Leominster Granite Works hauls stone slabs from the Burrage & Leavitt quarries off Granite Street in the early 1900s. Stone found in the Monoosnock hills was of excellent quality and was used for building purposes as well as curbing, paving blocks, and granite posts. Many of the city's older homes have exposed granite used in the foundations and steps. The quarries experienced a rebirth in the 1930s, when George Cheney's Monoosnock Quarries began supplying projects across Massachusetts and Rhode Island.

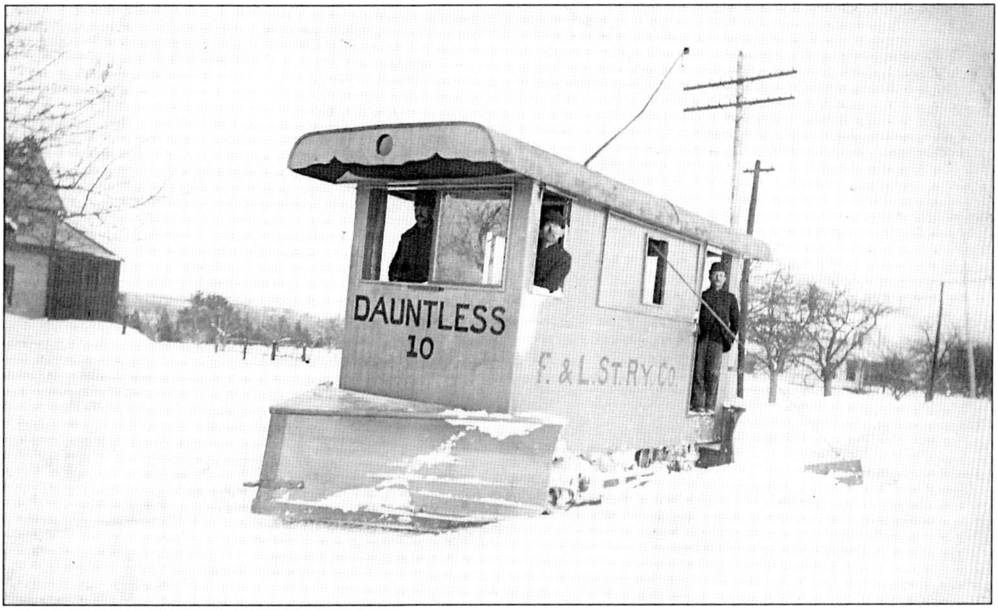

The "Dauntless" is seen plowing the tracks of the Fitchburg & Leominster Street Railway Company. The company was established in 1896. Its accomplishments were many: New England's first vestibule car in 1893, the first gasoline bus in 1922, and the first trackless trolley in Massachusetts in 1932. In 1893, they established Whalom Park; the amusement park on the Leominster-Lunenburg line remains a popular tourist attraction.

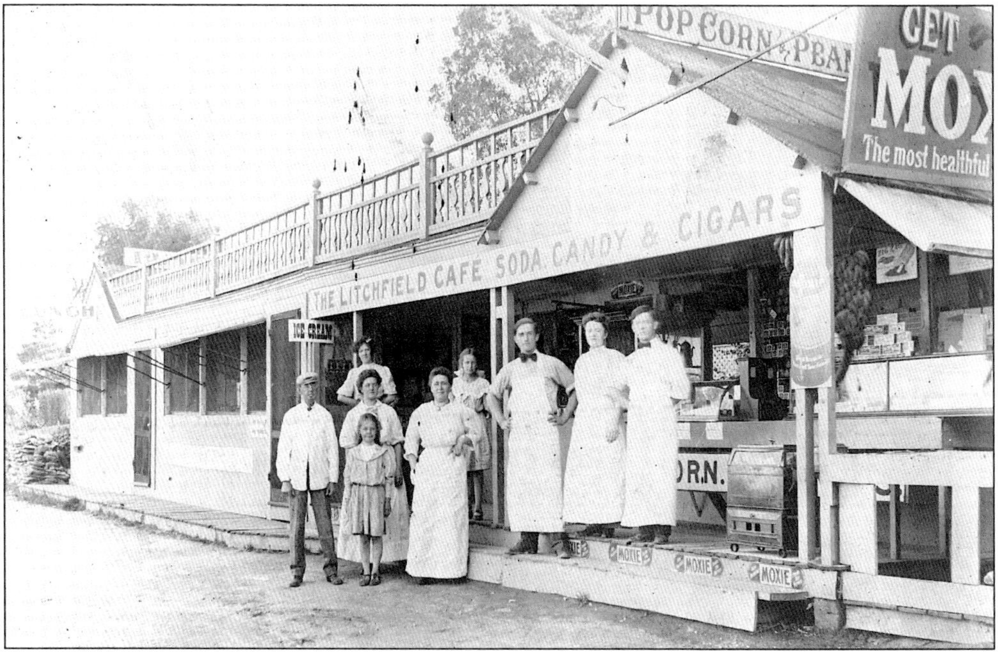

The Litchfield Cafe was located at Whalom Park and is pictured in this 1908 photograph. Proprietors Keller and Ducharme offered "box lunches put up to take out" primarily for people to enjoy in the park's picnic grounds. For 75¢ you could enjoy "fried chicken ala Maryland," one of the specialties on their full menu.

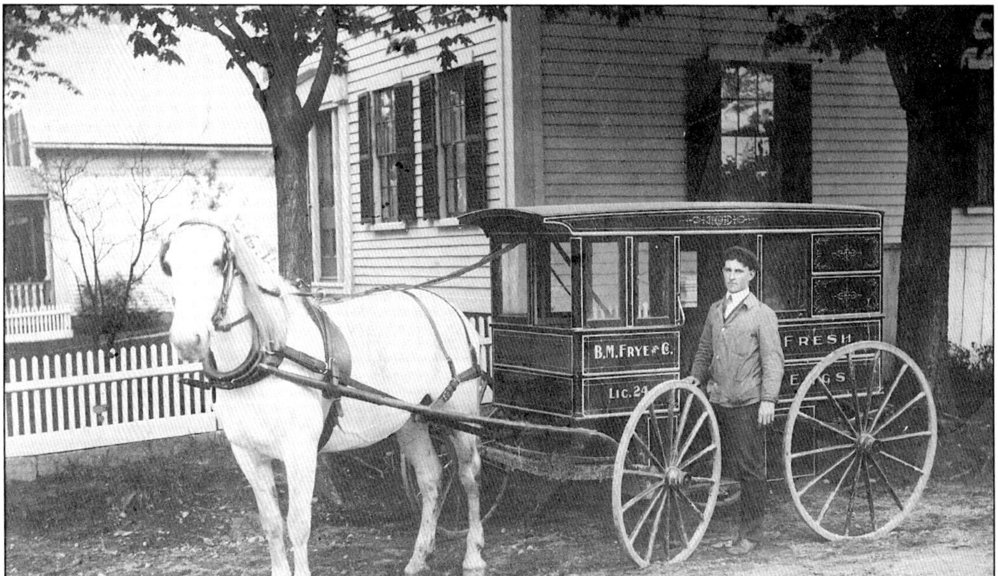

Frye's Dairy, known as Frye and Blanchard, was located at 102 Central Street. Mr. B.M. Frye began the business here c. 1903, advertising "milk, pure and sweet!" In 1906, the dairy delivered 70 cans and 560 quarts of milk daily in town, along with their best-selling "A-1 quality" butter. Both Frye and Blanchard personally went out on their routes to keep in close touch with their customers.

Specials advertised from Desrocher's Chicken Shop, located on Water Street can be seen here, c. mid-1940s. Maurice A. Desrocher owned and operated Desrocher's Poultry Farm on Tolman Avenue in North Leominster; he later went into the accounting field.

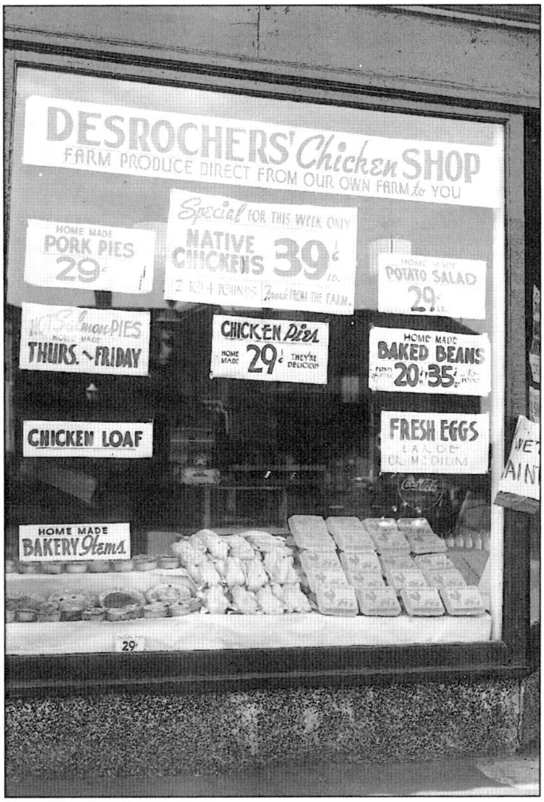

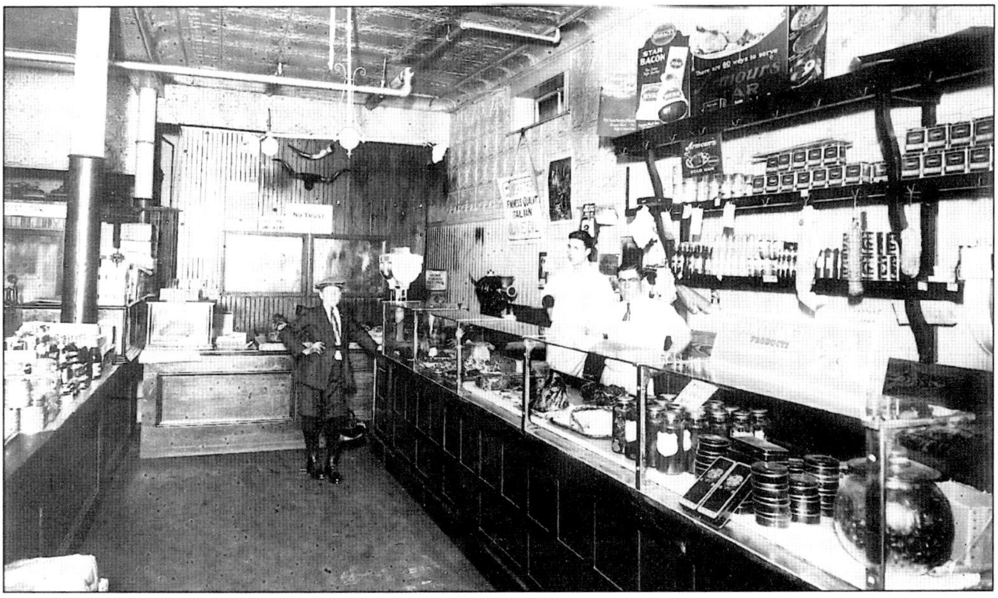

Victory Market was founded as a corner grocery store by Louis and James DiGeronimo shortly after World War I. They moved to 37 Mechanic Street, site of the present-day Plymouth Cafe, when their first store, located in the Kendall Block, was damaged by fire. In 1933, they relocated to 19 Mechanic Street. The modern supermarket on North Main Street opened in 1955 and the chain of Victory Supermarkets began.

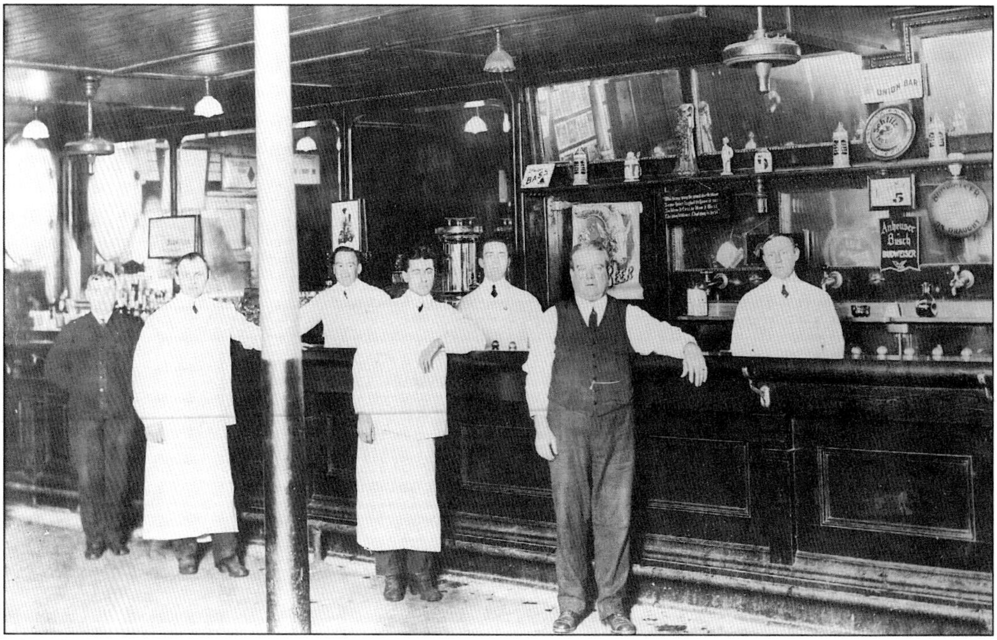

This bar was located in the former Columbia Hotel block on Merriam Avenue. It was known as the Columbia Cafe from 1926 to 1967. It then became Joe Smith's Bar from 1967 through 1987; it is currently operating as Michael's Pub.

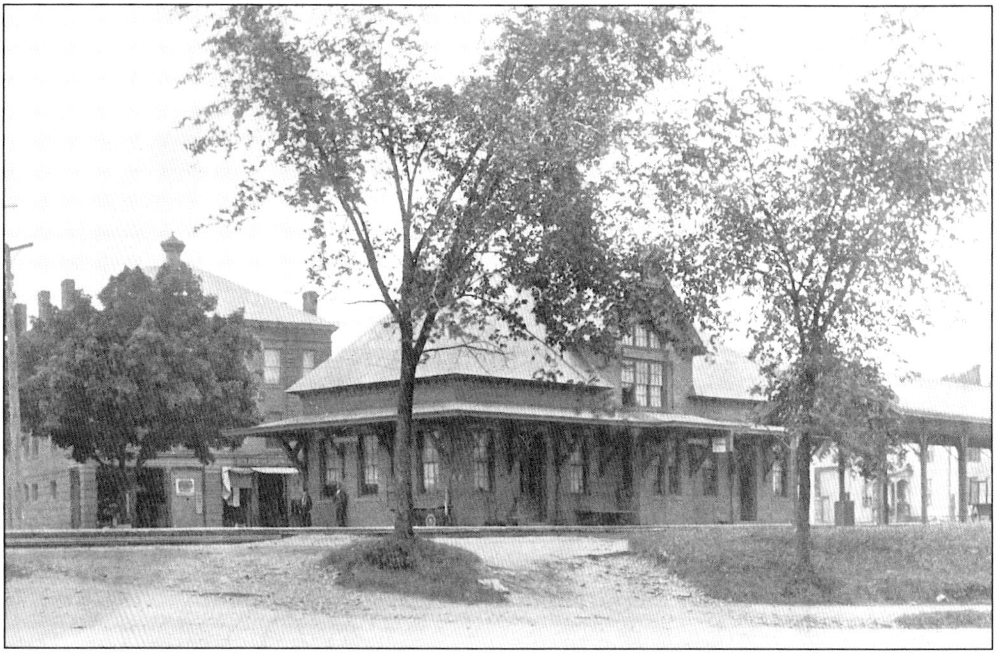

This Gothic-revival style station was built in 1878 for the New York, New Haven, and Hartford Railroad. The depot replaced a much smaller building on the east side of the tracks; it was used to carry passengers and freight until 1946. Many turn-of-the-century travelers came from New York on their way to summer homes in Princeton. The building today houses a model railroad shop, a liquor store, and the St. Jean Social Club.

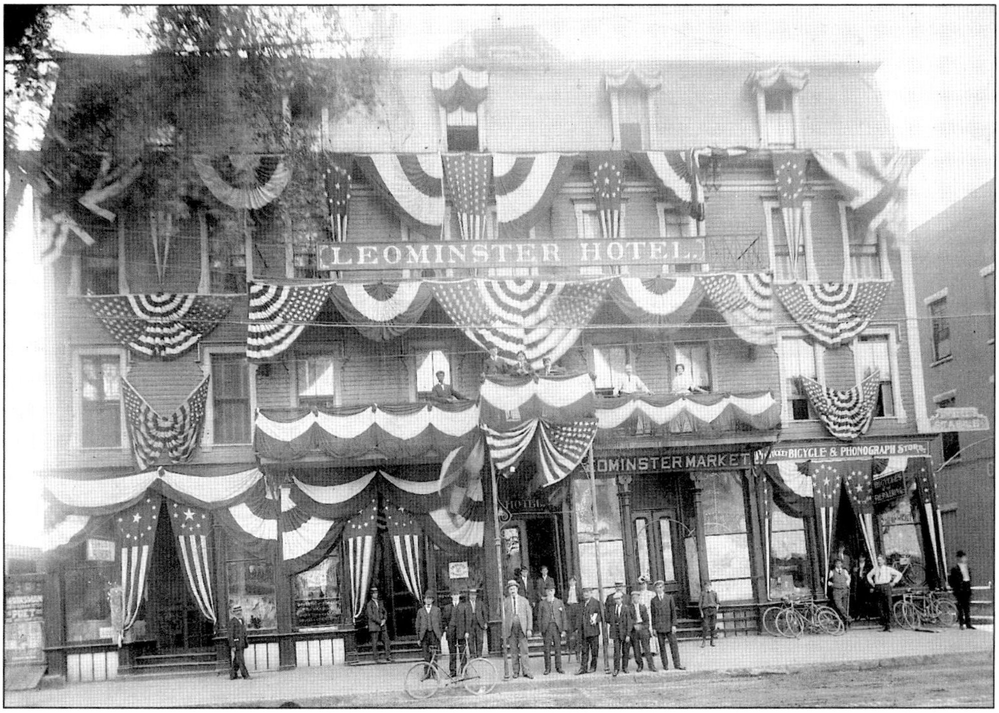

The old Leominster Hotel, decorated for July 4th, was located downtown just past the Monoosnock Brook. Owner Henry Sawtelle became Leominster's first mayor in 1916. His chair of office, marked with a brass plaque, is sometimes displayed at City Hall; at other times it is kept at the No. 6 Schoolhouse.

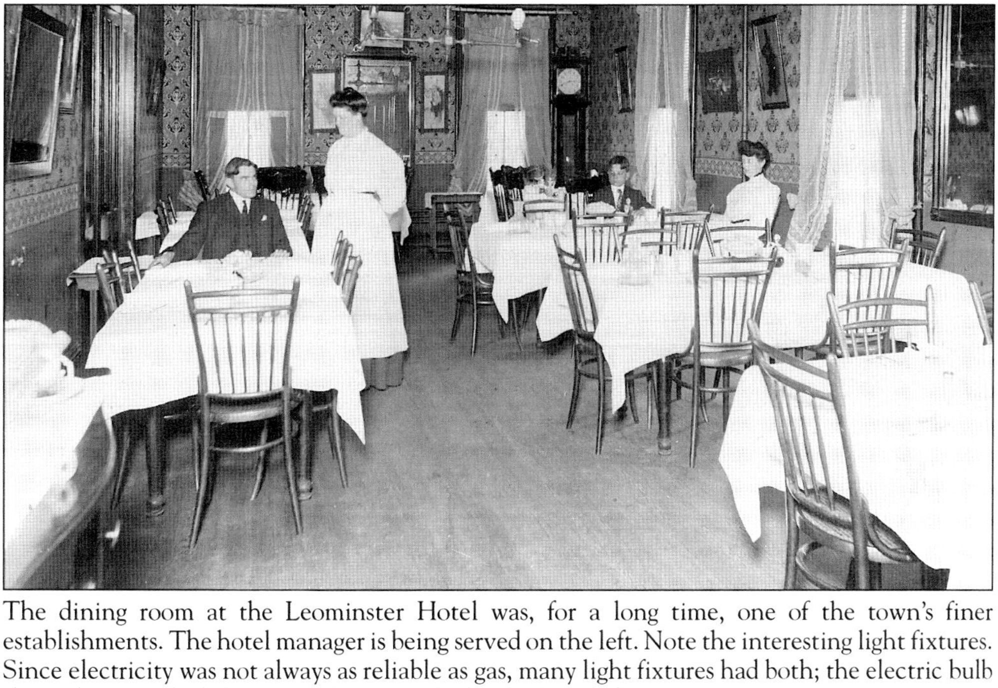

The dining room at the Leominster Hotel was, for a long time, one of the town's finer establishments. The hotel manager is being served on the left. Note the interesting light fixtures. Since electricity was not always as reliable as gas, many light fixtures had both; the electric bulb slants downward while the gas fixture with the shade stands up.

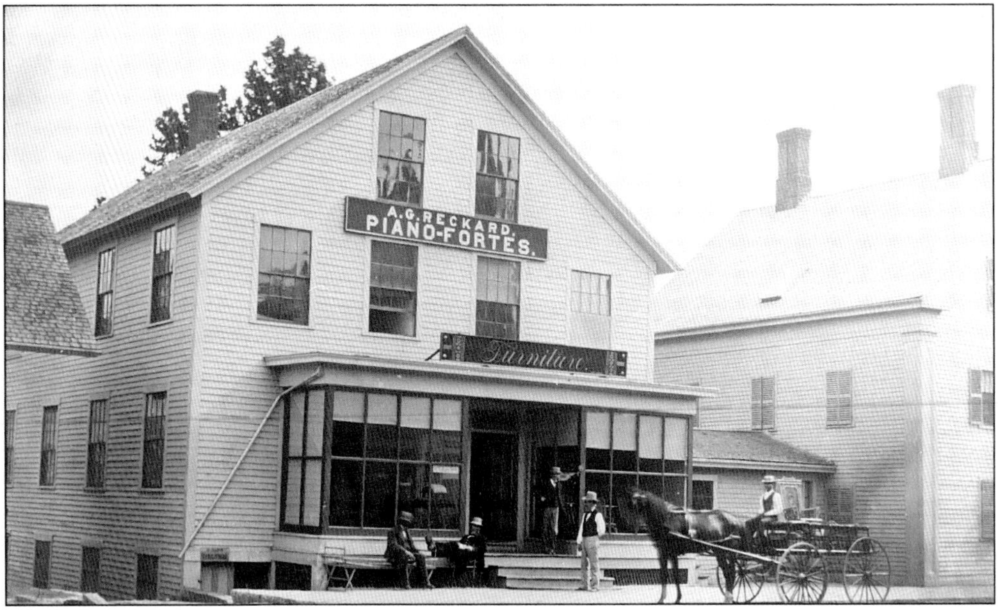

Andrew G. Reckard's shop at Church Street and Merriam Avenue can be seen here, *c.* late 1800s. Reckard has the distinction of being the first person in Leominster to veneer a piano case. Other important companies in Leominster's thriving piano industry were the Richardson, J.H. Lockey, Arlington, Jewett, and Wellington firms. In 1892, Leominster constructed 25% of all cases built in the United States; by 1906, the industry was doing a business of over $1 million annually.

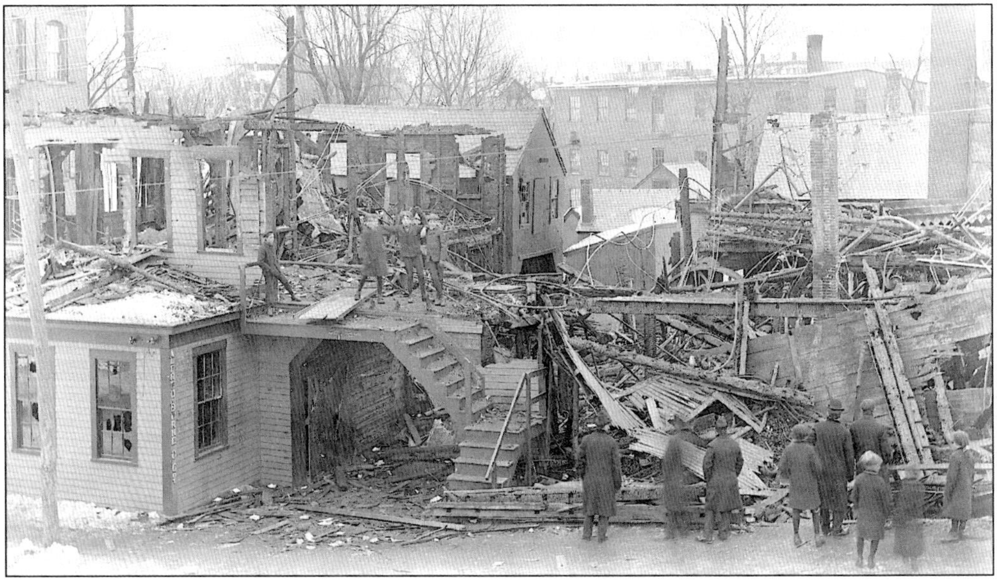

In 1896, the William S. Reed Toy Company on Summer Street was destroyed by the largest fire to strike the town since the Great Fire of 1873. The company relocated to Exchange Street by 1899. Toys manufactured by Reed included many wooden toys and games, which are eagerly sought after by today's collectors. The "Old Lady in the Shoe" cast-iron coin bank, one of only two reportedly made, sold at auction for over $200,000.

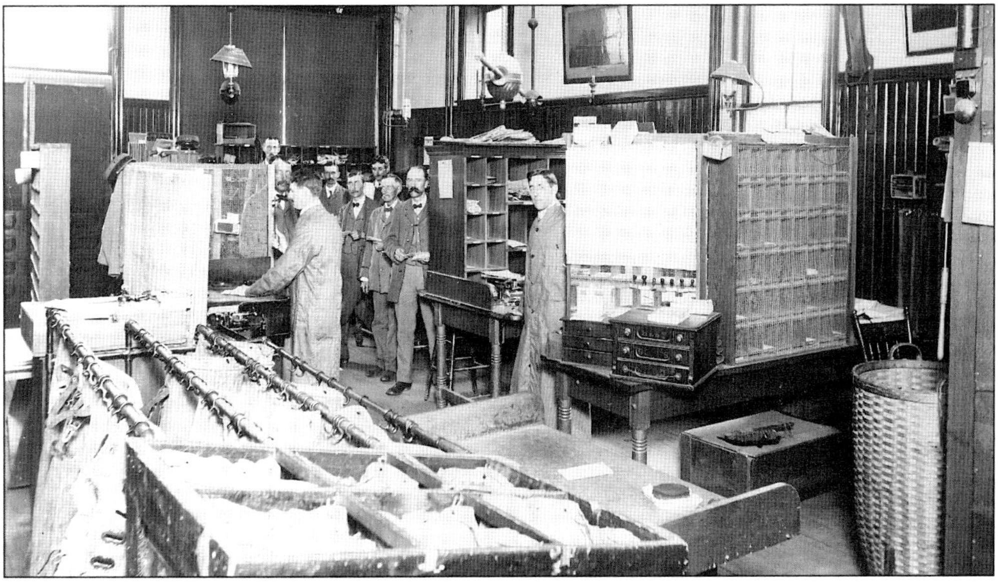

This 1907 photograph shows the post office mail room, located in the Bank Block on Main Street. Postmaster Thomas Hills was appointed in July 1874 by President Grant; he was reappointed by Presidents Hayes, Arthur, and Cleveland. He succeeded Charles Colburn, who served the community for over 40 years before retiring. The main post office has been in ten different locations since its establishment in 1789; it moved to its present location in 1929.

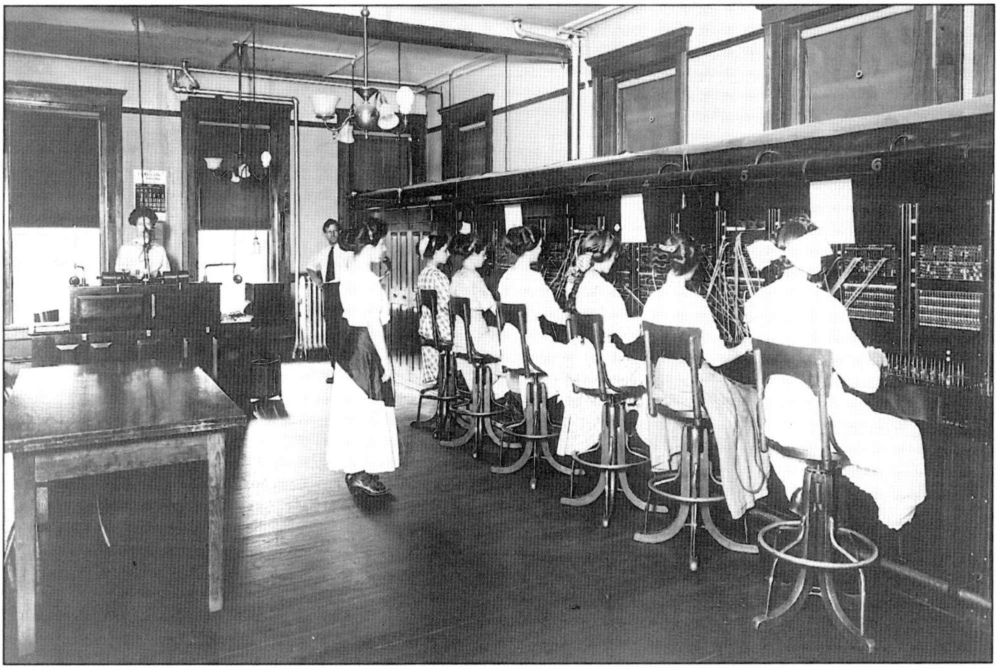

This photograph of New England Telephone Company switchboard girls was taken in July 1911. At this time, the office was located in the Richardson Building at 20 Main Street. The office had been in the Foster Block at 4 Main Street from 1885 to 1900 and at the Allen Block on the corner of Park and Pleasant Streets from 1901 to 1908. In 1906, there were 600 telephone subscribers in Leominster.

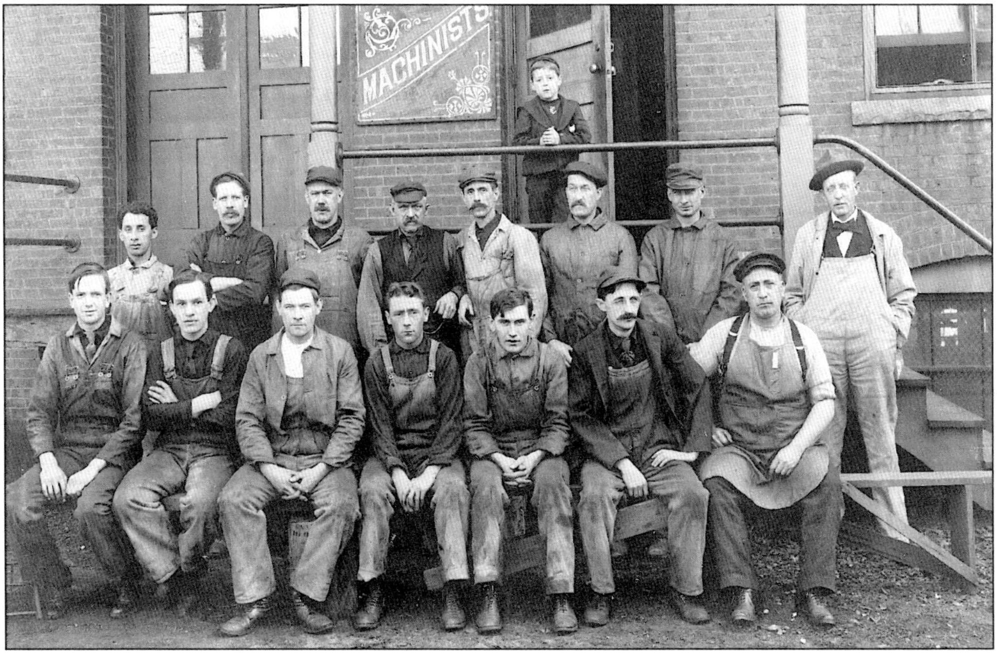

This 1897 photograph of the machinists of F.H. Cook and Company was taken in front of their shop on Water Street. They manufactured horn-working machinery and tools as well as machinery used to manufacture celluloid, tortoise shell and rubber combs, hair ornaments, and buttons. The business was especially proud of their "Gem Pencil Sharpening Machine." Standard Tool became their successor.

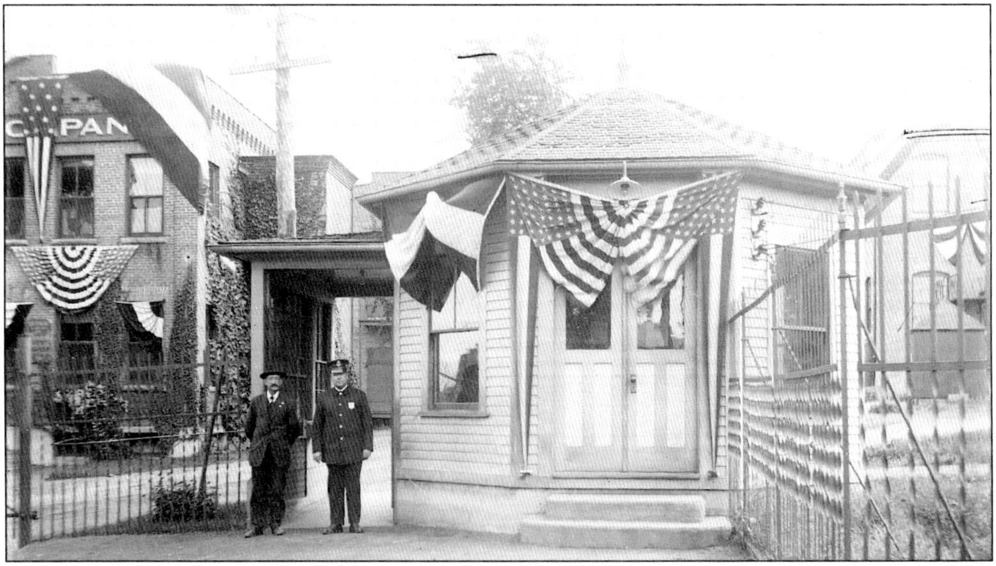

The gatehouse of the Viscoloid Company on Lancaster Street, like most major buildings in town, sports a patriotic look to celebrate the victory in WW I. Bernard W. Doyle was one of the founders of the company, established c. 1900 to manufacture hair ornaments from pyroxylin. "The Viscoloid" was one of Leominster's first plastics manufacturers, employing over 2,000 workers and boasting 106 buildings. In 1925, it was purchased by the duPont Company and later became Mi-Lor Manufacturing.

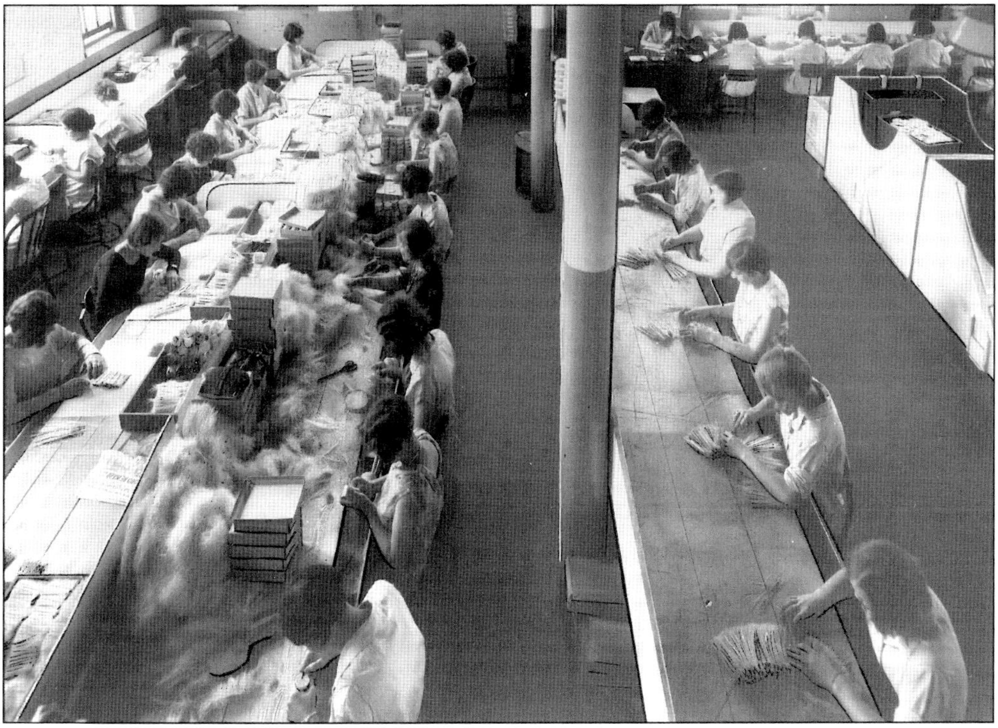

Young women put bristles in toothbrushes at the Doyle Works of E.I. duPont de Nemours's plant on Lancaster Street. The duPont Company, a giant in the plastics industry worldwide, was a progressive company: they offered one of the country's first pension plans and created a work council, which rewarded employees for suggestions and problem-solving. Proud of their safety record, the company celebrated 20 years without a lost-time accident with a sign outside the plant in August 1970.

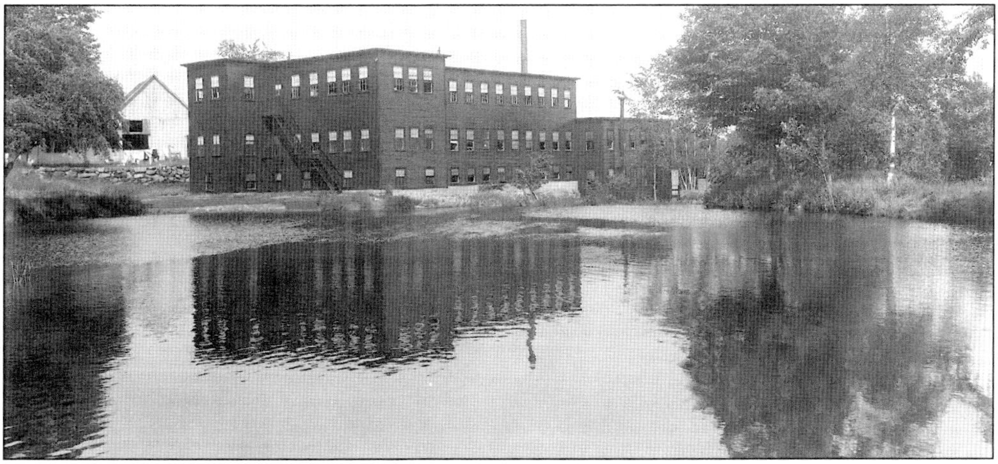

The E.B. Kingman and Company factory on Exchange Street is shown in this 1924 photograph. Edward B. Kingman founded the business in 1887, using horn from longhorn steers to manufacture combs at Spruce and First Streets. In 1914, the Howe family joined forces with Kingman and the transition from horn to celluloid began. By 1927, cellulose-acetate sheeting had been developed, overcoming the problems associated with celluloid's flammability. At present, the shop is closed and the small pond is virtually gone.

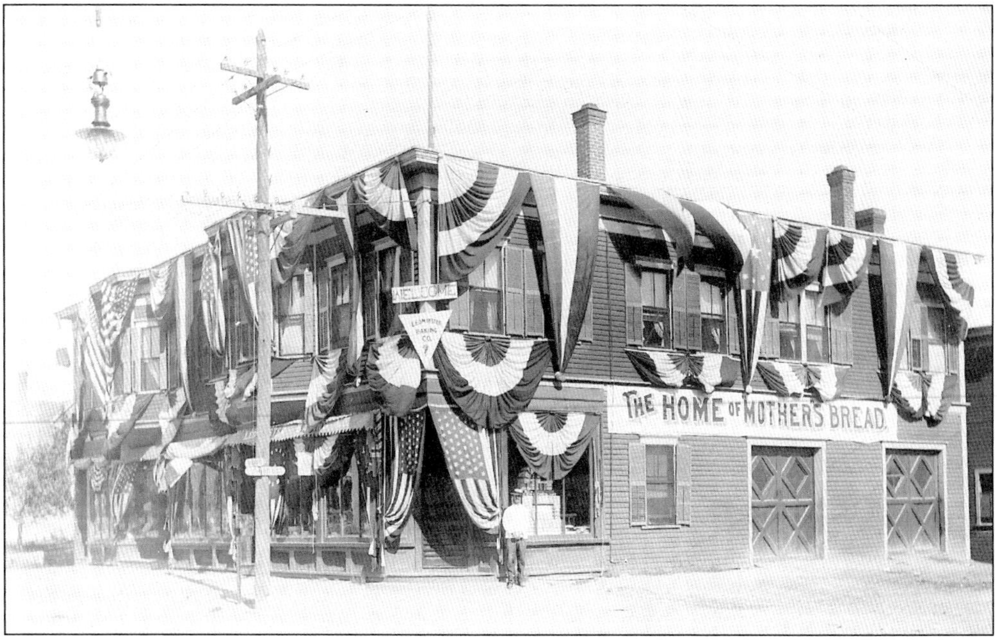

The Leominster Baking Company, "Home of Mother's Bread," at the corner of Spruce and Third Streets, is decked out in holiday bunting. The company was founded in 1898 by E.H. Nutting and B.F. Owens of Leominster and was considered a world-class bakery. Its success led to the establishment of the East Side Cafe, where it was claimed that every chair was filled at mealtimes!

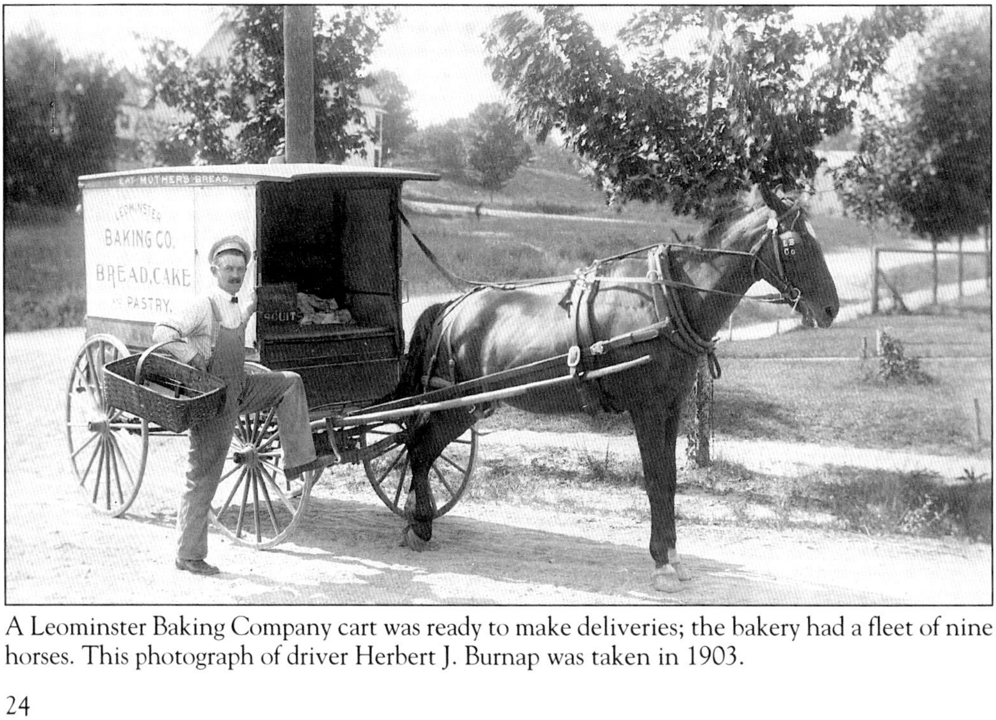

A Leominster Baking Company cart was ready to make deliveries; the bakery had a fleet of nine horses. This photograph of driver Herbert J. Burnap was taken in 1903.

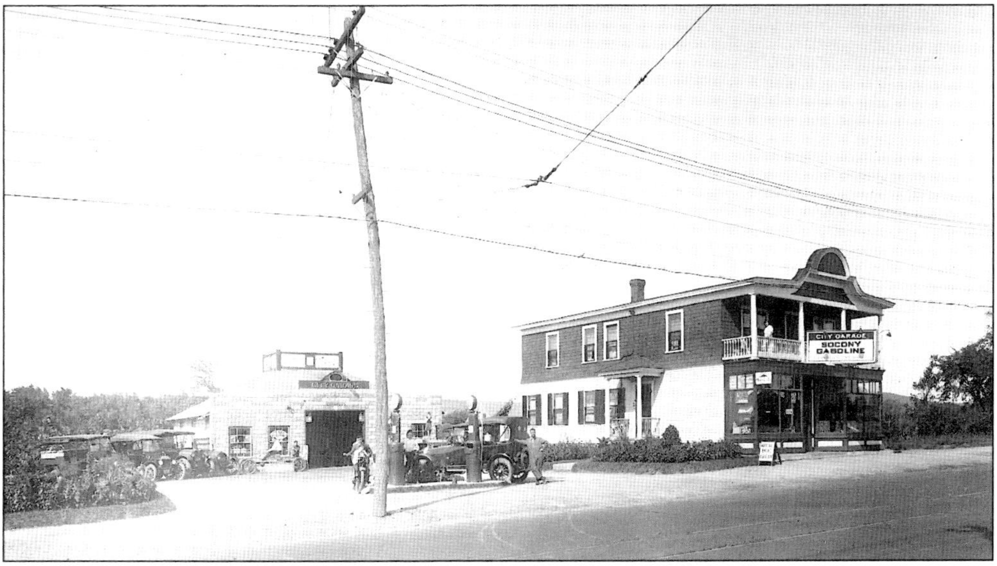

City Garage was located on Lancaster Street in this 1922 photograph. Eugene A. Lemire was the proprietor. In 1924, City Motor Car Company did business at this location. The present garage is located next to St. Anna's School.

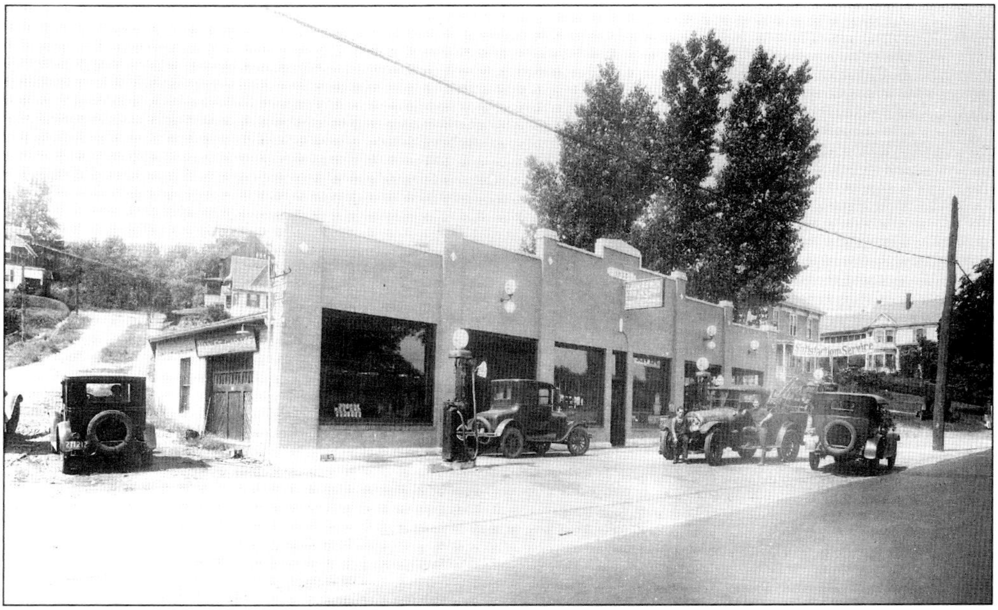

The Main Street Garage was built in 1925. The man leaning on the Main Street Garage truck in this 1930s photograph is Matt "Oscar" Johnson; he was employed as a mechanic by owner Avery Cousins. J&R Transmissions and NAPA Auto Parts are located there today.

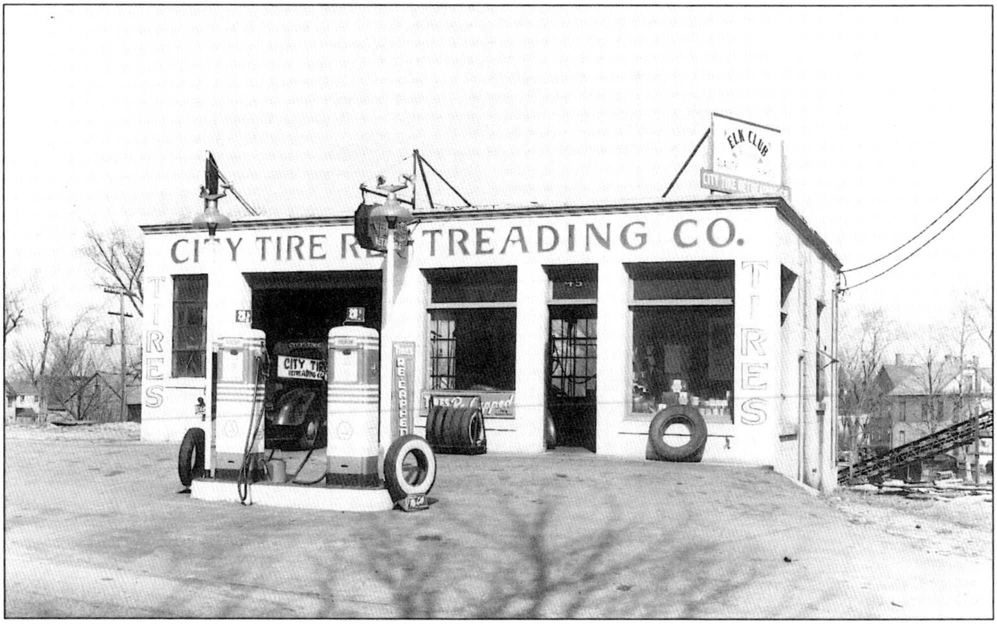

City Tire Retreading Company was established in 1932 by John and Larry Ferrera at Lancaster and Cedar Streets. The business was located across from the post office between 1936 and 1940, before it moved to the North Main Street location (shown here) in the 1940s. City Tire is now operated by John's sons, who expanded the building in 1980. Note the price of gasoline and the Leominster Elk Club Beverage sign.

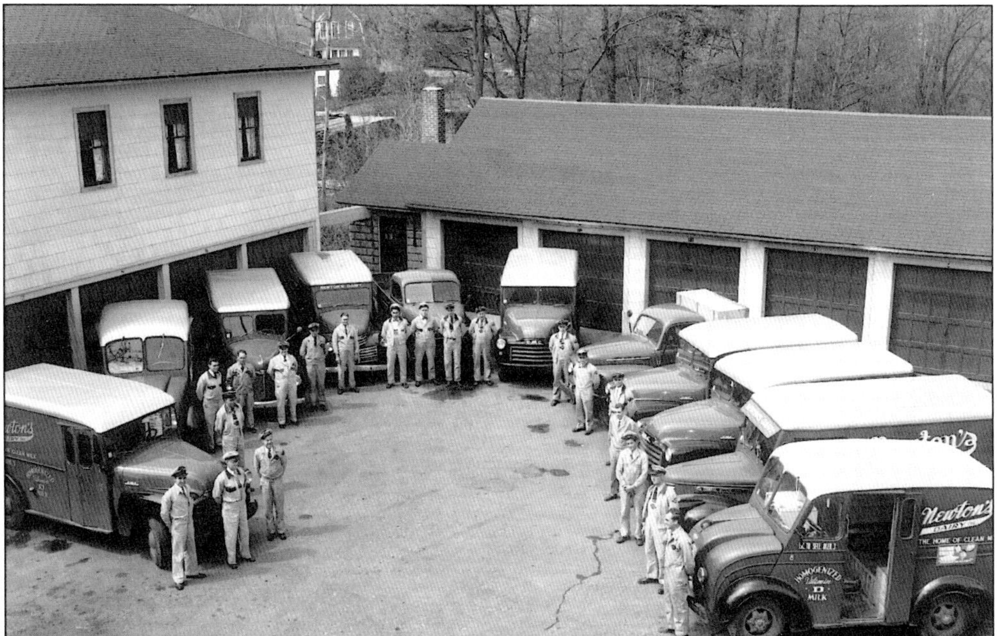

This 1953 picture of the Newton's Dairy delivery fleet was taken at their Manchester Street location. Home delivery of milk was still an important service at this time. The dairy, "The Home Of Clean Milk," later opened an ice cream bar that was popular during the 1960s.

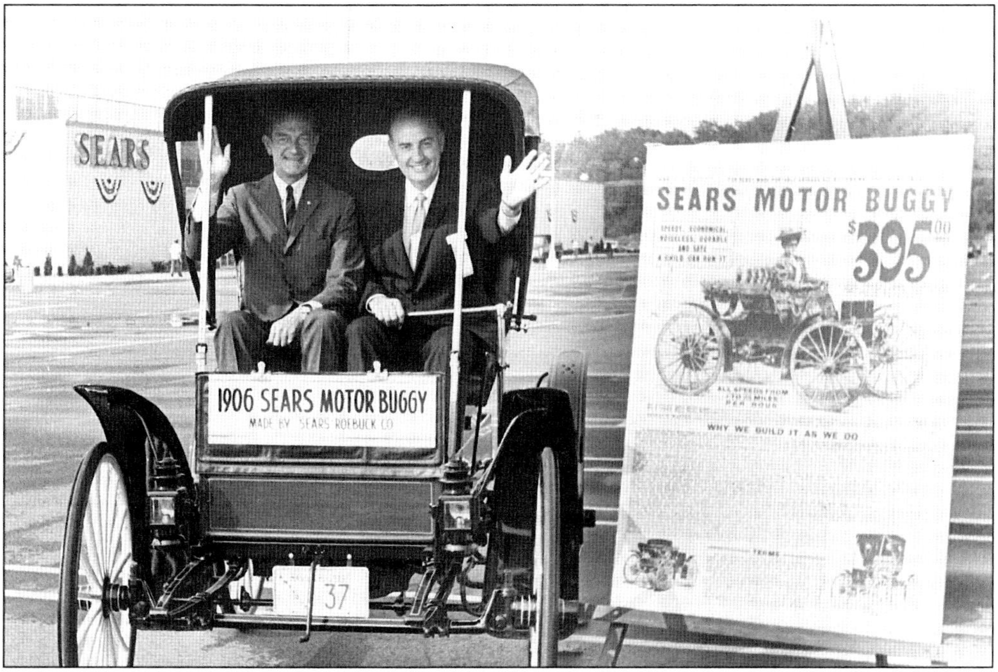

The Sears Motor Buggy makes an appearance at the grand opening of the Searstown Mall. The 1906 Buggy sold for $395 and was purported to be so safe "a child can run it!" The buggy toured the parking lot that day at speeds of 1 to 25 miles an hour, as advertised.

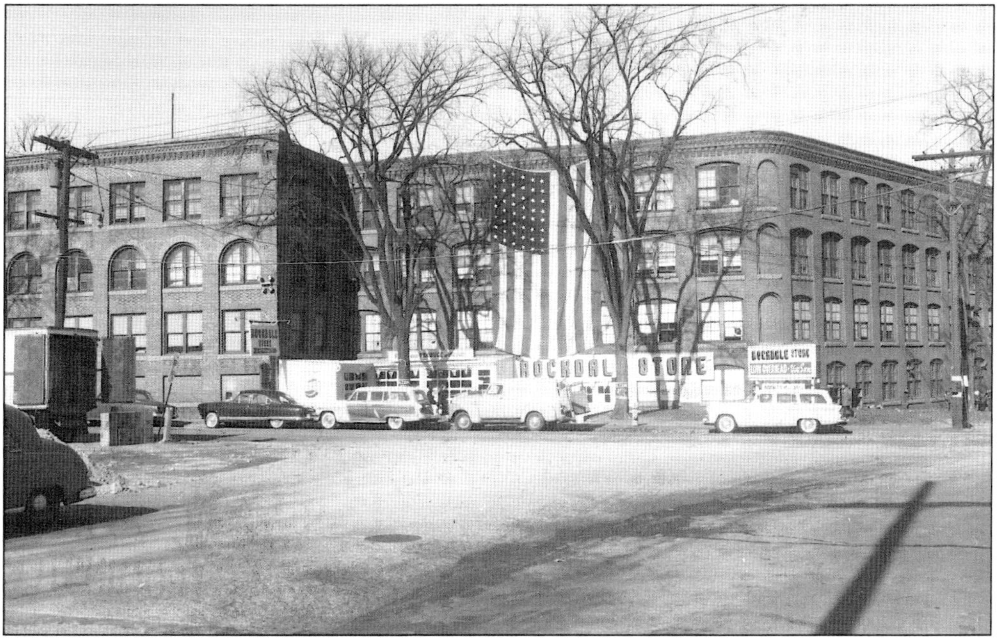

In August 1957, the Rockdale's Discount Department Store held their grand opening. Located on the corner of Whitney and Water Streets, the store was first managed by Jack Letteney and advertised having "Worcester County's best bargains!" The store was open daily from 10 a.m. until 9 p.m. and featured a restaurant, open-air fruit and vegetable stands, a bakery, and a dry cleaners.

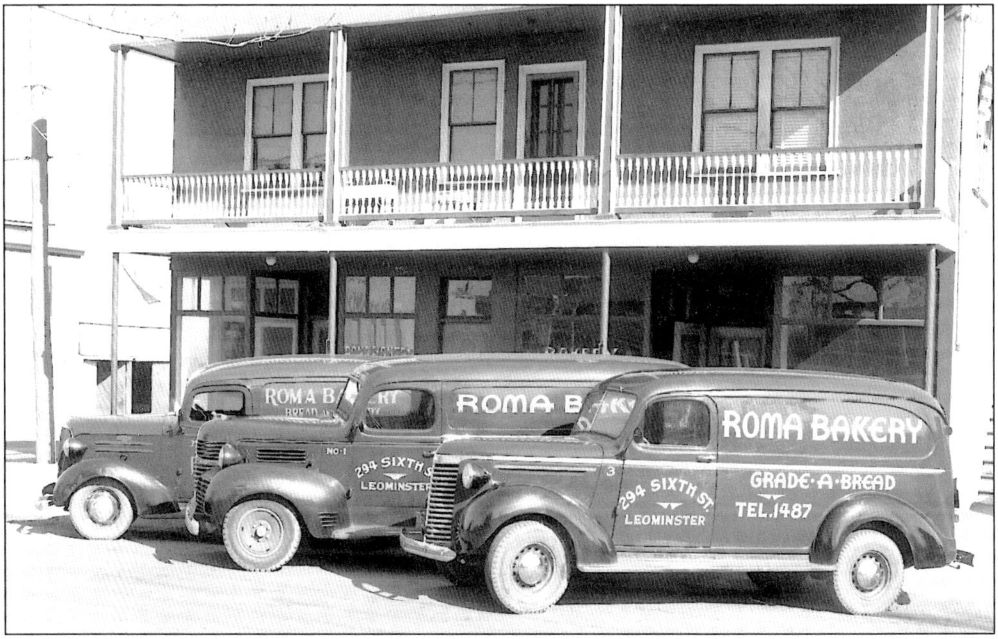

This 1940s photograph shows the Roma Bakery delivery trucks in front of the store at the corner of Middle and Sixth Streets. Their fine baked goods have been complementing meals since 1938, when Joseph Casacca founded the company. Casacca's son Norman was followed by his own sons, Bryan and Norman Jr., who are preparing to make "dough," carrying on the family tradition at the Northgate Plaza shop next to Victory Supermarket.

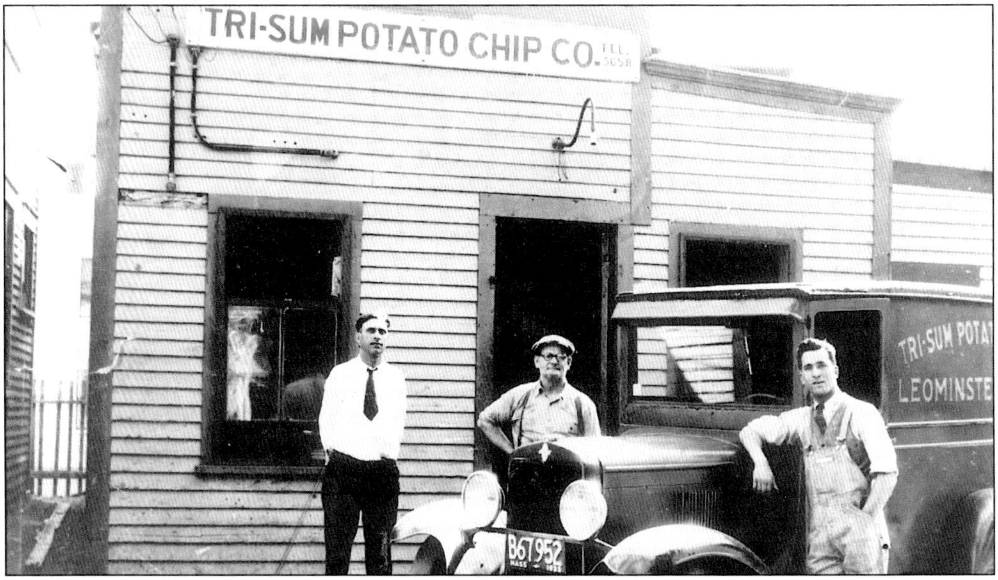

The Tri-Sum Potato Chip Company shows off their new name, selected via a customer contest. When the company was established in 1908 as the Leominster Potato Chip Company, their 8-mile route was covered by a horse-drawn cart. In this 1933 photograph, founder J.P. Duchesneau stands in the center with son Ernest; the picture was taken at their original Eighth Street location. Tri-Sum also operated on Mechanic Street, where they offered baked beans. In 1940, they moved to their current location on Carter Street. (Courtesy Pauline Duchesneau.)

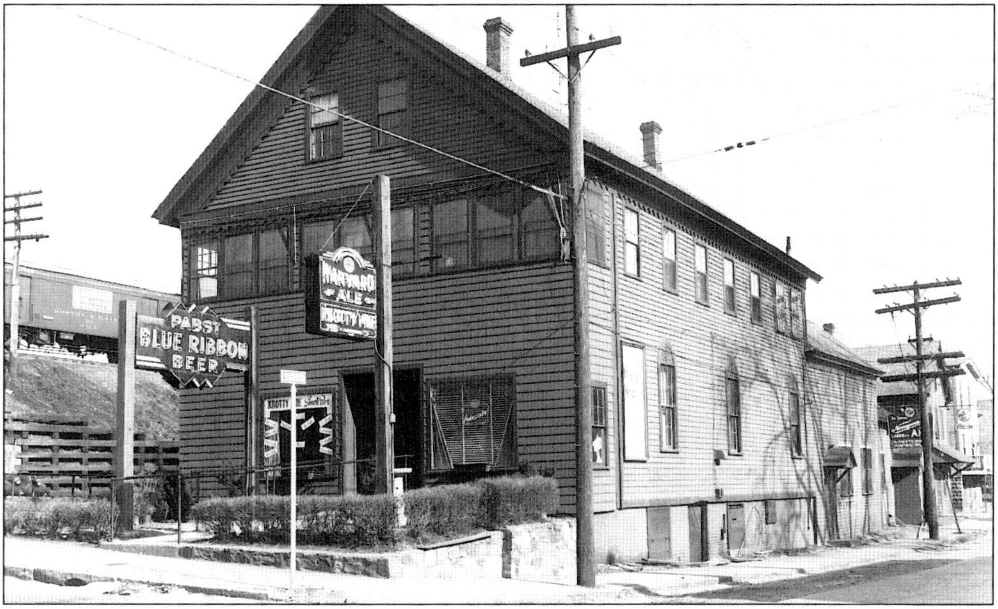

The Knotty Pine Restaurant and Bar was once located at the corner of Main and Nashua Streets in North Leominster, where Jiffy Lube operates today. Originally, it was the Number 10 Schoolhouse, located where Kendall Hall now stands. The building was moved across the street; a second floor was added in 1889, when the Pierce Street School opened. It then became Howe's Dry Goods Store until 1944, when James McKenna opened the Village Cafe, renamed the Knotty Pine in 1948. The 1970s saw two more colorful name changes: the "Devil's Workshop" and the "White Orange."

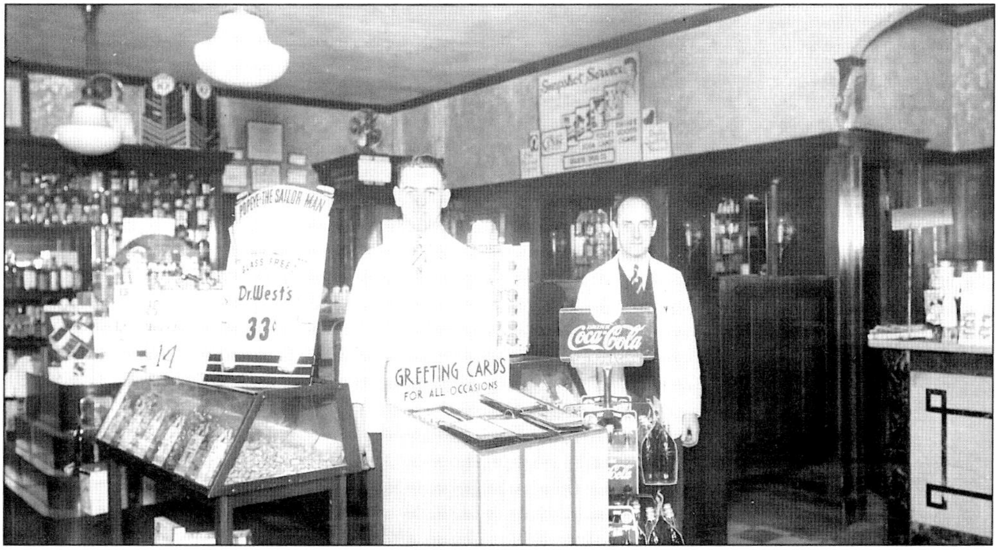

This early 1930s photograph shows the interior of Giguere's Drug Store on Spruce Street, established in 1903 by Alphonse Giguere. Ignazzio Carluccio, shown here with Amy Rheault, married Giguere's daughter and operated the pharmacy until his son Kent took over. The store was a real neighborhood gathering place; note the soda fountain on the right. The "Dr. West" toothbrushes on display were made at Leominster's duPont Company. The store closed several years ago.

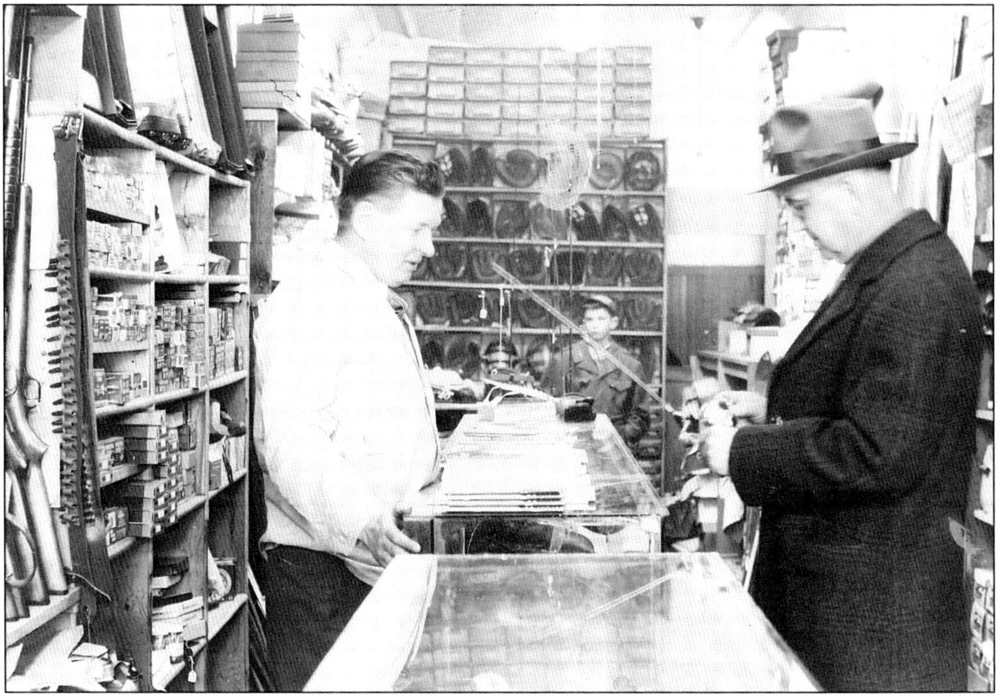

Many people fondly remember getting their first football, baseball, skates, or skis at Werner's Sporting Goods Company on Main Street. The store was established in 1946 by Werner Hytinen, shown here helping a customer. It was an era when downtowns were thriving, especially on Thursday nights when stores were open until 9 p.m. Malls and large chain stores have spelled doom for many shops on Main Street, including Werner's; the store is scheduled to close its doors for good in 1999. (Courtesy Werner's.)

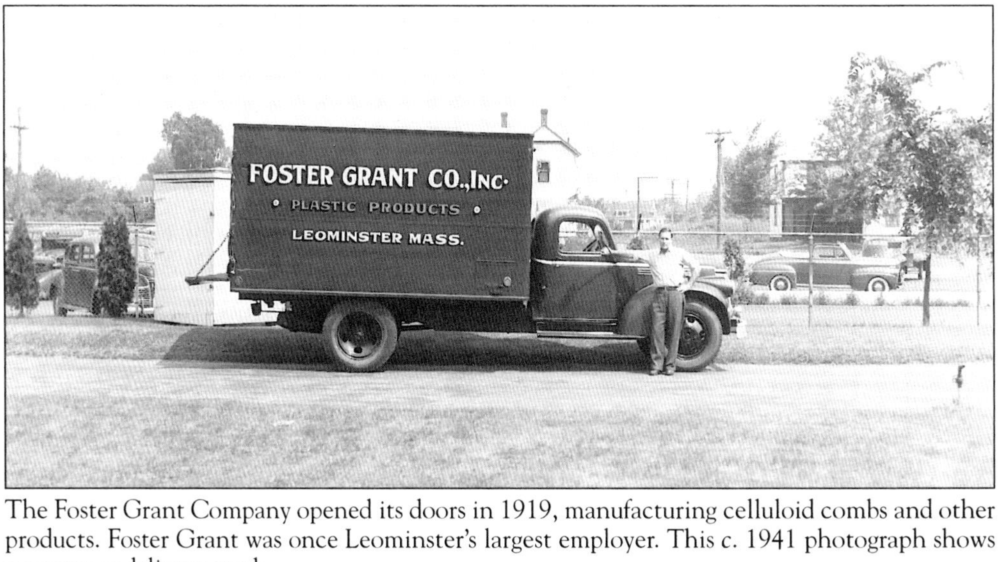

The Foster Grant Company opened its doors in 1919, manufacturing celluloid combs and other products. Foster Grant was once Leominster's largest employer. This c. 1941 photograph shows a company delivery truck.

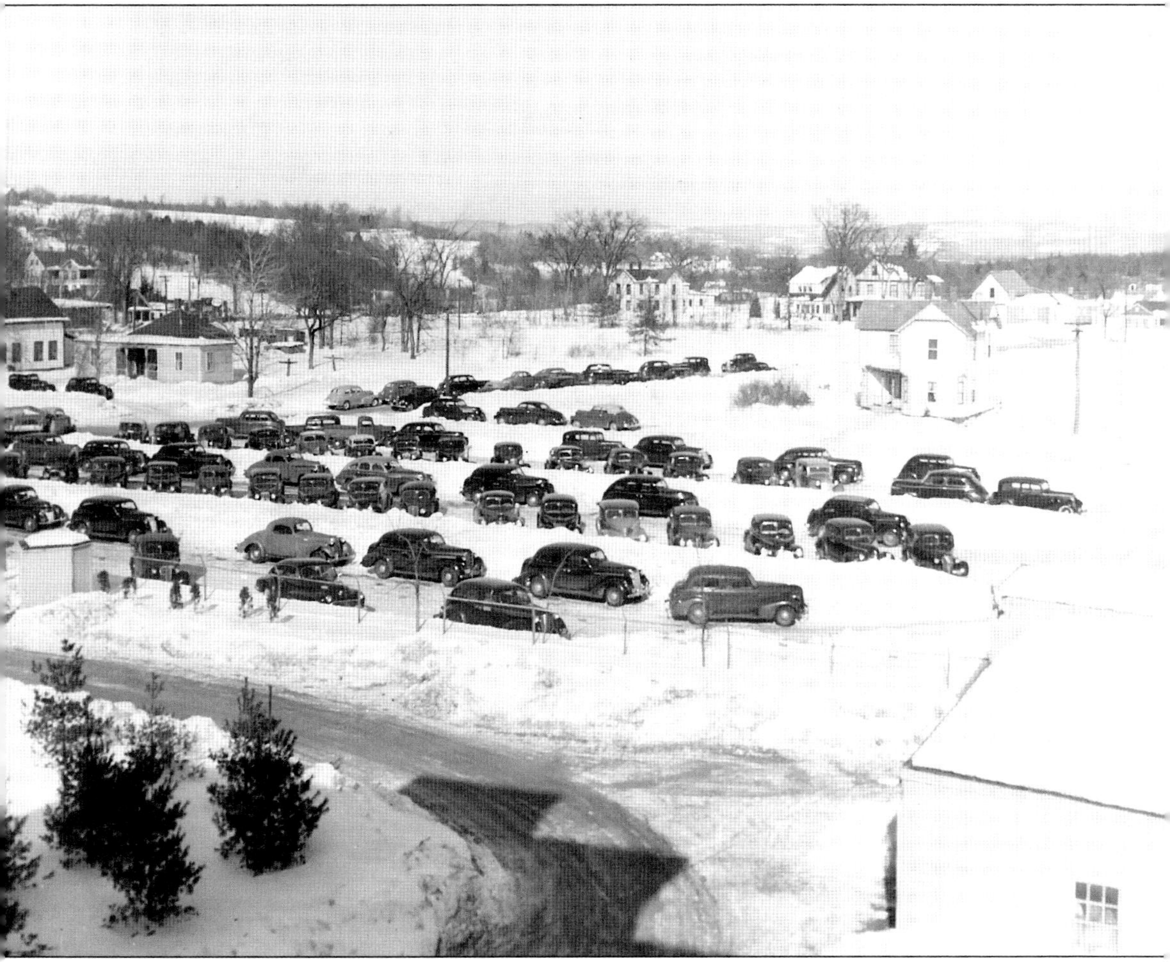

Under the leadership of founder Samuel Foster and his son Joseph, the Foster Grant Company grew into a complex organization, maintaining plants in six cities and two countries. A watershed event for the company and the industry occurred in 1930, when Sam Foster bought a new German machine designed for the injection molding of plastic. This manual, air-operated machine was then commercially impractical; Foster Grant technicians, however, succeeded where others had failed. They modified the machine and revolutionized an entire industry. The Foster family's generosity to the citizens of Leominster was matched only by the community's pride in "their" company. This photograph was taken from the parking lot at Foster Grant.

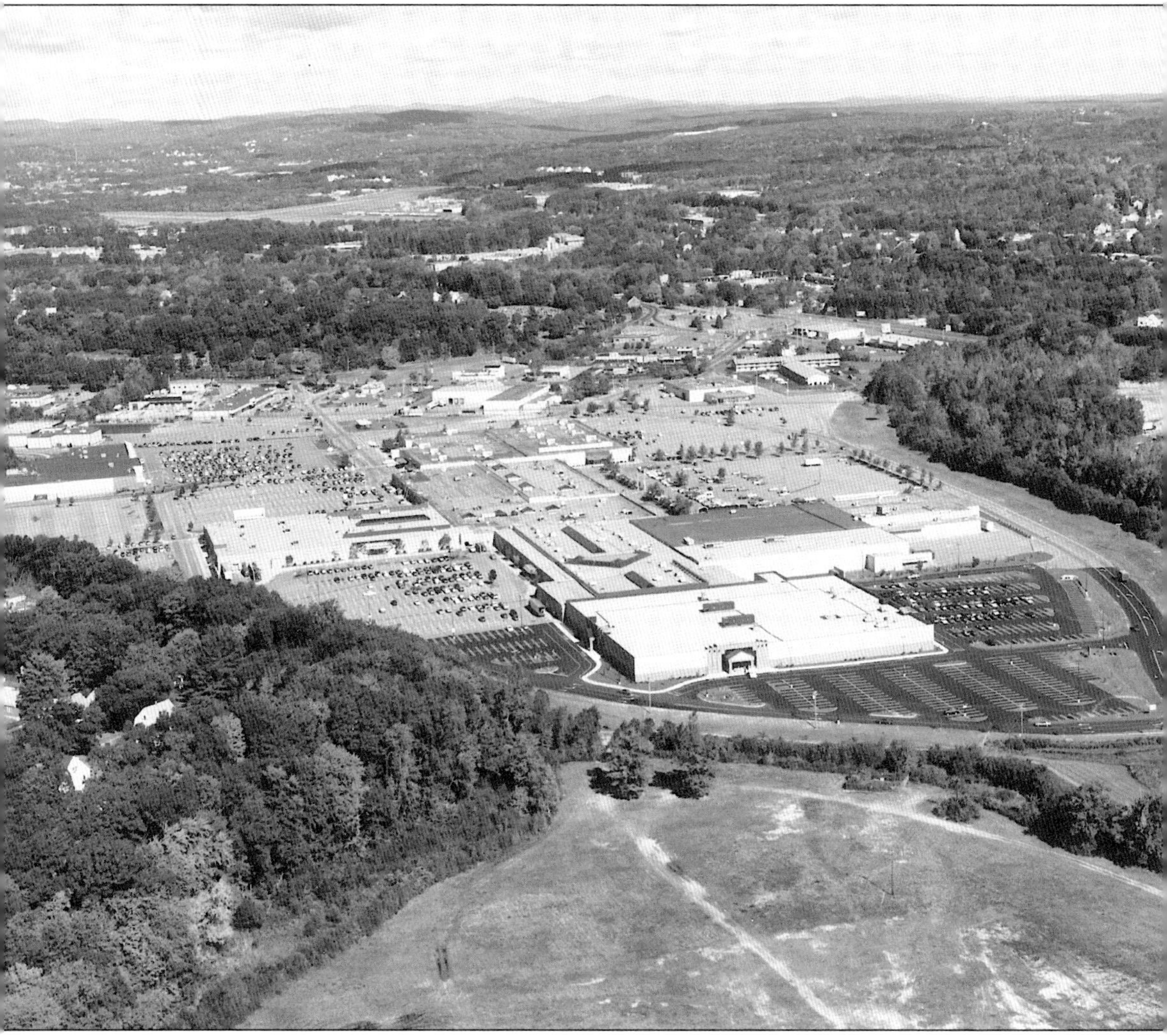

One of the greatest changes to Leominster was the establishment of the Searstown Shopping Center off Route 2 and Mill Street in the early 1960s. White-Acre Leominster Associates applied for the initial building permits; this was, and continues to be, the largest single building permit on taxable property ever issued by the city. In 1972, Kimco Development Corporation purchased Searstown Mall, shown in this current, aerial view. Today the mall employs over 2,000 people and remains Leominster's largest taxpayer. (Courtesy Kimco Development Corporation.)

Two

Street Scenes, Houses, and Neighborhoods

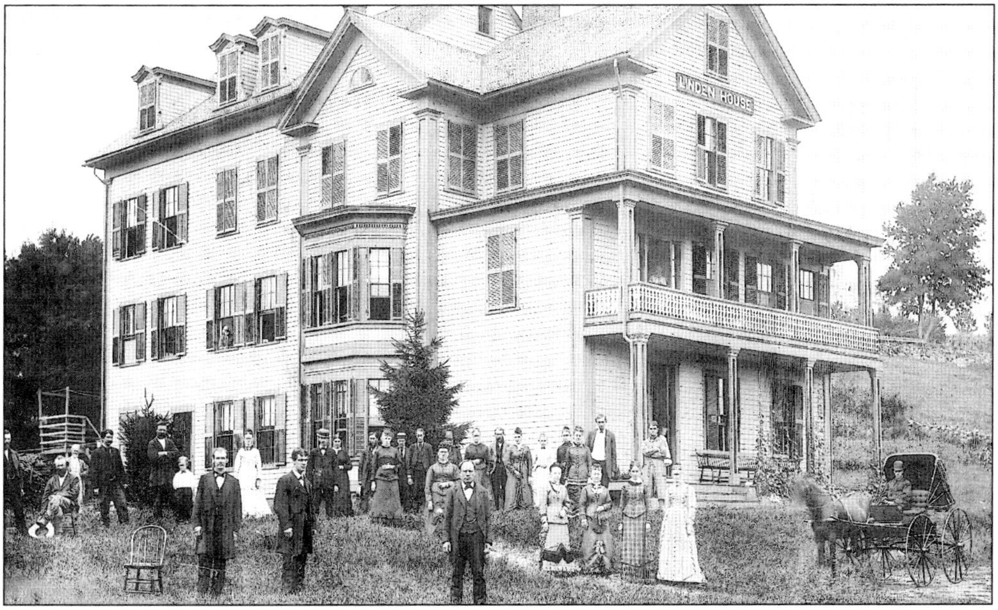

The Linden House, located on Church Street, was considered the town's "oldest hotel." George Bowditch leased the property from 1891 until 1900, when a Mr. McQuaid became the proprietor. It was rated as one of the state's first-class boarding houses, advertising "scrupulously clean, large, comfortable and airy rooms." In 1906, "transients" were charged $1 per day, while rates for "permanents" were fixed by agreement.

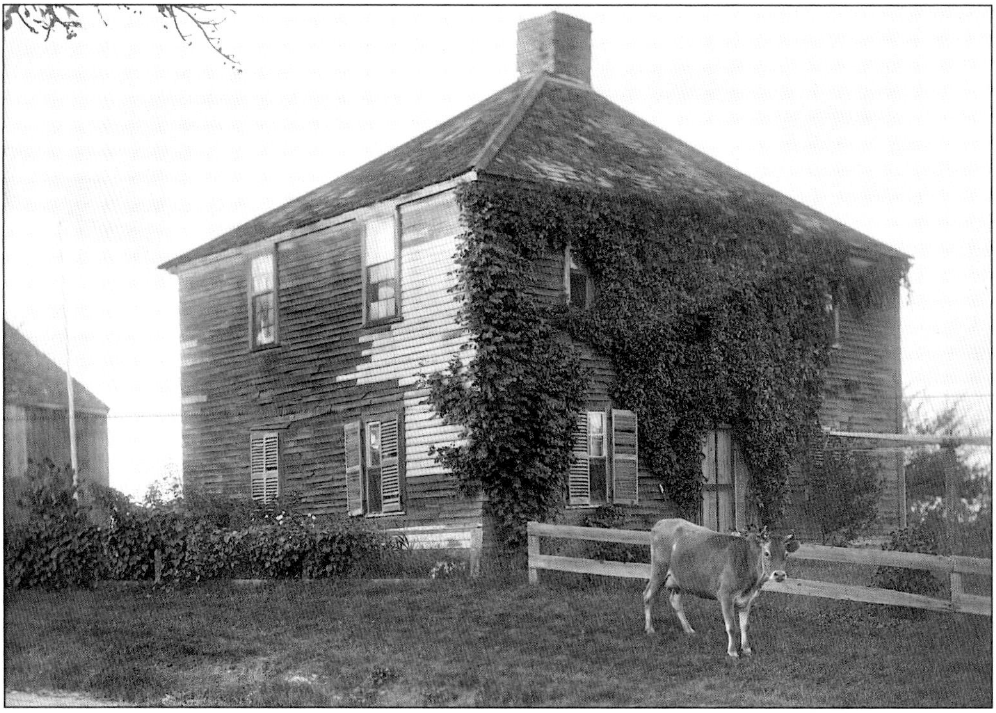

The Old Abbey, once located on Lindell Avenue, was built in 1738 by Josiah White. The sawmill owner built his house to last, using 3-inch planks in the construction. The building was named by Horace Cook for its fancied resemblance to a place described in an old novel. The Old Abbey was closely linked with Leominster's earliest history. In 1795, it became a tavern operated by Hopetele Leland; it was used to hide slaves in later years. The Old Abbey was torn down in the 1930s.

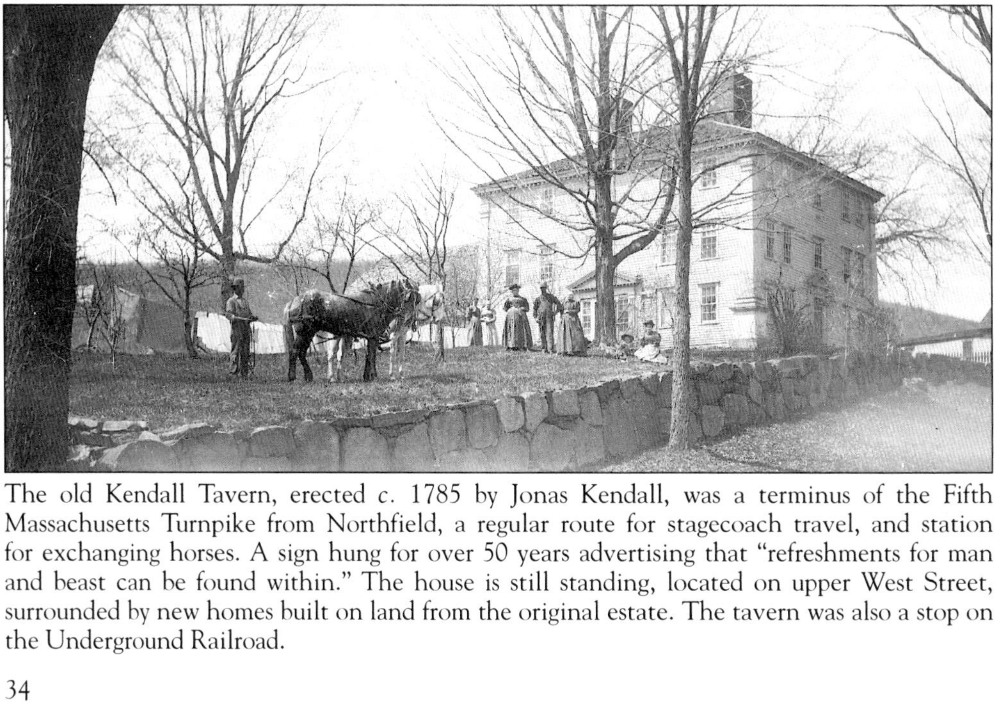

The old Kendall Tavern, erected c. 1785 by Jonas Kendall, was a terminus of the Fifth Massachusetts Turnpike from Northfield, a regular route for stagecoach travel, and station for exchanging horses. A sign hung for over 50 years advertising that "refreshments for man and beast can be found within." The house is still standing, located on upper West Street, surrounded by new homes built on land from the original estate. The tavern was also a stop on the Underground Railroad.

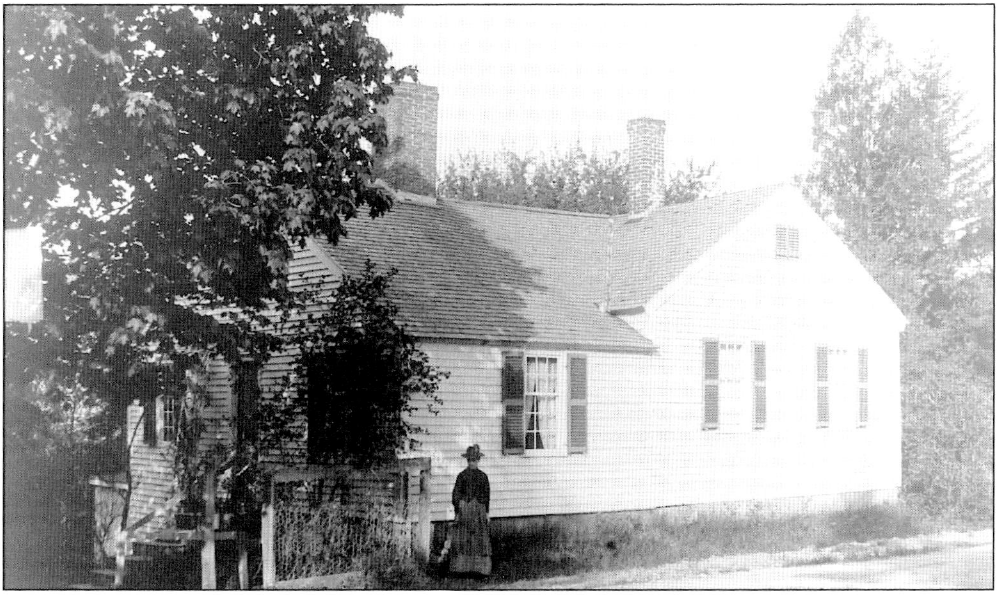

Historian Mary Tolman stands in front of her home at 140 West Street. One of Leominster's oldest homes, it was owned by Oliver Carter, whose father gave Carter Park to the town. The house was a 1763 addition to a tannery already on site. Carter sold the house and tannery to Benjamin Hawks, whose habit of setting traps to catch his neighbors' chickens was the origin of the nickname "Chicken Harbor." The "little red house by the road" is still standing.

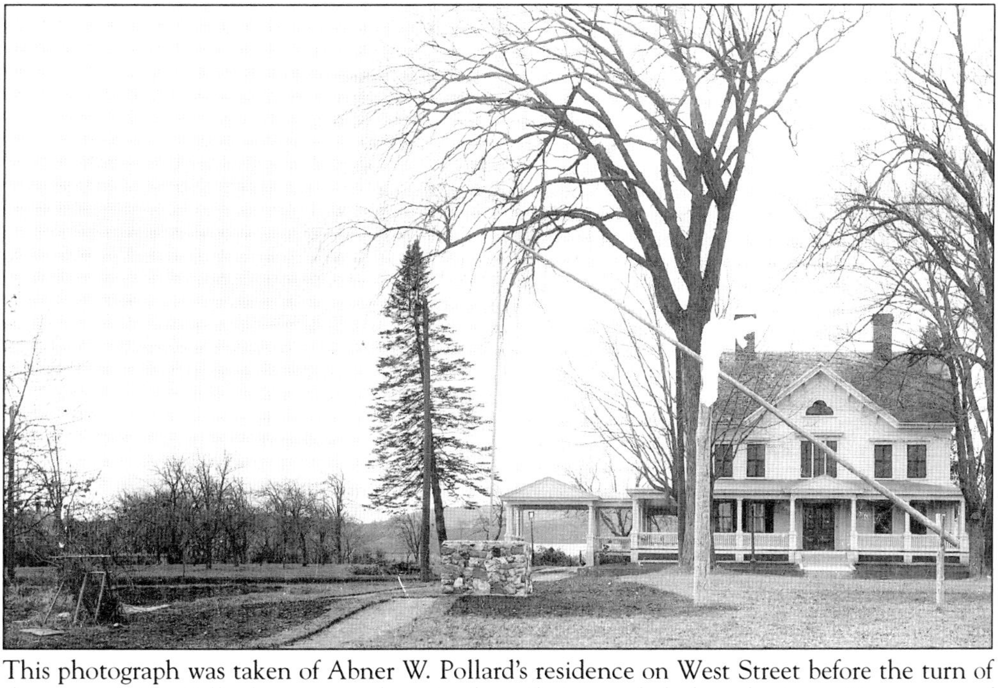

This photograph was taken of Abner W. Pollard's residence on West Street before the turn of the century. Mr. Pollard was a merchant in the tailoring and clothing business. He was one of the founders of the largest fashion publishing company in the world and served as its treasurer for 30 years. This home stands today opposite the Carter Junior High building. The sweep well and front yard are now part of West Street.

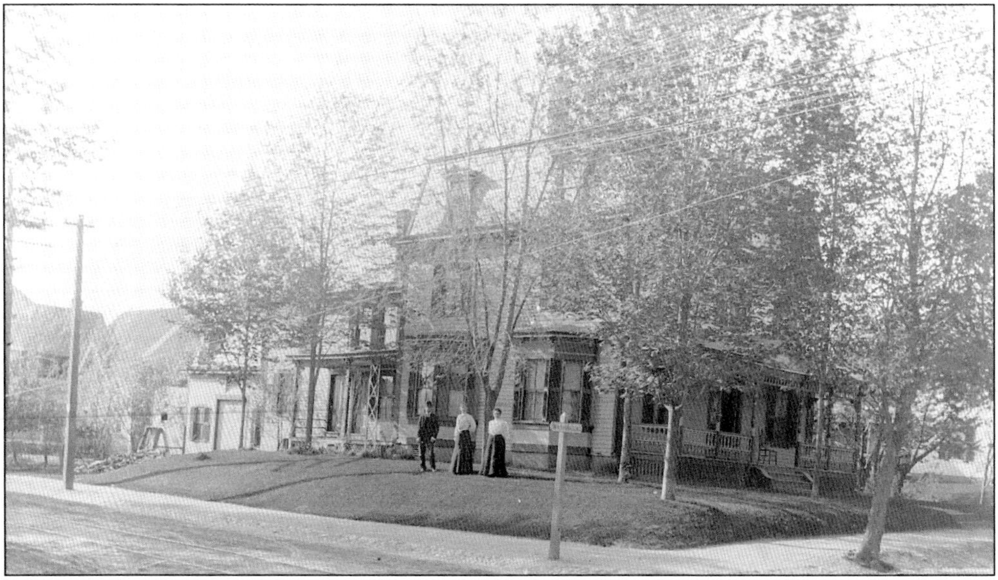

The Henry M. Bosworth residence at 32 Washington Street was built between 1870 and 1890; Henry Bosworth, a painter, moved here between 1891 and 1892. His widow, Georgia, continued to live in the house until 1920 and had it converted into a three-family dwelling. The house still stands today at the corner of Washington Street and Merriam Avenue.

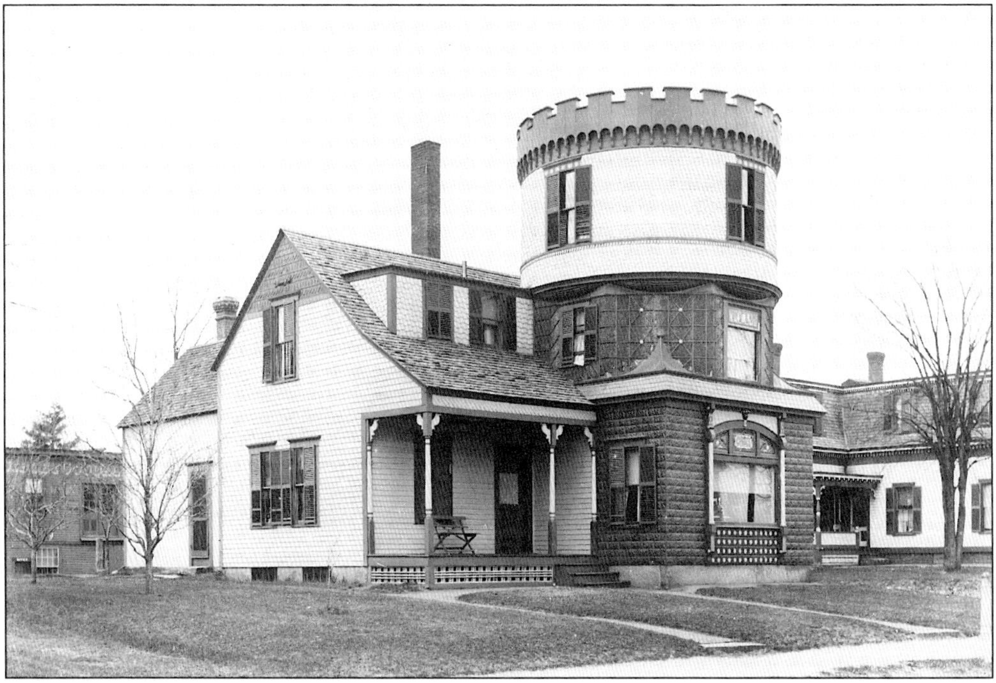

A turn-of-the-century view of Leominster's three-bay "wedding cake house," also known as the Houde House after its builder, carpenter and mason Adolphe Houde. This wonderful and unusual home was built in 1891 as an "advertisement" for Houde, who designed it to feature the variety of construction styles and techniques he could offer his customers. It has been recently renovated and still stands today at 87 Union Street.

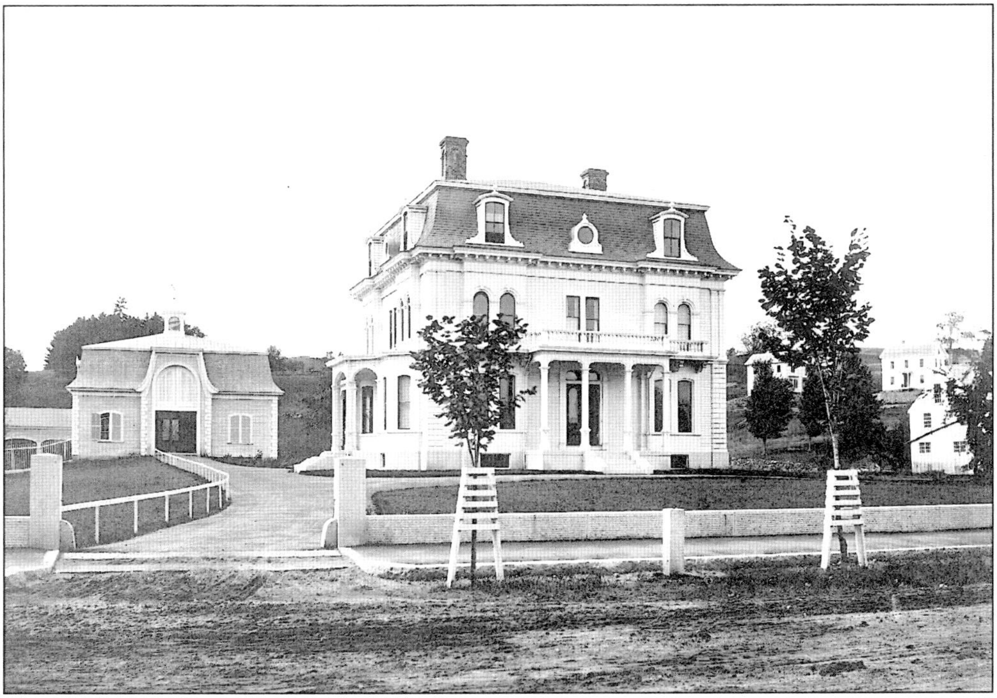

This beautiful, three-story colonial building, now St. Leo's Rectory, was part of the former Phelps estate. Located on Main Street, it was renovated from attic to cellar by the Reverend Michael Slattery, who served as pastor in 1930. The round, stained-glass window set in the front of the building is the old Massachusetts state seal. St. Leo's Church was completed in 1900.

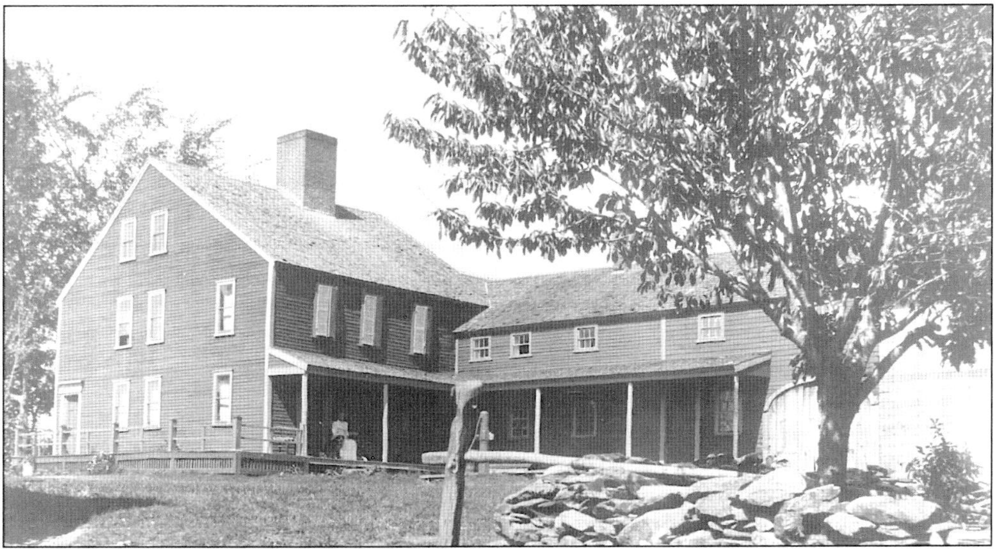

This view is of the Wilder Homestead on Lake Whalom. The Wilder family was one of the original Proprietors of Leominster; their land extended from the lake almost to the Fitchburg train station. The house, no longer standing, was located on Wilder Road, at the fork where the road divides. An original garrison house, built for protection against Native Americans, stood across from the homestead.

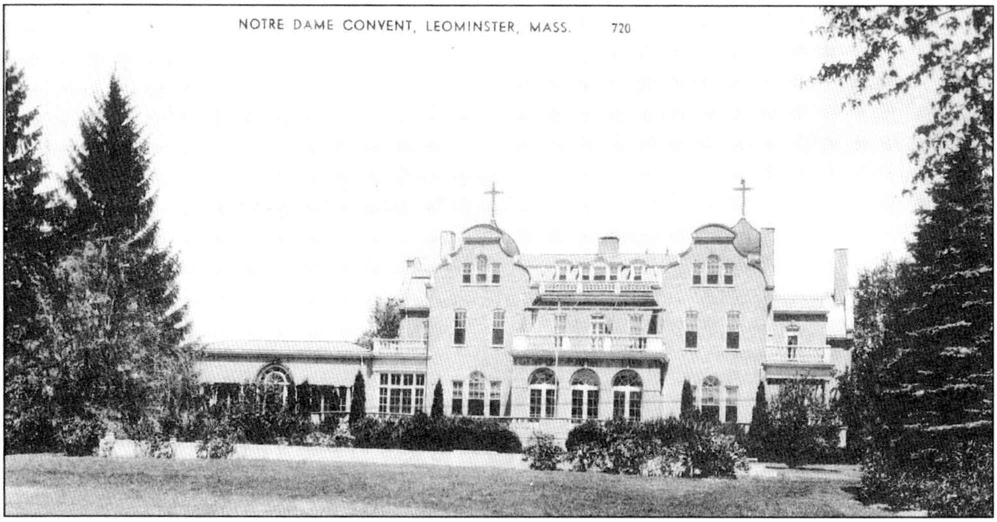

"Grayling Hall," located at the corner of Merriam and Lindell Avenues, has a wonderful history. The land was originally purchased by Timothy Kendall. His house was moved down Lindell Avenue on logs when Joel Crosby, once General Washington's bodyguard, purchased the property in the 1790s and built a large federal house there. In 1905, industrialist Harry Pierce built Grayling Hall. The next owner was Mr. Ewing, known as the "Tapioca King," who sold the estate to the Sisters of Notre Dame when his wife died. The postcard shows the convent.

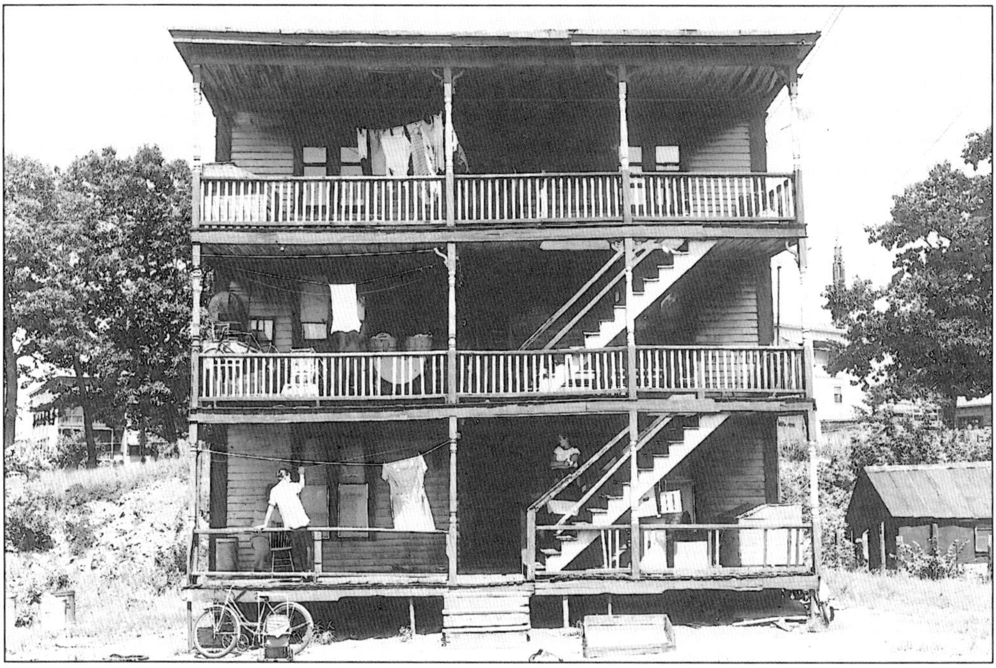

This "French Hill" three-decker has seen better days; it is not representative of most of the homes found today, which are owner-occupied and kept up quite well. This was one of the most heavily populated areas of town. Many people walked to their jobs in the plastic factories and machine shops from their homes on "The Hill." The steeple of St. Cecilia's Church can also be seen in this 1940s photo.

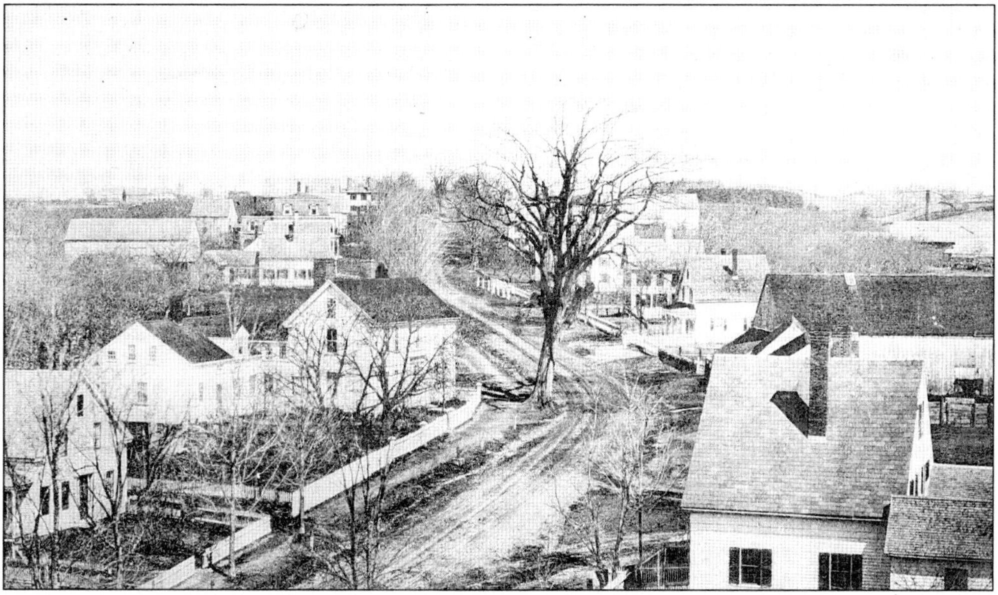

This interesting photograph of Main Street in North Leominster was taken in the 1860s from the Congregational Church steeple. It solves the puzzle of why the turn in the road exists just after the railroad underpass. It seems the large elm tree in the picture belonged to a prominent citizen who refused to let the tree be cut down. The tree remained and the curve in the road is noticeable today to all who use this heavily traveled road.

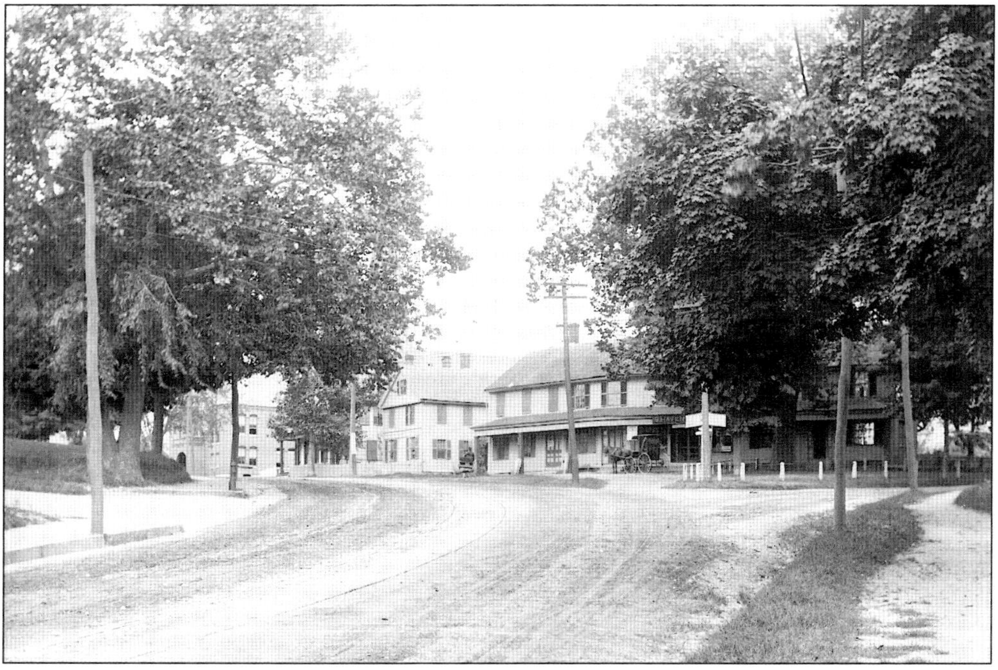

This quiet and peaceful intersection of 1901 has become today's traffic nightmare at Main and Prospect Streets. Pierce Street School is at the left and the store behind the sign post is S. Haven and Sons Groceries at 565 Main Street.

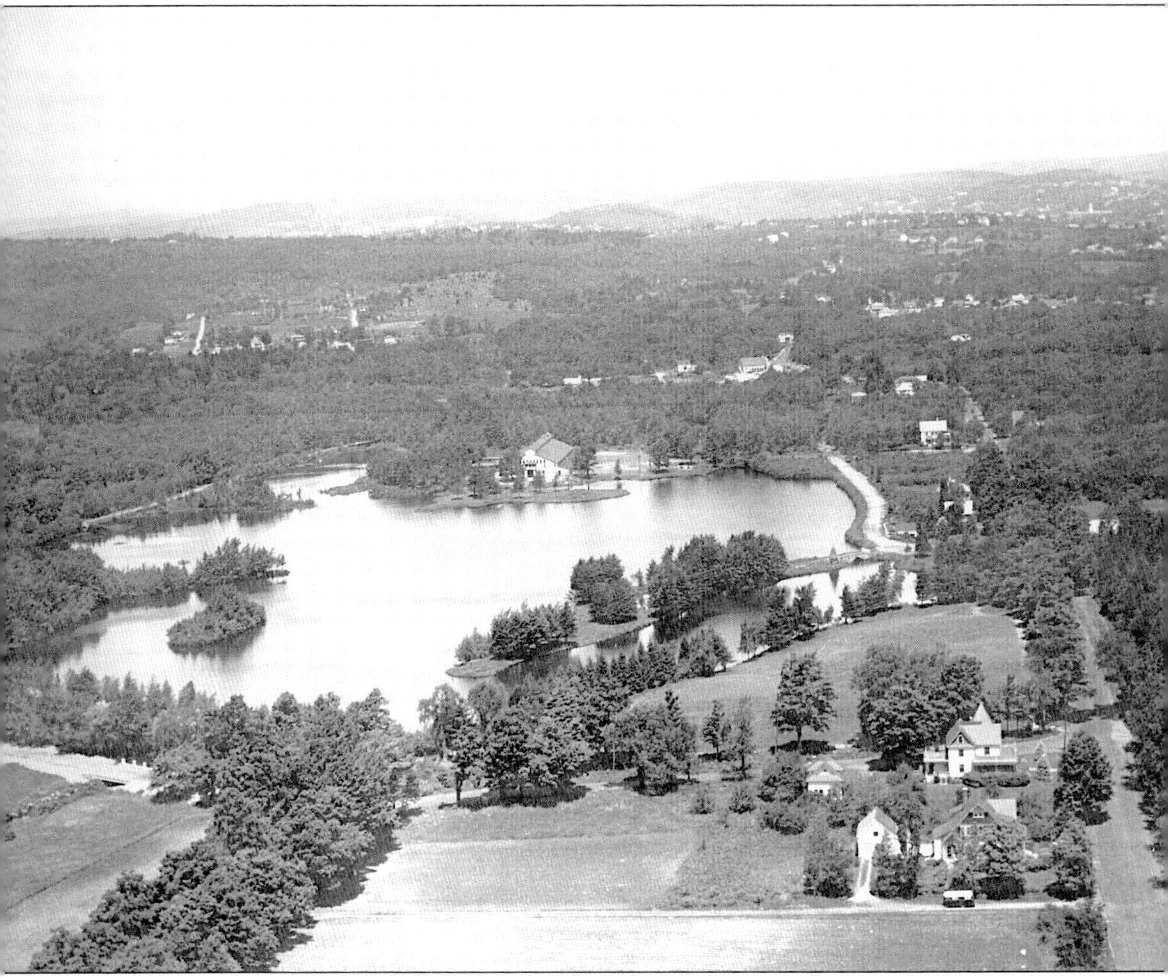

Harry K. Pierce created the man-made Pierce's Pond as a backdrop for his riding path and large stable. In this aerial view, you can see Lindell Avenue on your right; at this time, it ended at Merriam Avenue. Grayling Hall is out of view on the right. Pierce's estate was a showplace; if it were built today it would cost $3 million! He built an attached glass building for his Southern-born wife's "Palm Court" so she could enjoy her palm trees through the New England winters. When he sold the mansion to Mr. Ewing, the "Tapioca King" filled the mansion with priceless works of art from all over Europe. Today, the Julie Country Day school utilizes the garage and small stable building; Grayling Hall is in disrepair and set to be demolished.

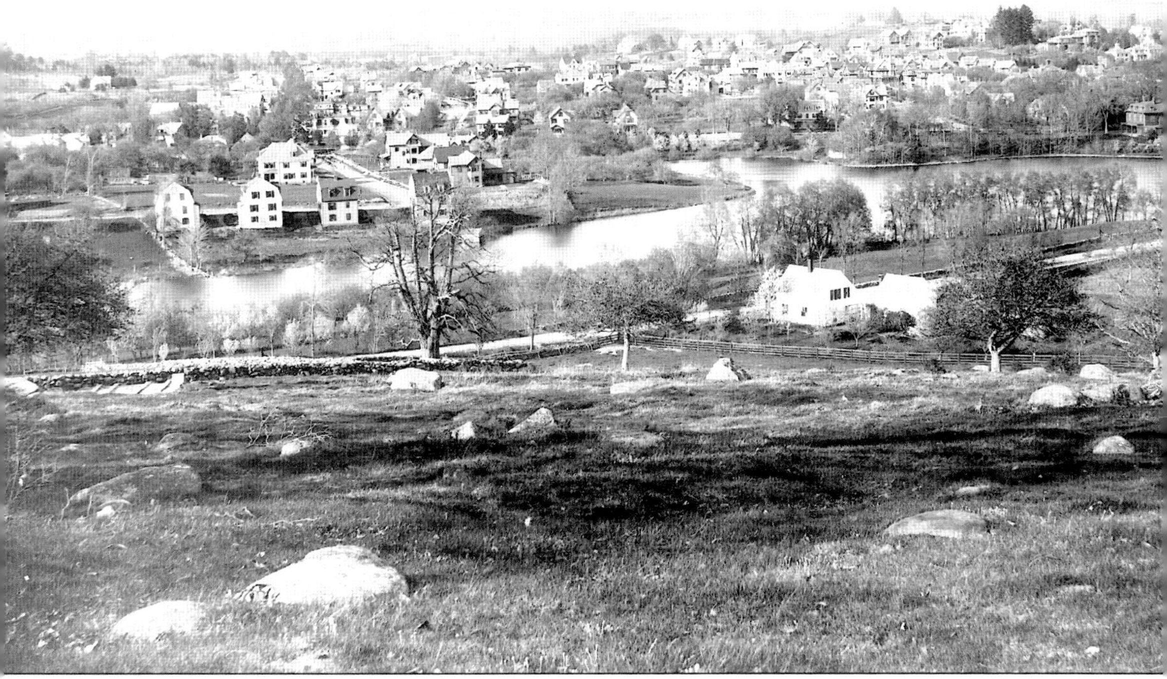

This photograph of Leominster at the turn of the 20th century was taken from Gardner Hill. Rockwell Pond can be seen as well as the Salisbury Mansion on the far right. Elm Street is in the foreground, at the foot of the hill.

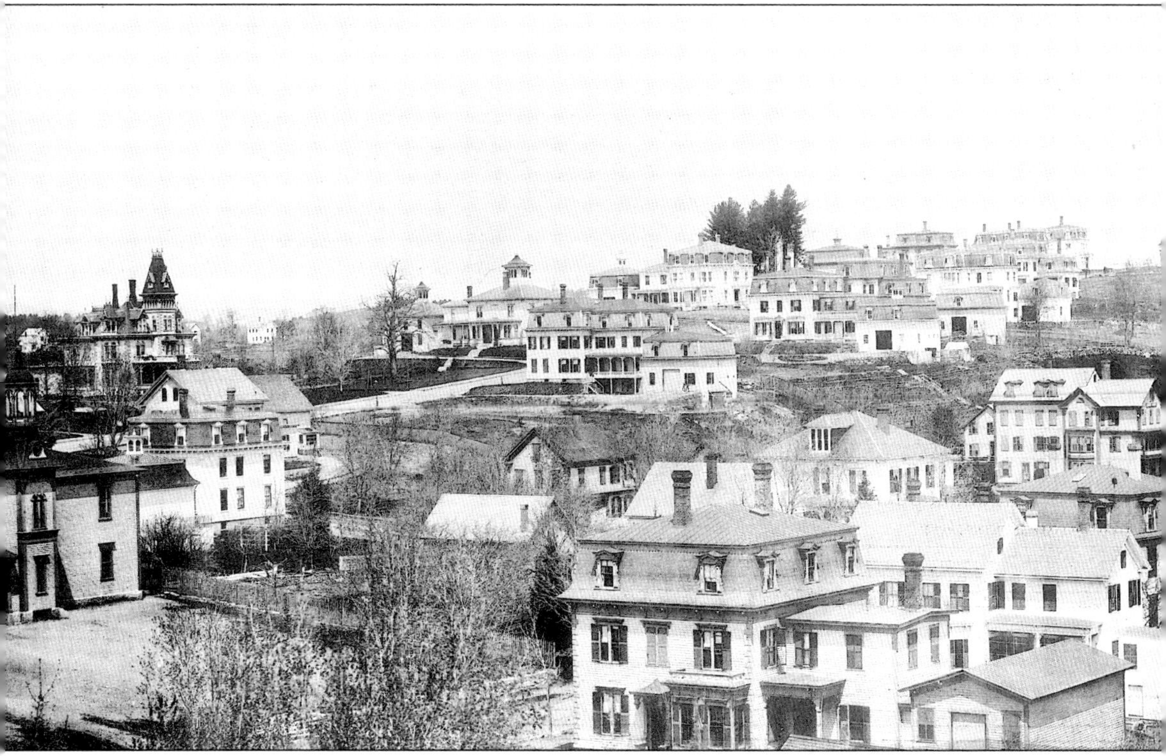

This photograph is a view from the Unitarian church, which shows Grove Avenue. These elegant homes were owned by many of Leominster's leading industrialists. Note the absence of trees, especially larger varieties. At the time these homes were constructed, the land was virtually cleared of trees.

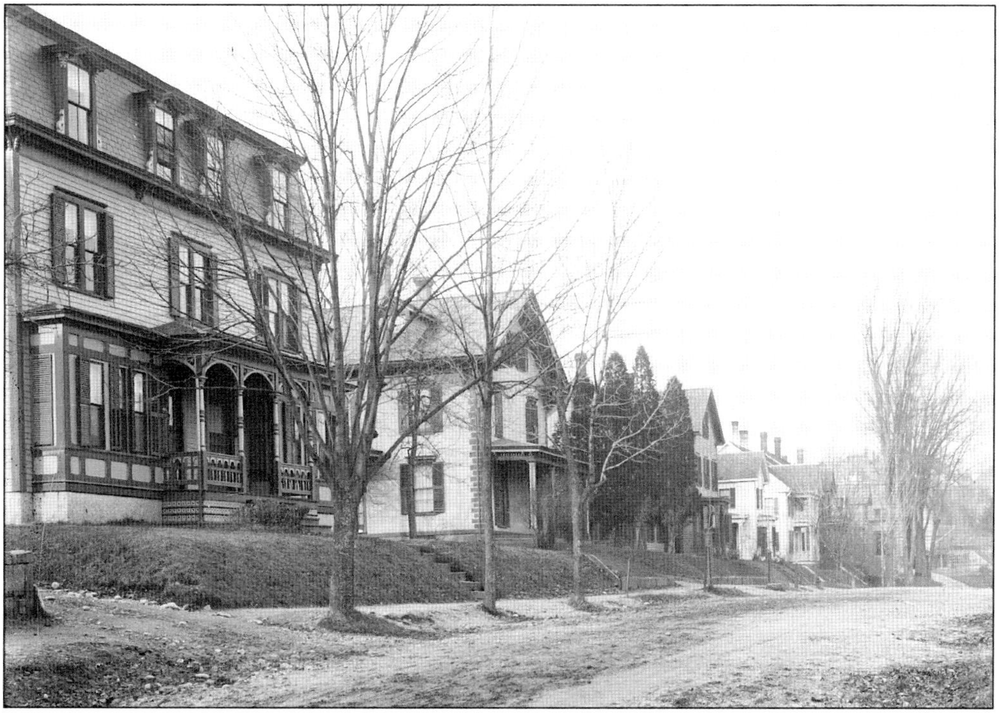

This view of School Street from West Street shows the homes in 1895. All of the houses shown are still standing; the Gallagher Junior High School building at the end of the street is now the courthouse. Many of the homes have been converted into attorneys' offices. The second house in the photograph was the residence of Arthur C. Merriam.

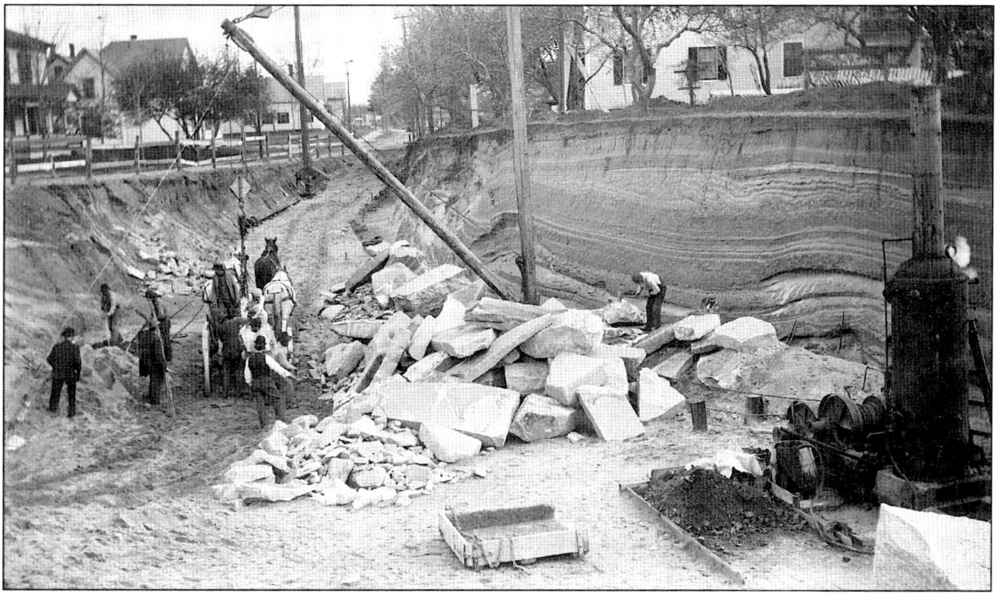

This 1897 photograph shows the use of animal and steam power to lower the grade at the intersection of Lancaster and Graham Streets. The railroad bridge built at this site caused problems for many tractor-trailer trucks in the 1980s; they got stuck under the low clearance underpass.

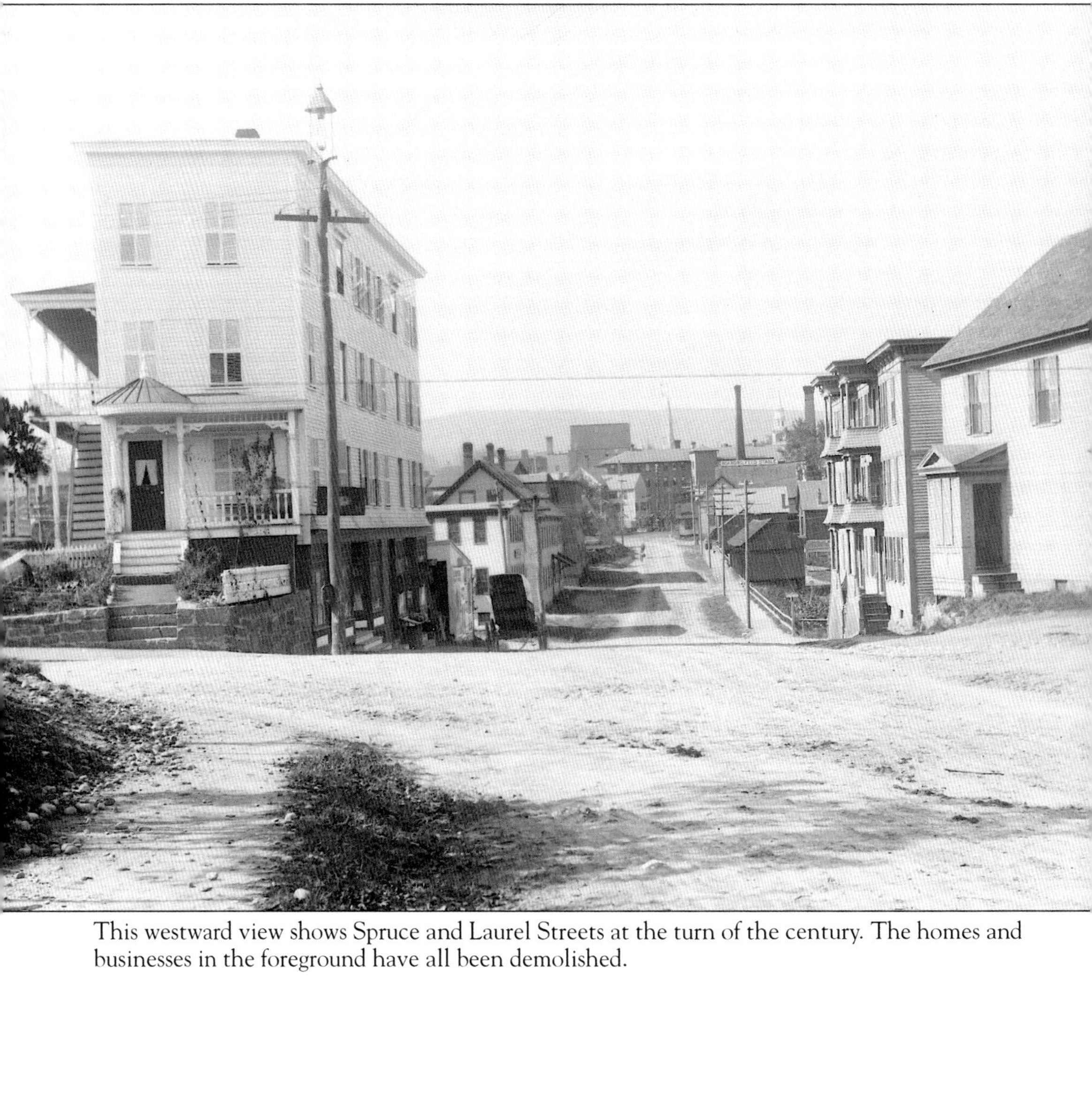

This westward view shows Spruce and Laurel Streets at the turn of the century. The homes and businesses in the foreground have all been demolished.

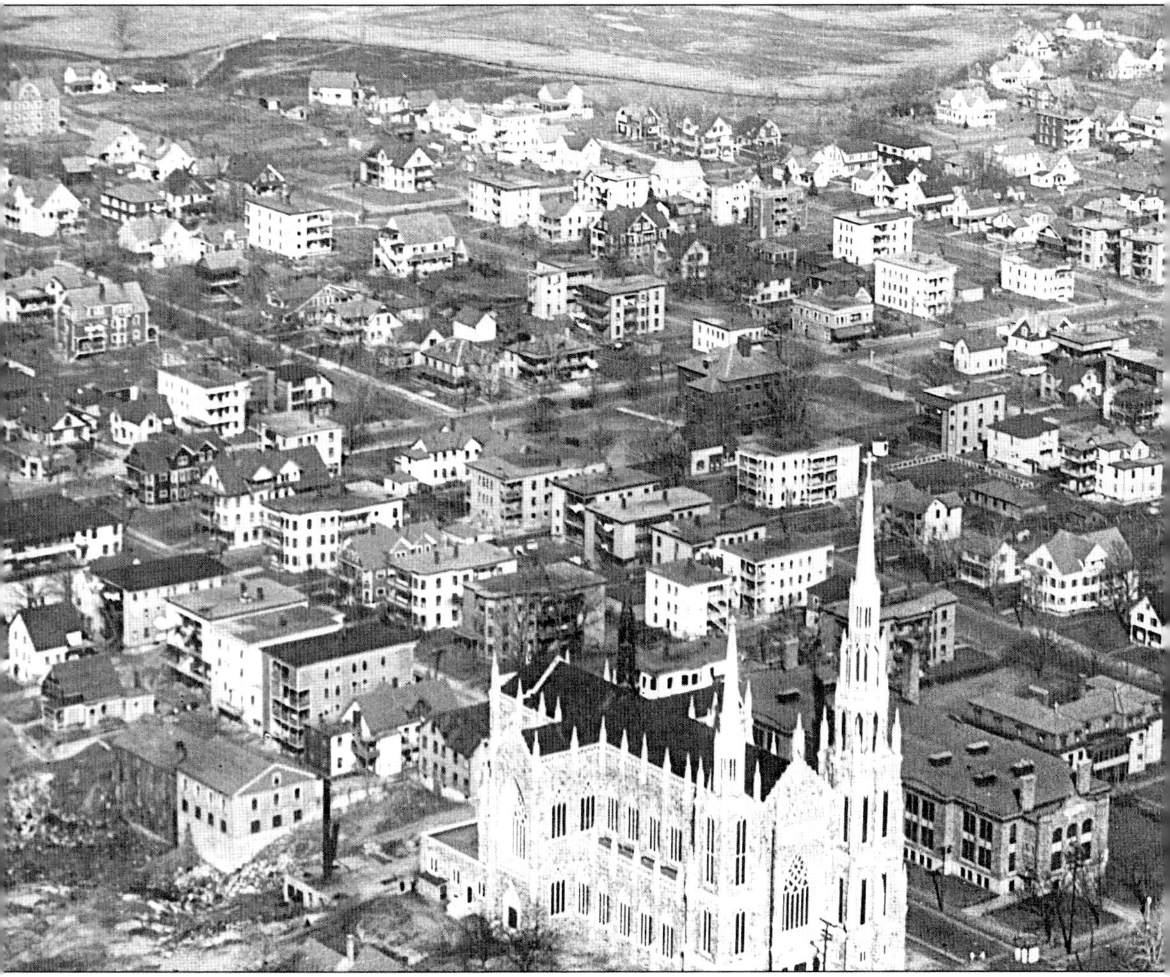

This aerial view of Leominster's East Side (the "French Hill" section) was taken in the mid-1930s. Buildings seen here, from bottom left to right, are Lamothe's Hall, St. Cecilia's Church, the former St. Cecilia's parochial school, and the former Spruce Street school, replaced by the Mathias Lapierre Senior Citizen High Rise apartments. Whitney Field (now Searstown) is at the top of the picture.

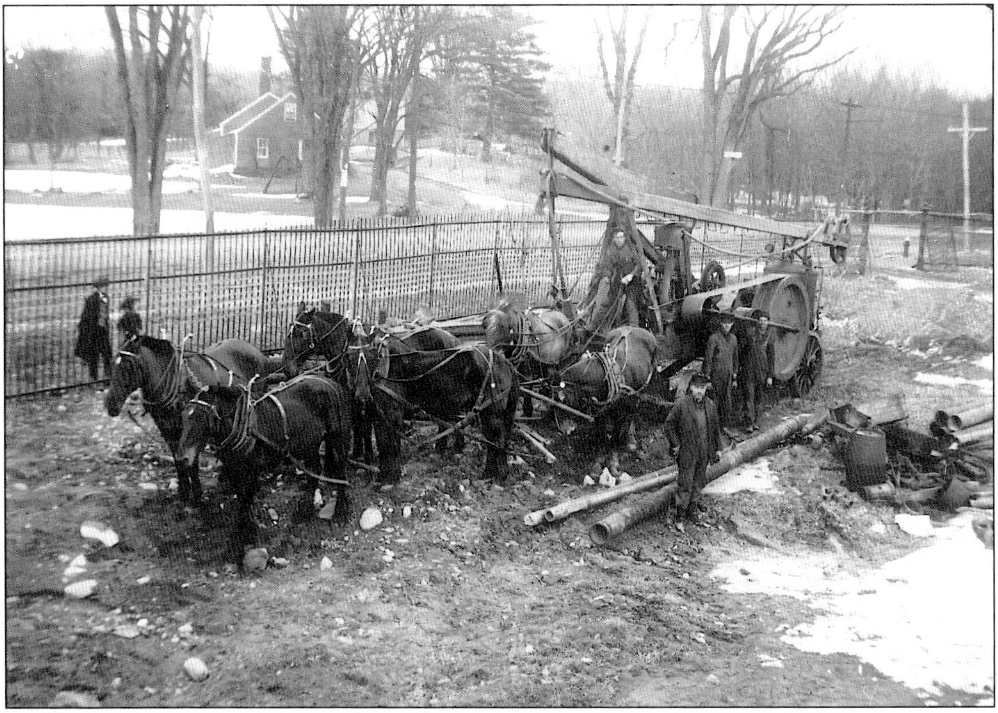

Drilling for water wells was important work; this photograph shows the six-horse team needed to haul a drilling rig. The location is Viscoloid Avenue; Paul Gates's house is in the background.

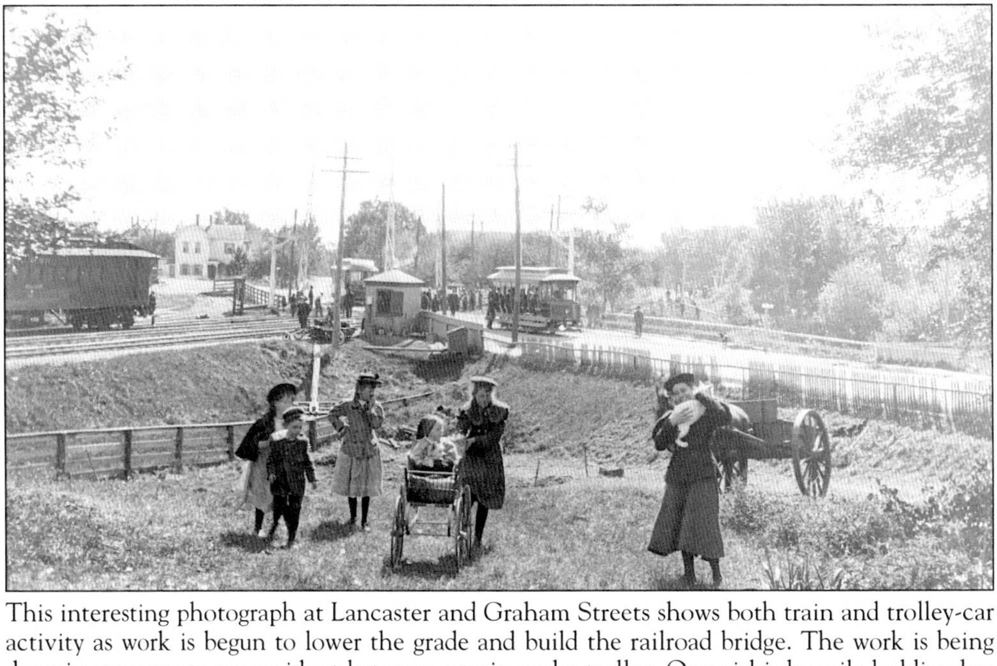

This interesting photograph at Lancaster and Graham Streets shows both train and trolley-car activity as work is begun to lower the grade and build the railroad bridge. The work is being done in response to an accident between a train and a trolley. One girl is happily holding her cat in front of a pony cart; another girl pushes her little sister and her puppy in a Whitney carriage. The lone boy in this picture probably wishes he could join the workmen!

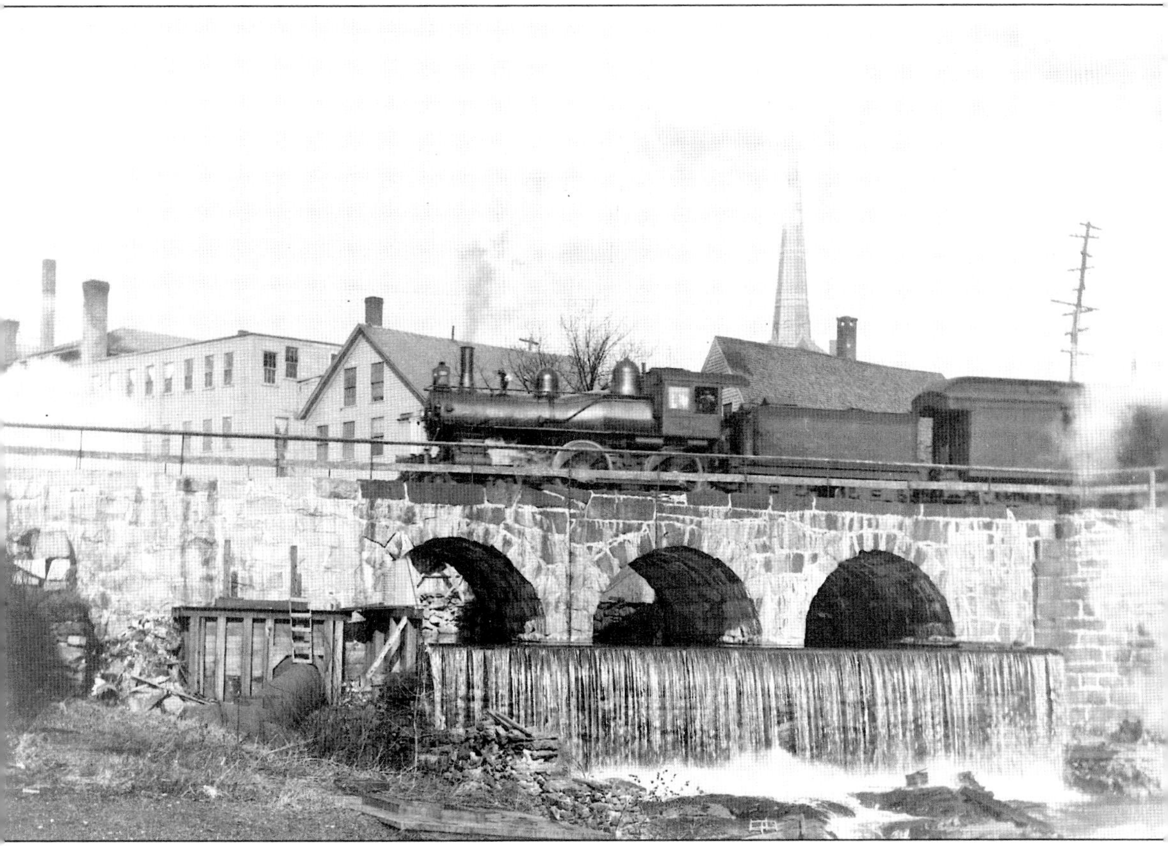

The Water Street Bridge saw heavy train traffic in and out of the Depot Square area. This bridge, like others of its day, was built to withstand the test of time. Many of them remain in use today. The Water Street Bridge was built in 1847 and was used by the New York and New Haven Railroad for passenger and freight traffic until 1946; it used the rail for freight only from 1947 to 1955. Conrail and other companies then used the track until service was discontinued in the late 1970s. At present, there is talk of re-establishing rail service; the bridge, still in excellent condition, would be ready!

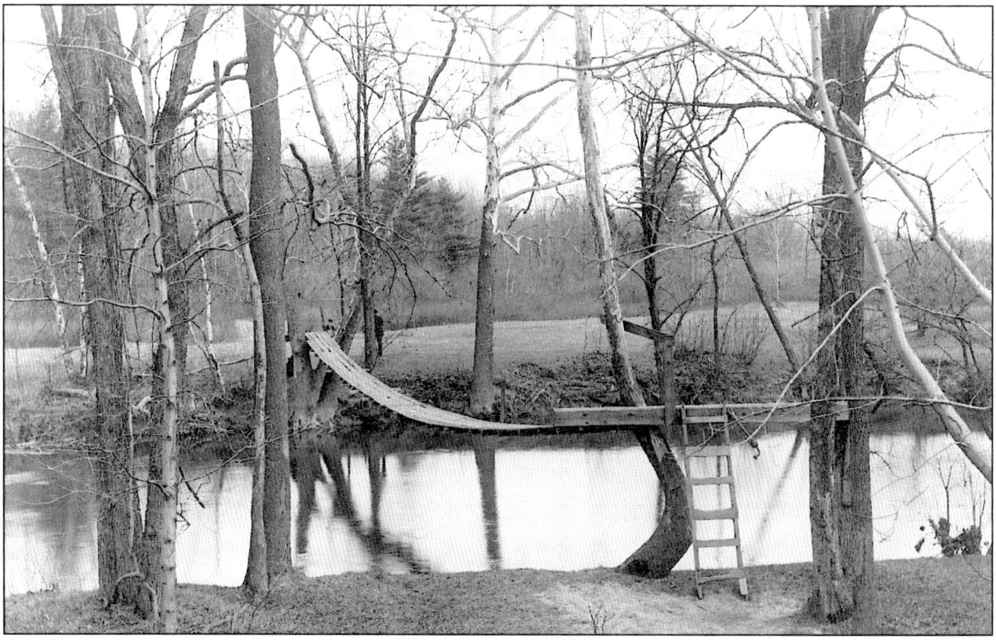

The old swing bridge in North Leominster ran across the Nashua River. Workers used it as a shortcut to get to work at the Leatherboard Company. It was not designed for the faint hearted!

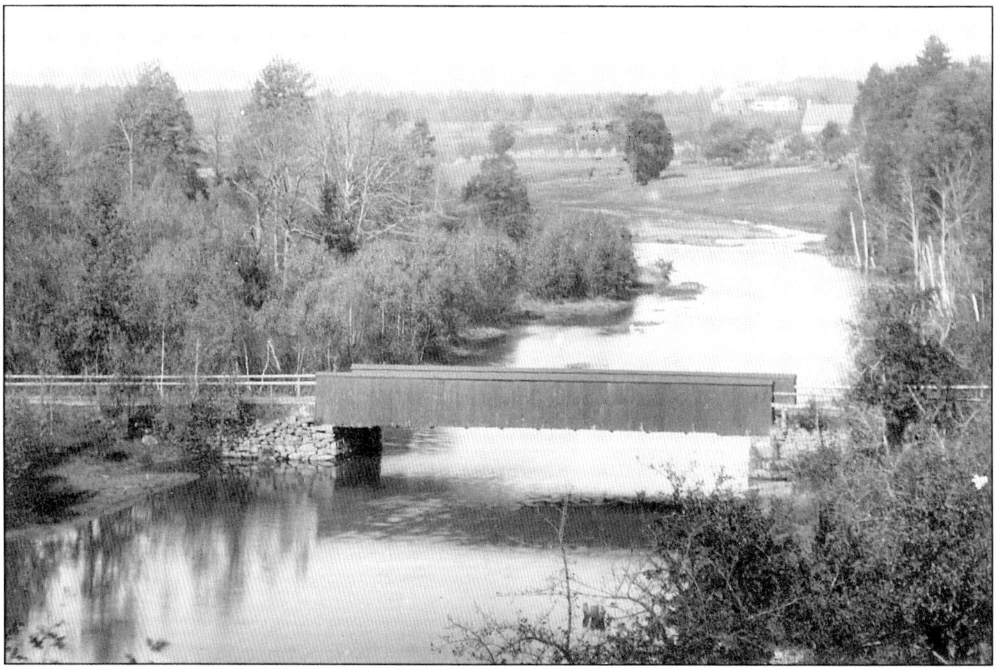

The "Red Bridge" once spanned the Nashua River on Mechanic Street near Johnny Appleseed Lane; it was a wooden construction that was painted red. In 1925, Mayor Sawtelle recommended to the City Council that the bridge be replaced, as it was built in the era of horse-drawn vehicles and was too narrow to accommodate increasing automobile traffic. When the new bridge was washed away in the flood of 1936, the current bridge was built in 1937.

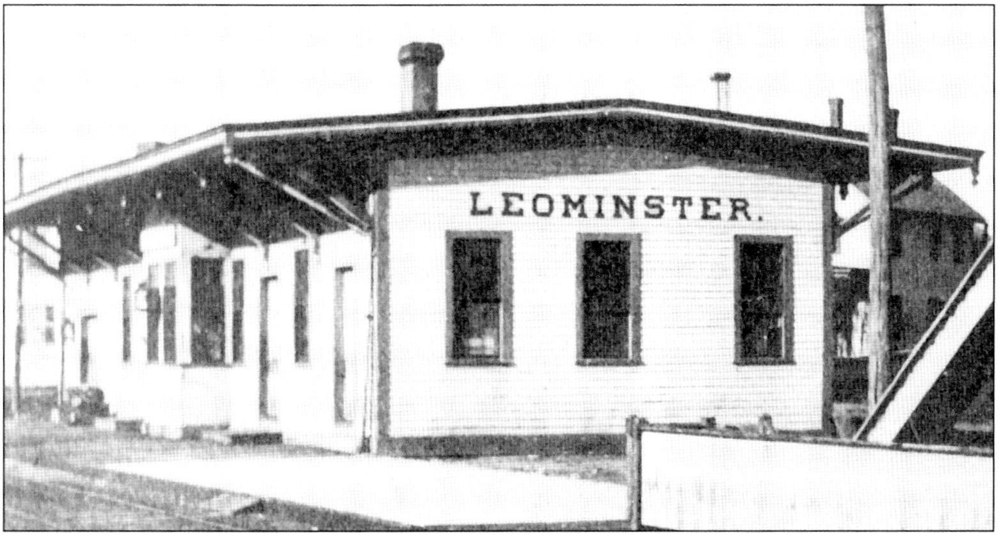

This photograph of the second North Leominster Station in the 1870s was taken from the bridge, looking at the rear of the station. There were three depots on this site. The first one burned; the second building was eventually leveled and the lumber was used to build Fairview Farm. The last depot, built in 1899, was replaced by Wyman's Package Store.

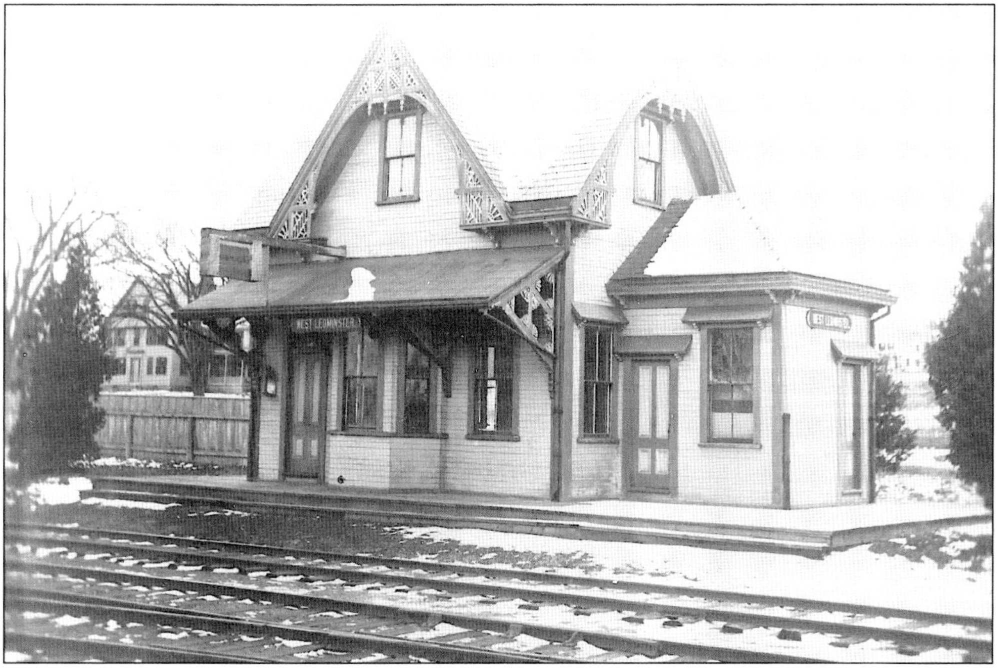

The West Leominster Depot was located on North Main Street, near the junction of Hamilton Street. When rail service was discontinued, the depot was moved from this site to 16 Nelson Street and converted into a single-family home. The house was sold to the McDonald's Corporation in 1976 and razed to make room for their new restaurant.

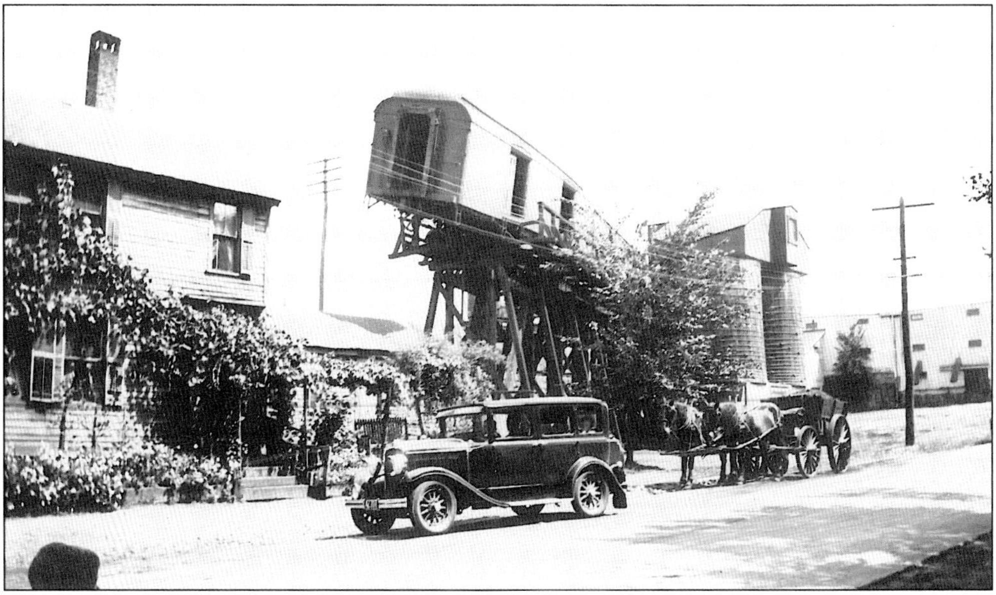

This unusual photograph was taken in North Leominster, approximately a quarter-mile from the North Leominster railroad bridge and depot. While the train was unloading, the support structures gave way, creating this scene. Amazingly, no injuries were reported and the elevation supports were replaced by a fill-type incline approach to the bridge that remains in place today.

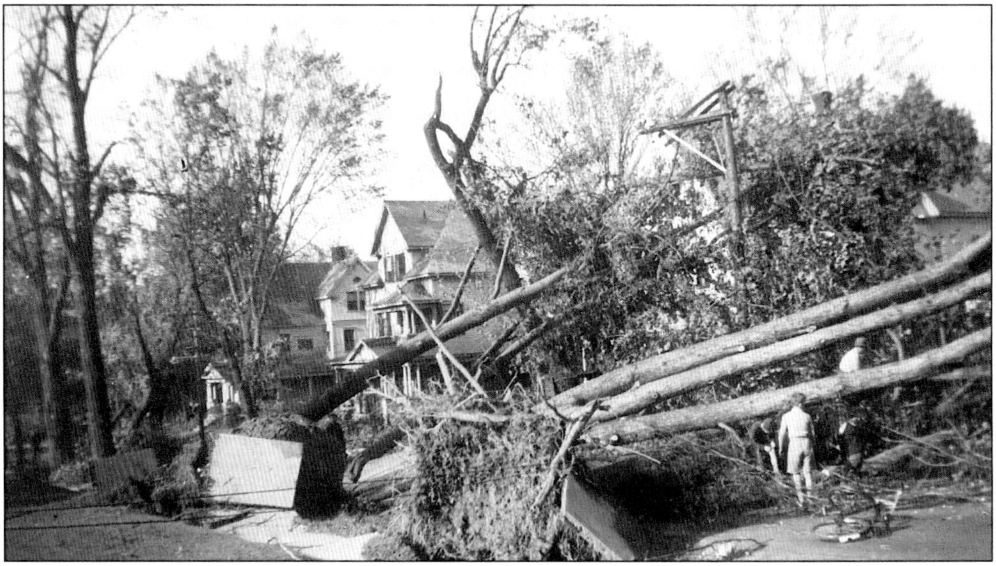

The worst storm in city history struck on the evening of September 21, 1938. The hurricane's screeching winds toppled trees and chimneys, downed electric and telephone lines, shattered glass, ripped through buildings, and tore off roofs throughout Leominster. Roads were blocked by uprooted trees in every section of the city. Hundreds worked feverishly to restore order and repair damage, including City departments, the WPA, and the U.S. National Guard. In this photograph, Washington Street is impassable.

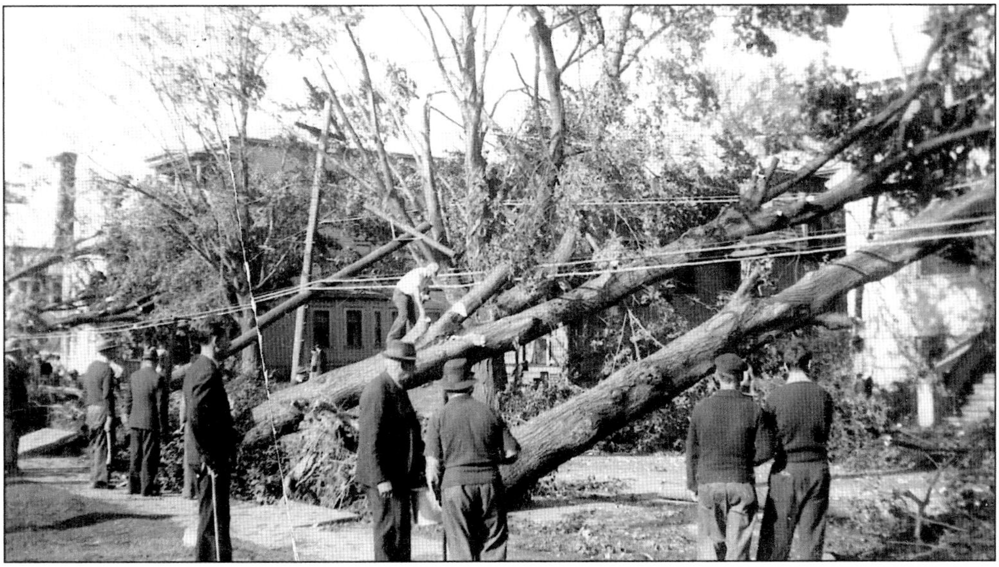

Trees and downed power lines block Pleasant Street in front of the Leominster Heating Company. Telephone and electric services were crippled, with estimates of over $1 million in storm damage. Many stately elms and maples on the West Side and the Common were lost, as well as 500 pine trees, whose possible removal had been the source of major controversy between Mayor Sidney Bell and the planning board.

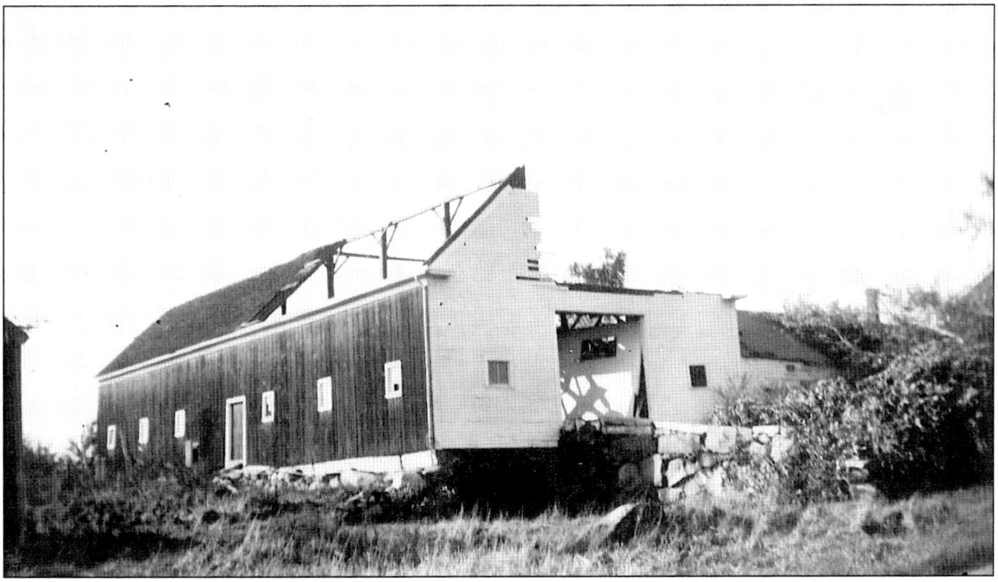

The roof and hayloft of Paul Washburn's barn at Sholan Farm is sheared off. Miraculously, no serious injuries were reported during the hurricane, other than a 60-year-old man who suffered a fatal heart attack. The storm's aftermath, however, claimed the life of 10-year-old Harold Hildreth when a fallen limb pinned him to a tree trunk as he played near his home on Adams Street.

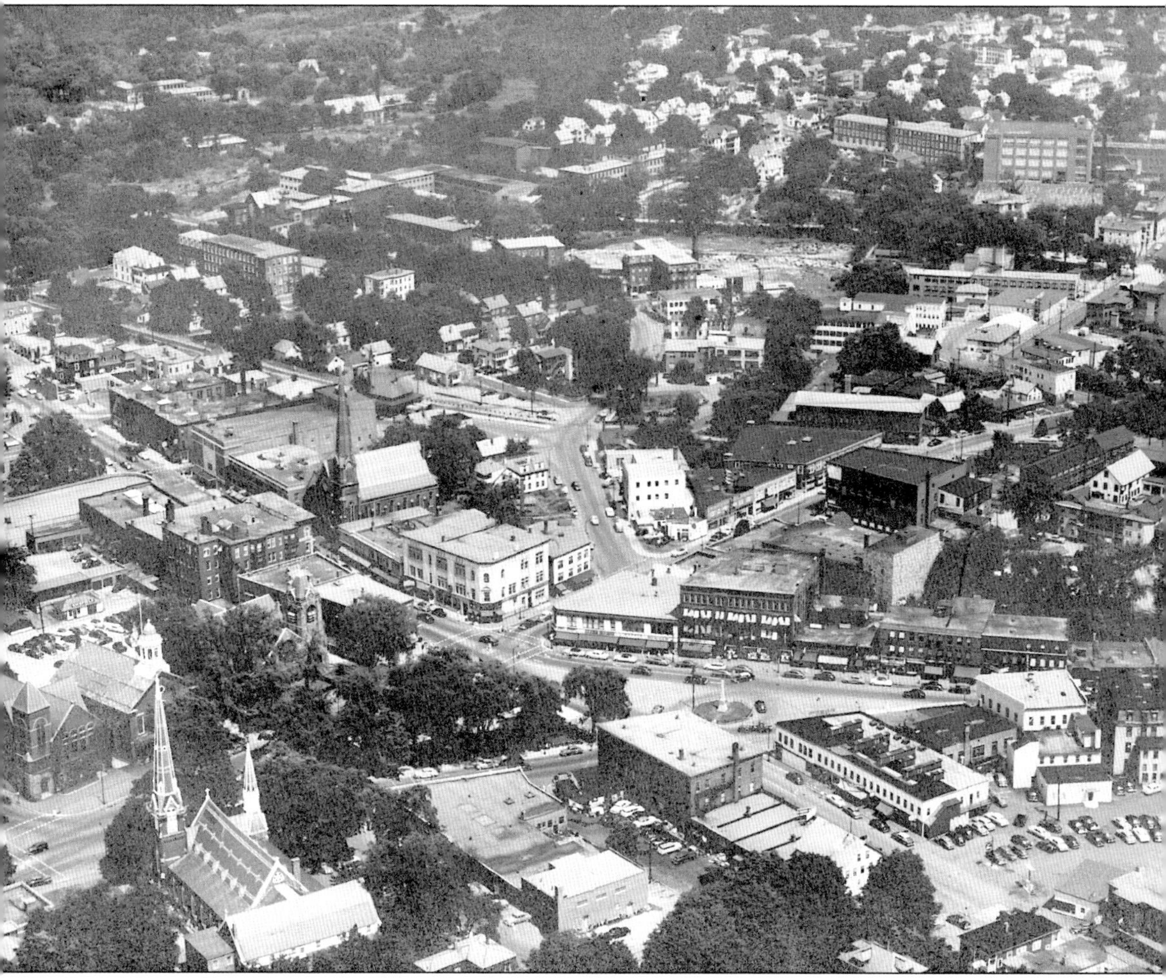

This excellent aerial view of the city was taken in 1953. The photograph shows over 20 easily spotted changes to downtown and the surrounding area. Can you identify them?

Three

DOWNTOWN

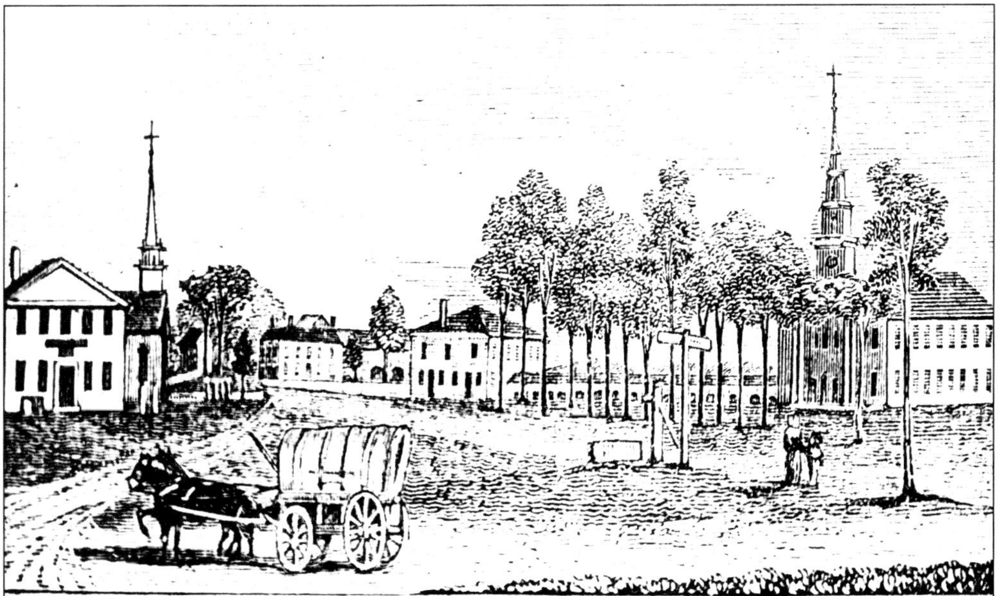

South-eastern view of the central part of Leominster.

This early view of Leominster Center dates to *c.* 1838; the drawing was made from a spot where Pleasant Street and Monument Square join, looking across land that will eventually become the Common. The first building on the left was Henry Allen's store on Park Street, where he "sold everything from whale oil to cambric needles." Next is the Orthodox church, which burned in 1872. After the trees is the Johnson home on West Street; the large square building is the First Town House. Horse sheds extend over to the first Unitarian church, built in 1823. The water pump and sign were replaced with the Civil War monument.

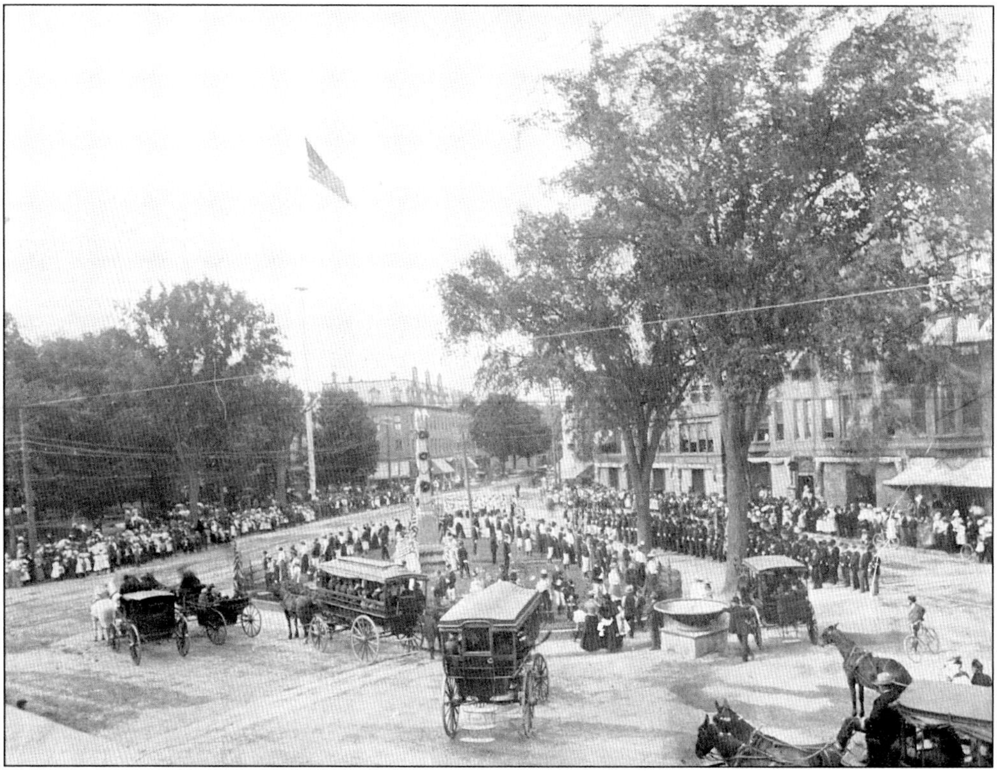

This view of the Memorial Day celebration of 1900 in Monument Square was taken from a rooftop at the corner of Pleasant Street. Members of the GAR and the Leominster Cadets stand guard next to the decorated Civil War Soldier's monument. Note the large circular watering trough.

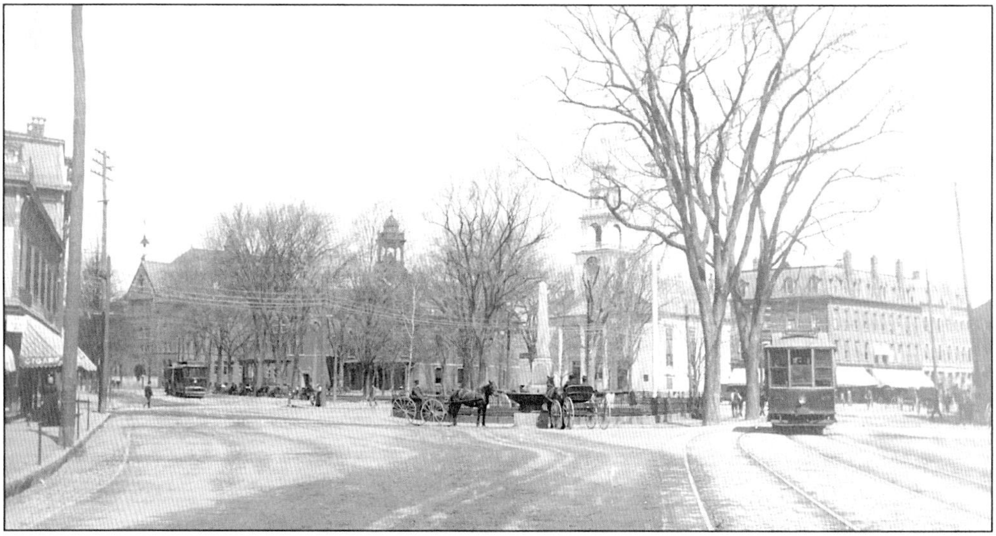

This view from the south side of Monument Square, looking northeast, dates from the turn of the century. A trolley approaches from the right; on the left, cobblestones can still be seen in the street. The elegant white steeple of the first Unitarian church soars above the Common, graced by the stately elms which came down in the Hurricane of 1938.

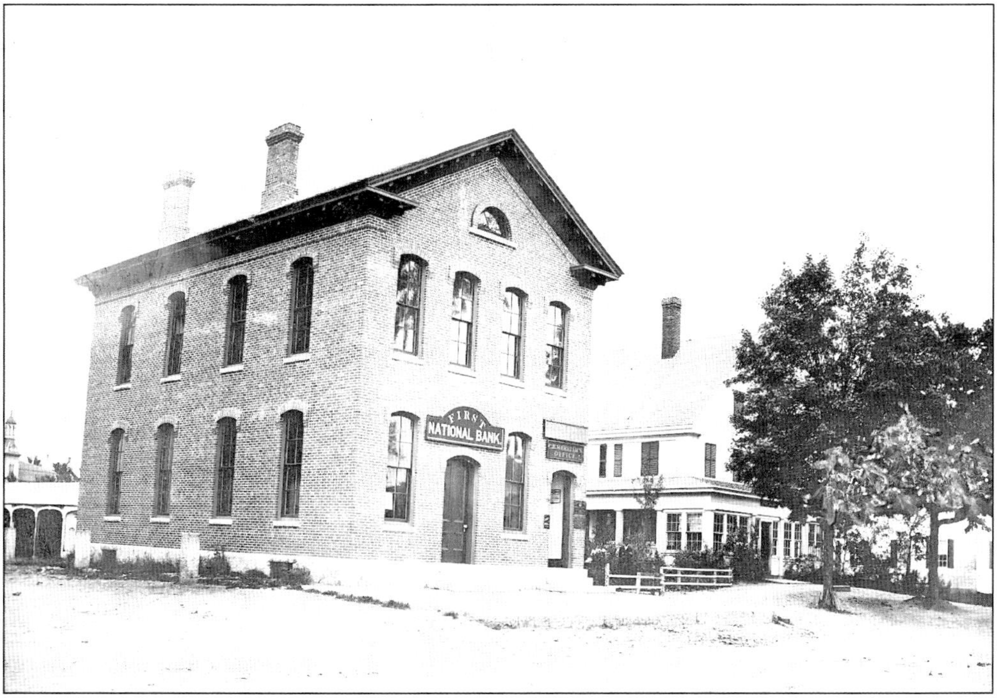

This view is of the corner of Main and Mechanic Streets. where West Street begins. The Foster Block was not yet constructed. The First National Bank was established in 1864; it stood next to the home of Charles Colburn, who sold dry goods and patent medicines. When Colburn became the postmaster, the building also served as a post office. Note the tower of the Field High School on Church Street and the stables of the Unitarian church (left).

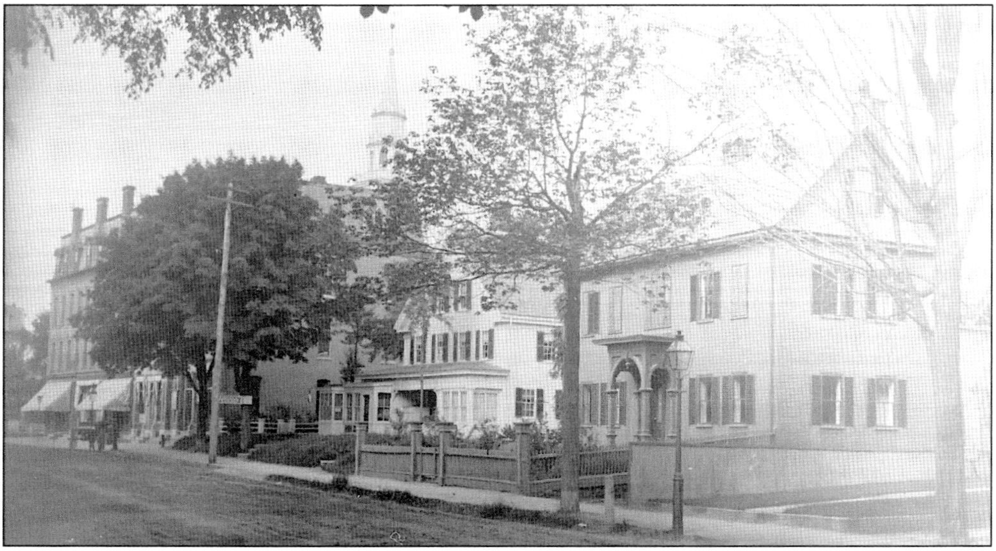

This view looks southwest down Main Street, towards the common. The brick house on the right was the home of James Bennett; in old photograph books of Leominster, he can be seen sitting in his doorway. Further on the left you see the new Foster Block and the steeple of the Unitarian church.

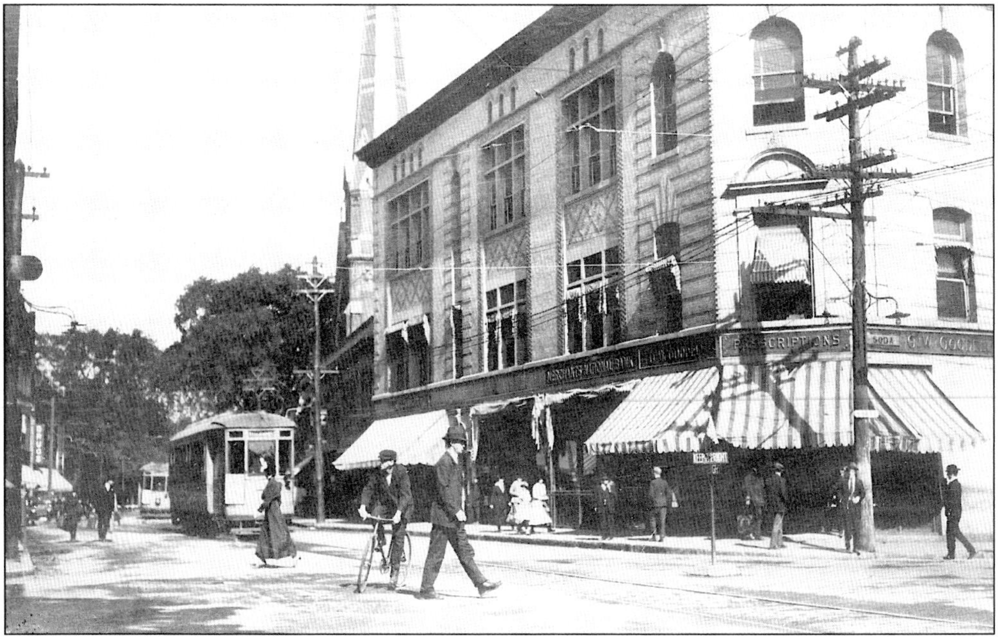

This photograph, taken from the Common, looks north down Main Street. The second McGrath building, presently home to BankBoston, is located on the corner of Mechanic Street. During the 1960s, many young men knew its location well: the offices of the selective service "draft board" were located upstairs.

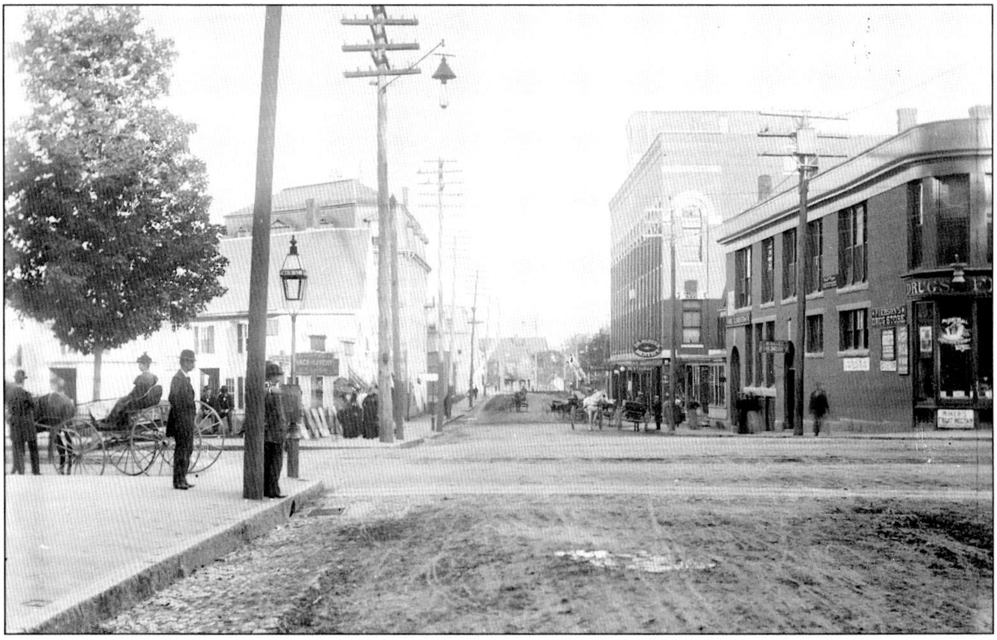

This picture looks south down Mechanic Street at the corner of West and Main Streets. The first McGrath Building is on the right, followed by Kendall Block—the imposing brick structure housing shops, offices, and the Music Hall. Note the gas lamppost on the left and the electric light hanging high above the intersection.

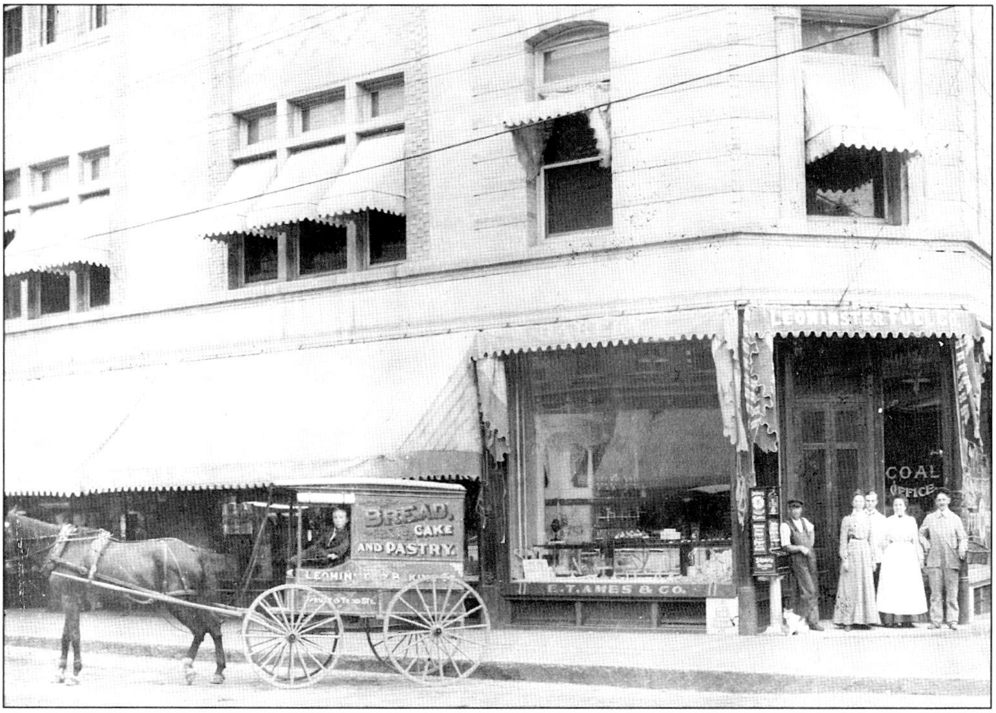

The Leominster Fuel Company was located in the second McGrath Building at the corner of Main and Mechanic Streets. The building has housed a variety of businesses over the years.

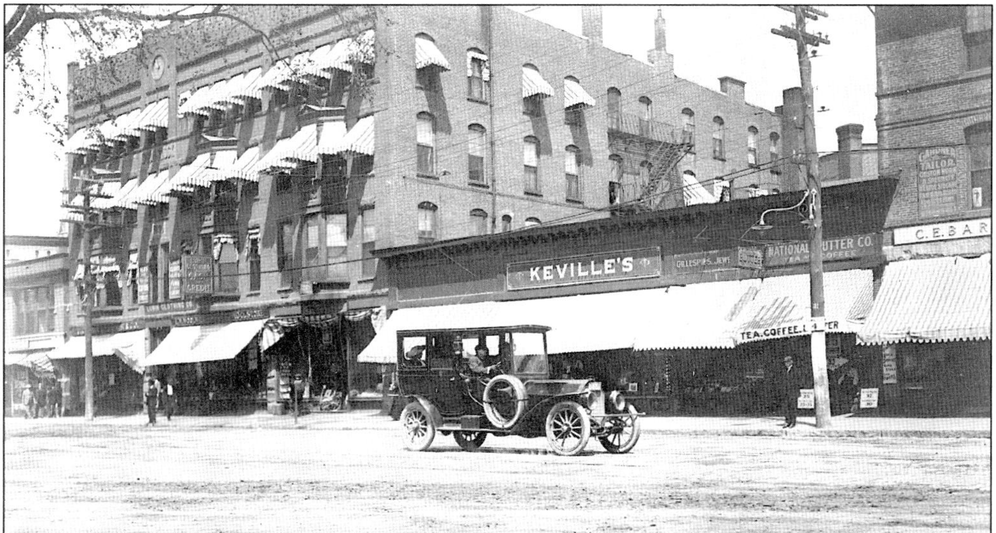

Looking across Monument Square, one can see the Wood Block and its awnings, c. 1915. This area of shops was previously called Collins Row; all the buildings were of wooden construction.

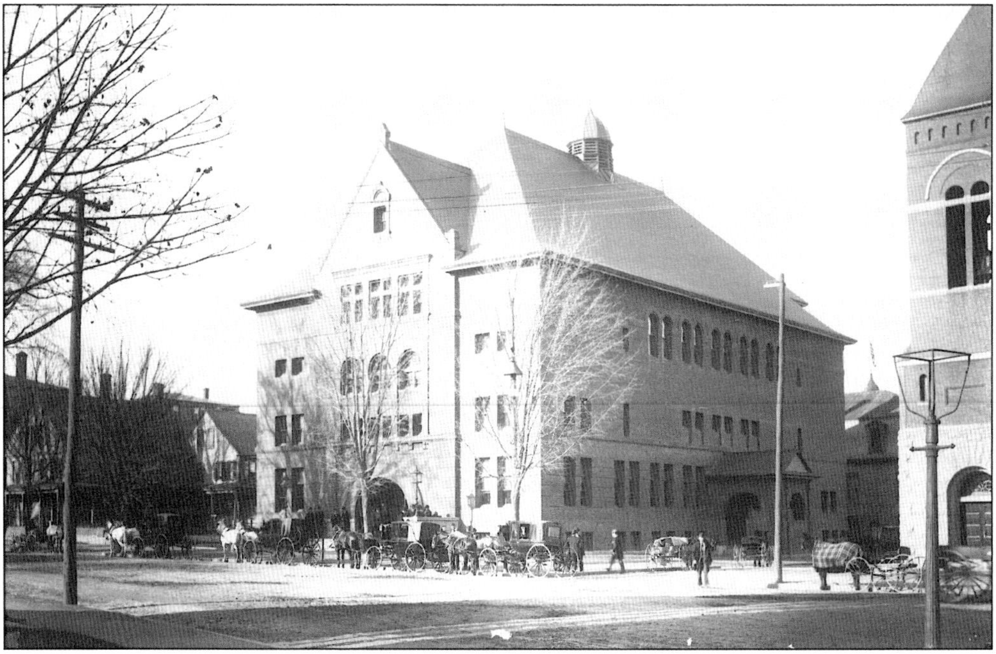

This Davis photograph shows Leominster's fifth town hall. Built in 1895 of a gorgeous, dark red brick, the building boasted a magnificent auditorium and stage and featured luxurious, quartered-oak trim. When it burned down in 1909, town offices moved back into the 1851 Old Town Hall building until 1915, when the present-day municipal building was completed.

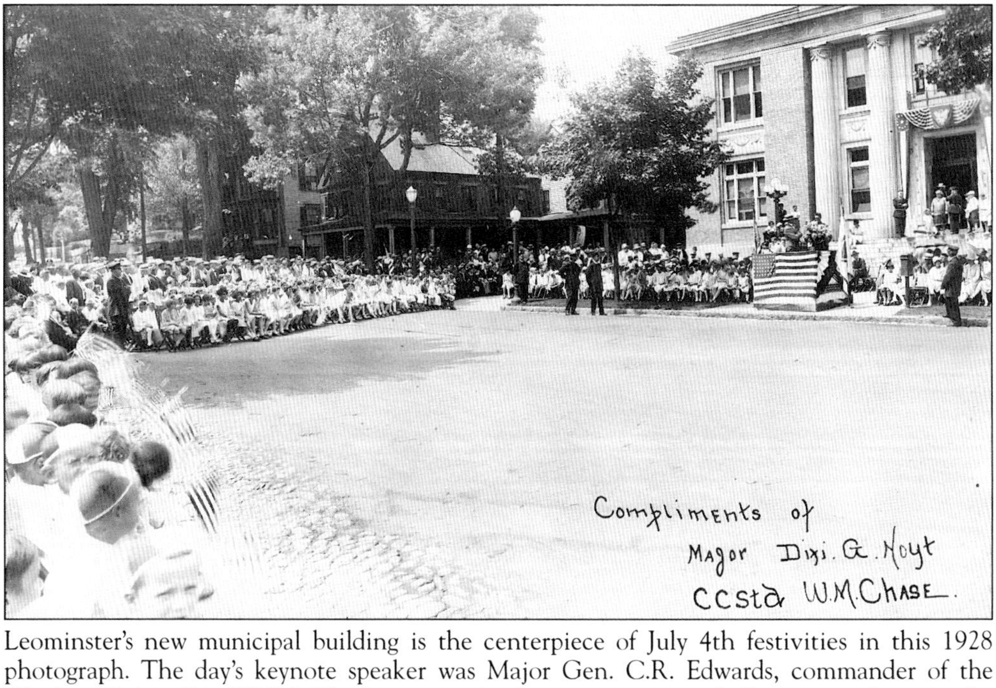

Leominster's new municipal building is the centerpiece of July 4th festivities in this 1928 photograph. The day's keynote speaker was Major Gen. C.R. Edwards, commander of the "Yankee Division" in WW I. The large rooming house next to city hall was torn down in the 1940s to make way for a parking lot; it was the residence of "Popcorn" White.

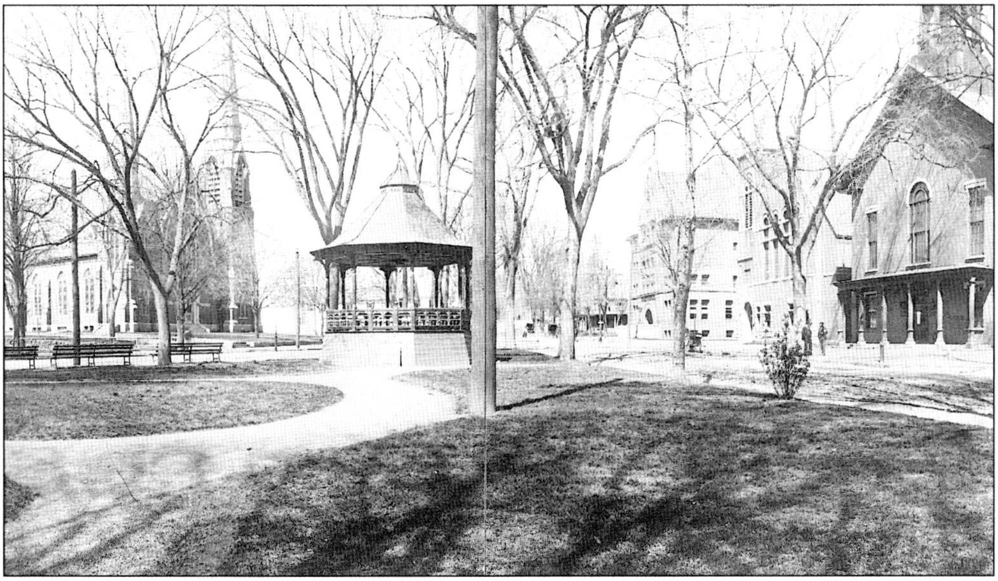

This view across the Common was taken prior to 1909. On the left is the Pilgrim Congregational Church; on the right are the Old Town Hall, the Baptist church, and the New Town Hall.

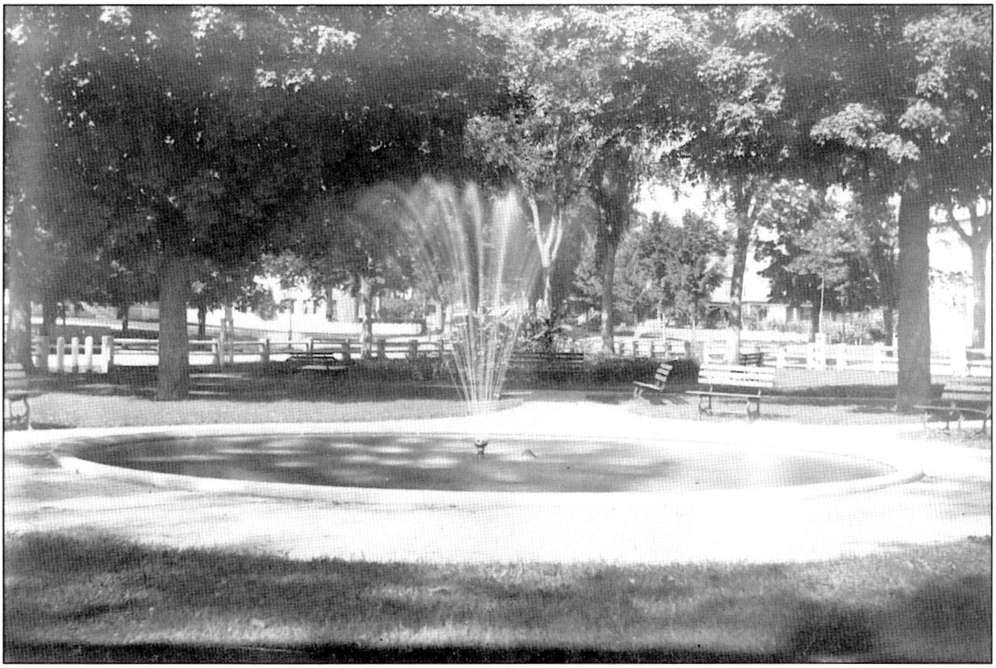

This fountain and pool was located on the Common, close to the West Street side of the park and near the site of one of the five city wells used to fight fires. On Memorial Day, flowers were floated in the pool in memory of those who died at sea. Today that tradition is carried on at Rockwell's Pond behind the Veteran's Quarters.

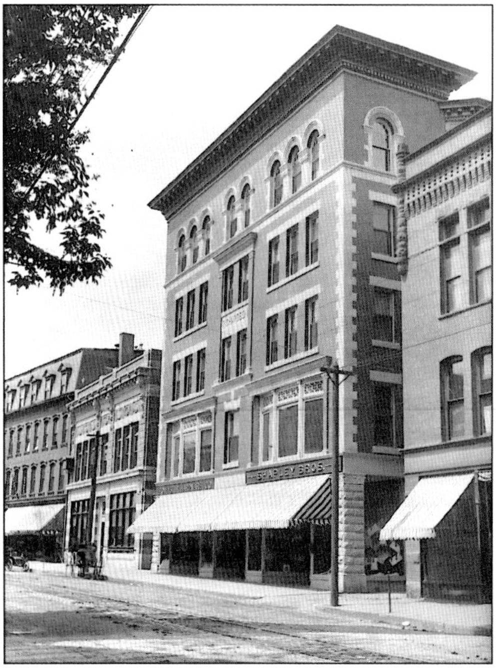

The Richardson Building on Main Street was built in 1904 by H.B. Richardson, owner of the Richardson Piano Company. The outside is done in the Renaissance-revival style of brick and cut stone. The building's interior featured fine wood carving, elaborate moldings, marble stairways, and a cast-iron elevator. The commercial space and apartments were devastated by fire in 1989 and again in 1994, but owners Ben Fini and Morris Schwartz have restored and updated this downtown gem.

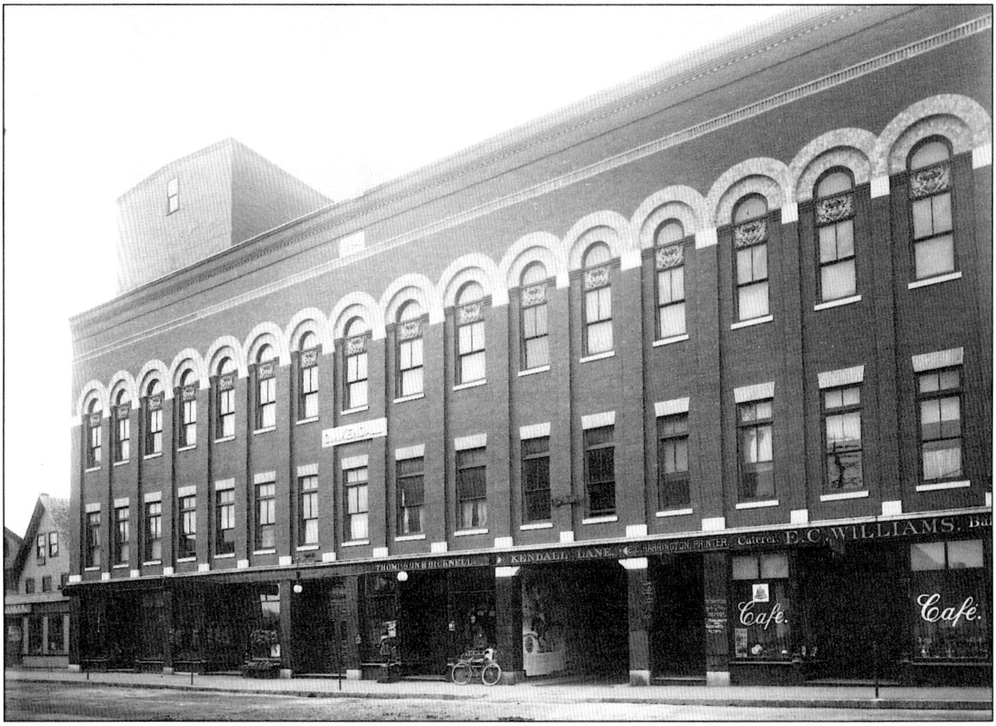

This block was erected on Mechanic Street in 1894 by George M. Kendall, a businessman known as "The Cucumber King." The four-story brick building contained stores on the ground floor, including the first Victory Market; offices and the Music Hall Theatre occupied the upper floors. The McEvoys purchased the Music Hall in 1924. When the block was destroyed by fire in 1927, they built the Plymouth Theater, naming it for Mrs. McEvoy's birthplace in England.

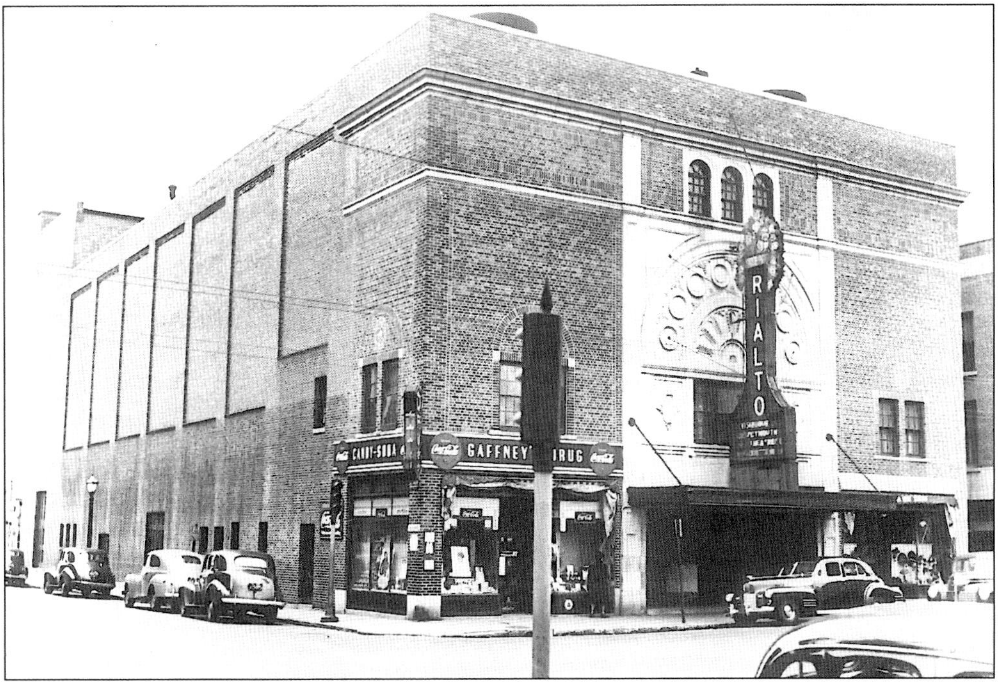

In 1923, Rosina and Thomas McEvoy opened their elegant showplace, the Rialto Theatre. Boasting a huge chandelier, a miniature fountain and goldfish pond, and a $15,000 Robert Morton electric organ; the Rialto cost over $200,000. It was the first movie theater in the area to show "talking pictures" and, for an additional dime, it offered reserved seating. The Rialto closed in 1933; the building was used as the city's recreation center from 1950 until 1969 and has housed the YMCA in recent years.

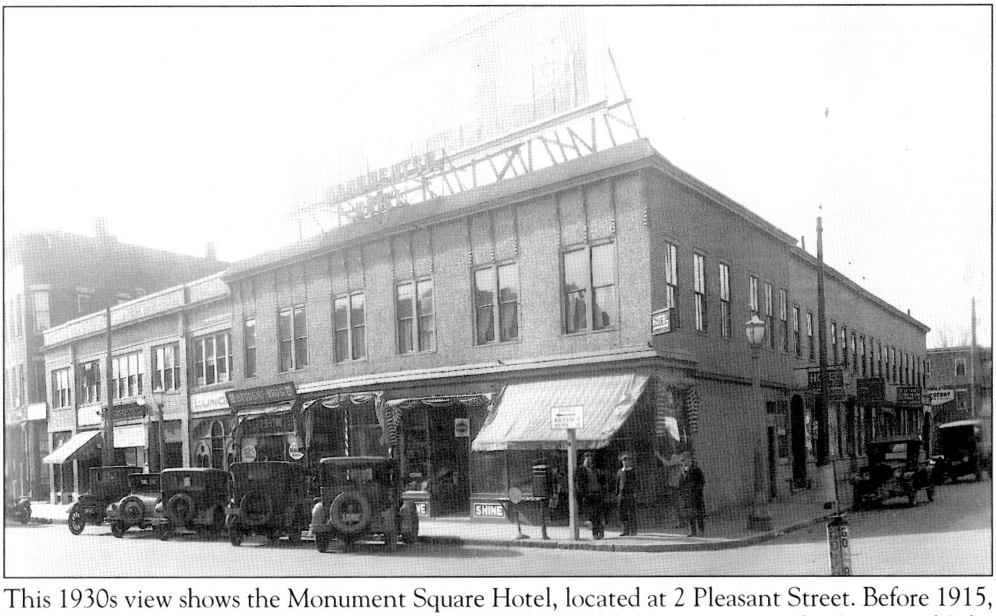

This 1930s view shows the Monument Square Hotel, located at 2 Pleasant Street. Before 1915, it was known as the Monument Square House. The establishment was run by Anne and Julia Keating. Note the sign on the roof advertises "Coke Fuel," not "Coca-Cola!"

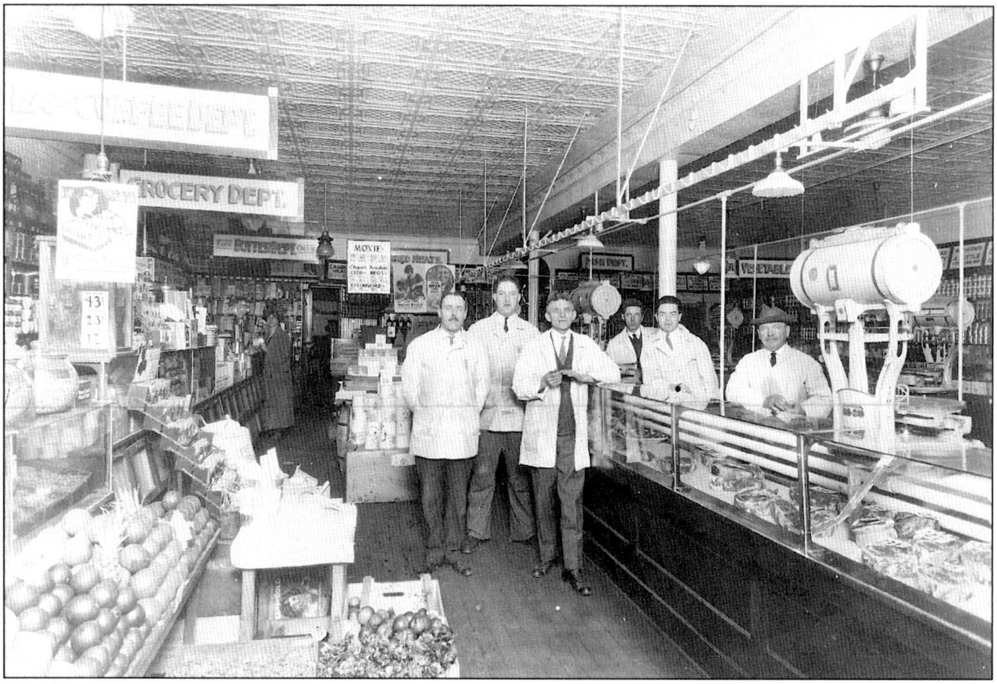

Brockleman's Market at 8 Monument Square was begun in 1919 by Anton F. Brockleman; his brothers later joined him in business. The store featured groceries, a meat market, and a bakery. Leominster historian Evelyn Hachey remembers taking her children to Brockleman's on Saturday mornings for fresh doughnuts; people could watch the doughnuts being made through the store's front window. The business closed in 1950.

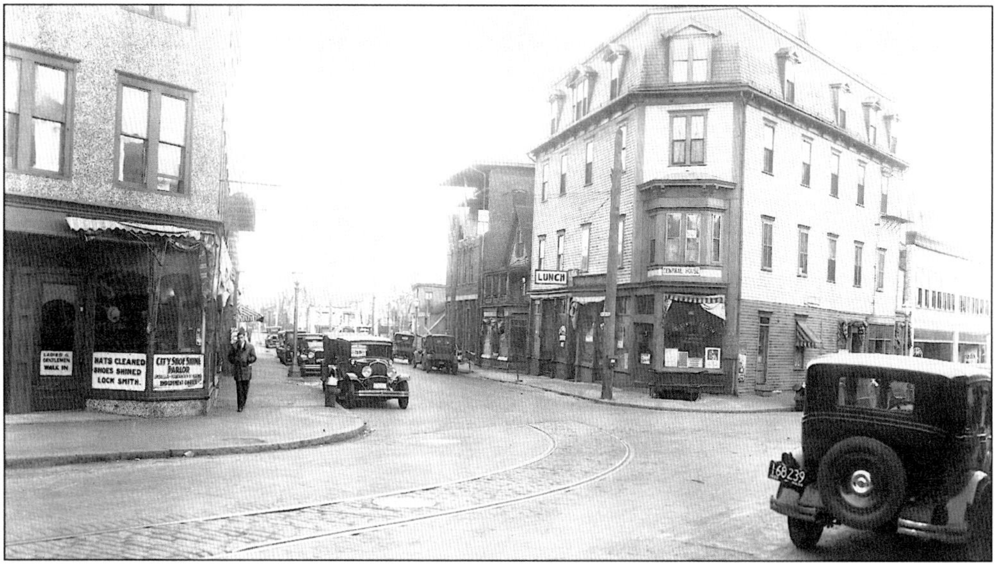

This photo was taken looking north down Water Street at the Mechanic Street entrance to "Cat's Alley," a narrow lane running behind the Wood Block from Mechanic Street to Manning Avenue. The Central House Hotel is in the right corner, next to a meat specialty shop called the Public Market. The left-hand corner is now the site of the BankBoston parking lot.

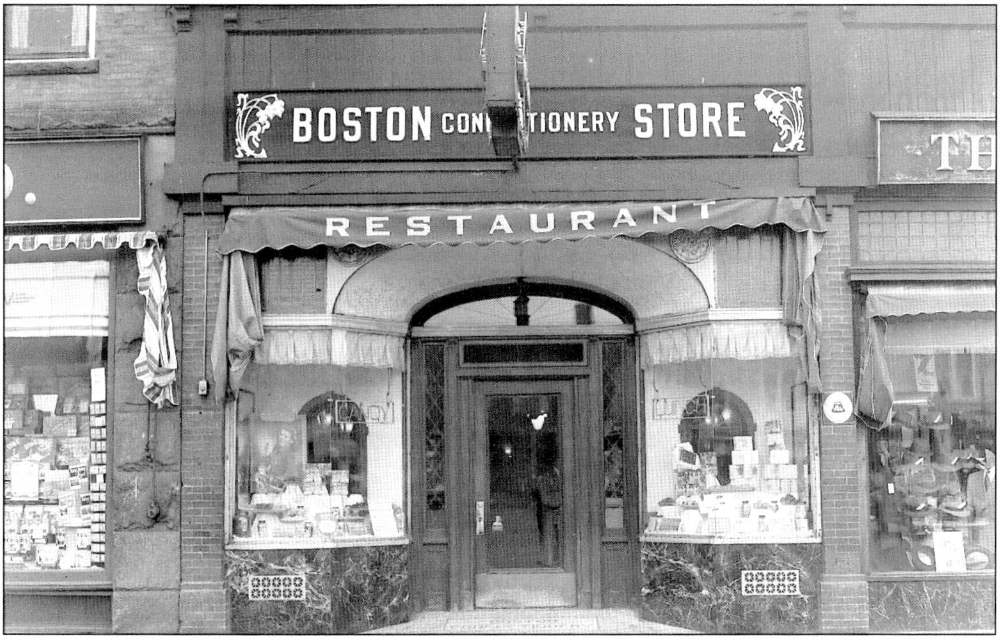

The Boston Confectionery Store, located at 20 Monument Square, was a thriving business and a Leominster tradition for over 40 years. Greek-American owners Becrelis and Moskos opened the store in 1913 and served a variety of candies, sweets, nuts, and ice cream. In 1952, the "B.C." was sold to Louis Dellechiaie and Carter Kalustian; it was completely destroyed, along with eight other businesses, in a spectacular fire in 1956. The business never reopened.

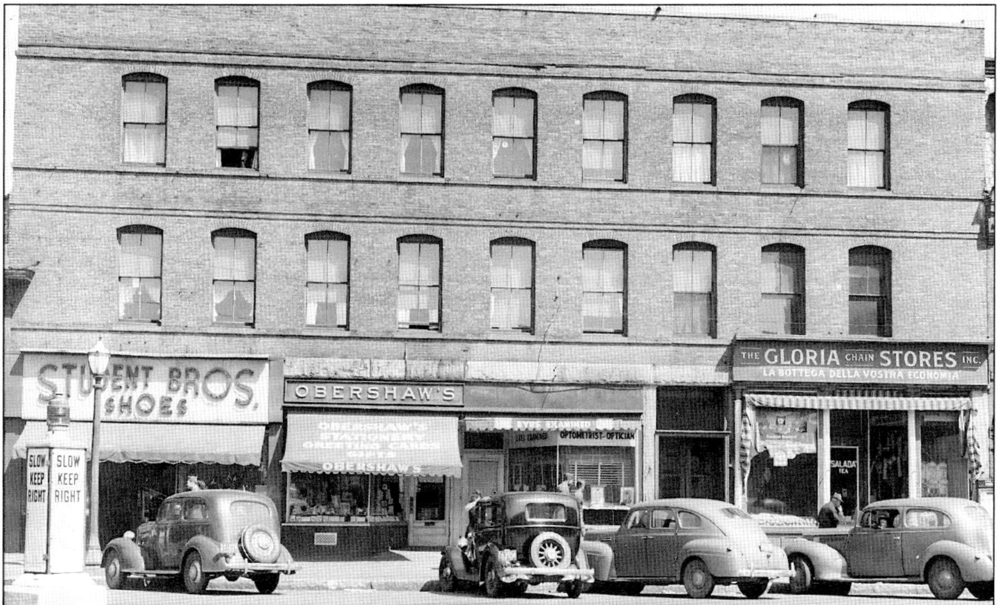

This view of downtown in the early 1940s shows 26-34 Monument Square. Obershaw's was a stationery and gift store; Gloria Chain Stores Inc. were specialty grocers catering to the Italian population. The Chevrolet automobile has wooden spokes (notice the spare tire). Army personnel were also a common sight at this time. Friendly's Restaurant now occupies this space.

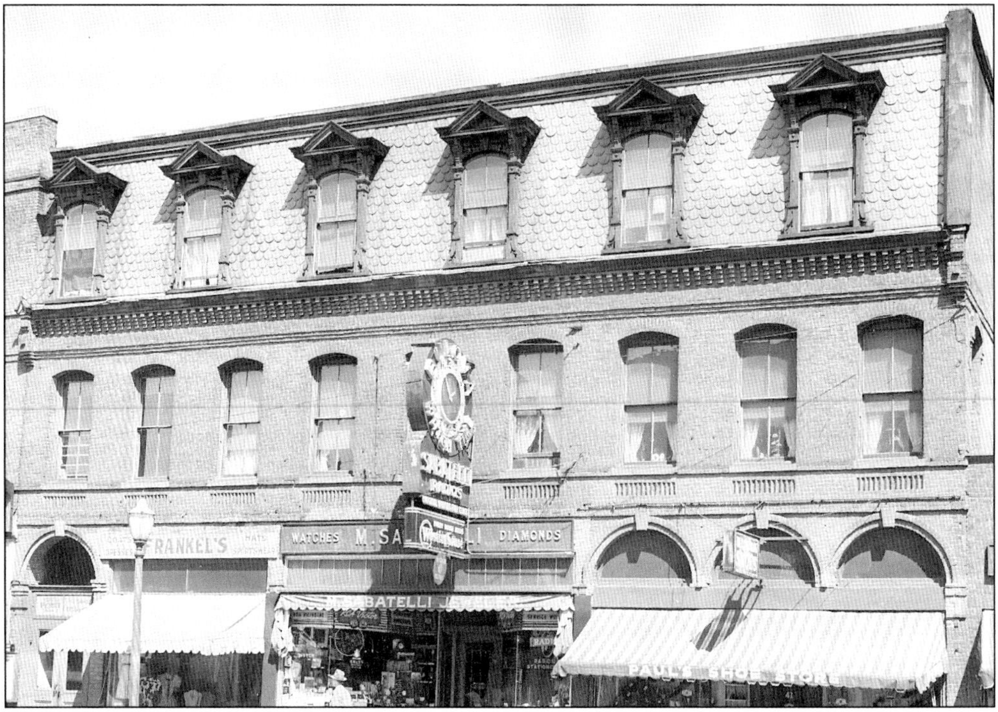

This is a 1944 view of 36-42 Monument Square. The Perry Insurance Agency occupied the second floor; at street level, Frankel's featured women's clothing, while Sabatelli's specialized in jewelry, clocks, and radios. Paul's Shoe Store was replaced by Russell's Shoe Store. By 1955, Sabatelli's had expanded to 42 Monument Square.

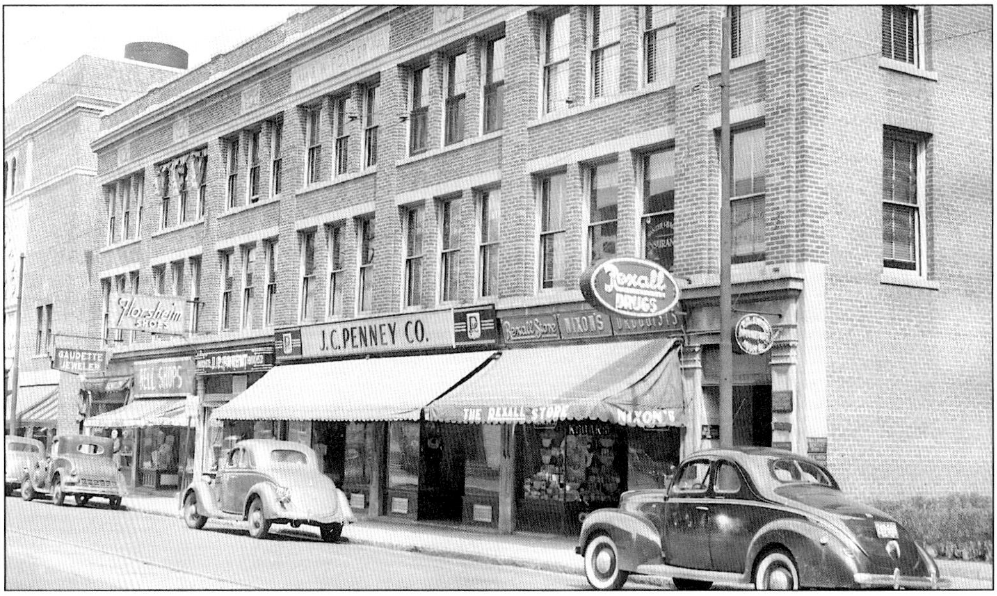

This 1940 view of the R.W. Foster Block illustrates the variety of businesses and specialty stores established in the "golden era" of downtown. Shopping on Thursday nights, when stores were open late, was a real social event; in the 1950s, it was the "cruising night" for the high school crowd.

The Methodist church on Main Street is shown in this 1940s photograph. The church was built in 1871 and prospered on this site for more than 90 years. The steeple, a well-known landmark for several generations, was badly damaged in the 1938 Hurricane. It was finally declared unsafe by 1955 and reluctantly taken down. The congregation moved in 1965 to its present location at Merriam Avenue, Hall Street, and Willow Street. The historical society collection features a pew from the old church.

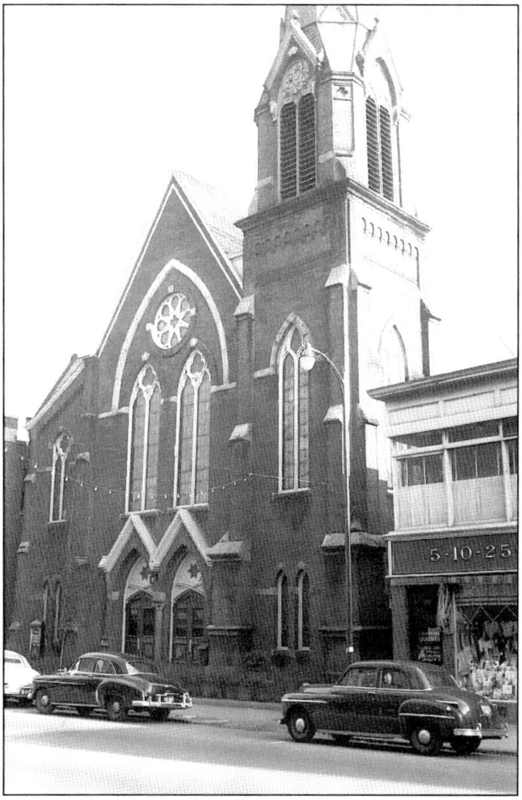

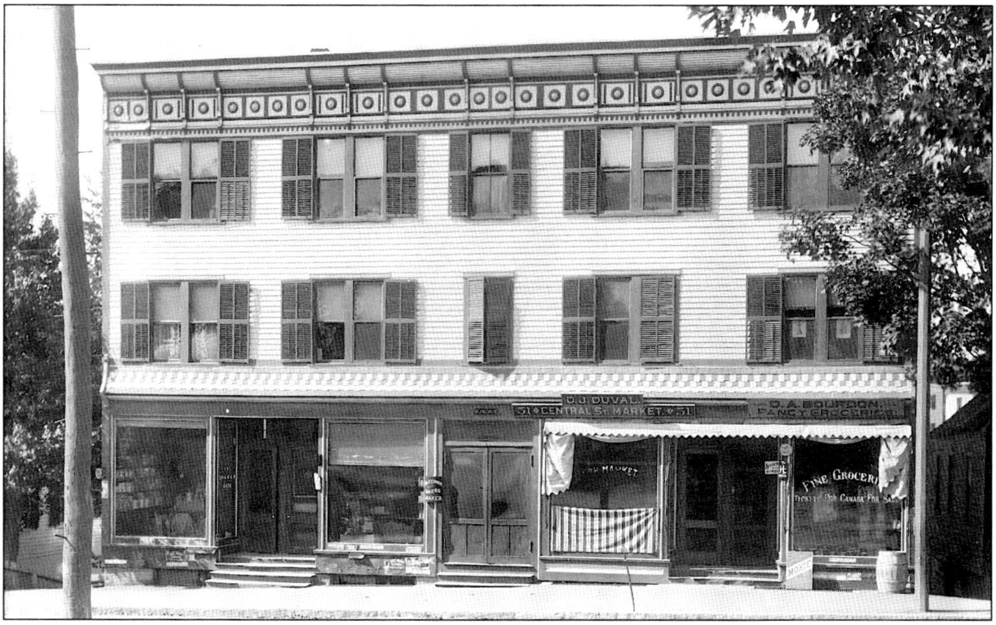

The Duval Block, established in 1893, was located at 51-53 Central Street. This 1897 photograph shows the Central Street Market, owned by D.J. Duval, who maintained that his store was "the best in town, with the best refrigerators." He employed two assistants. The second floor was occupied by Mrs. V.S. Verette, a dressmaker.

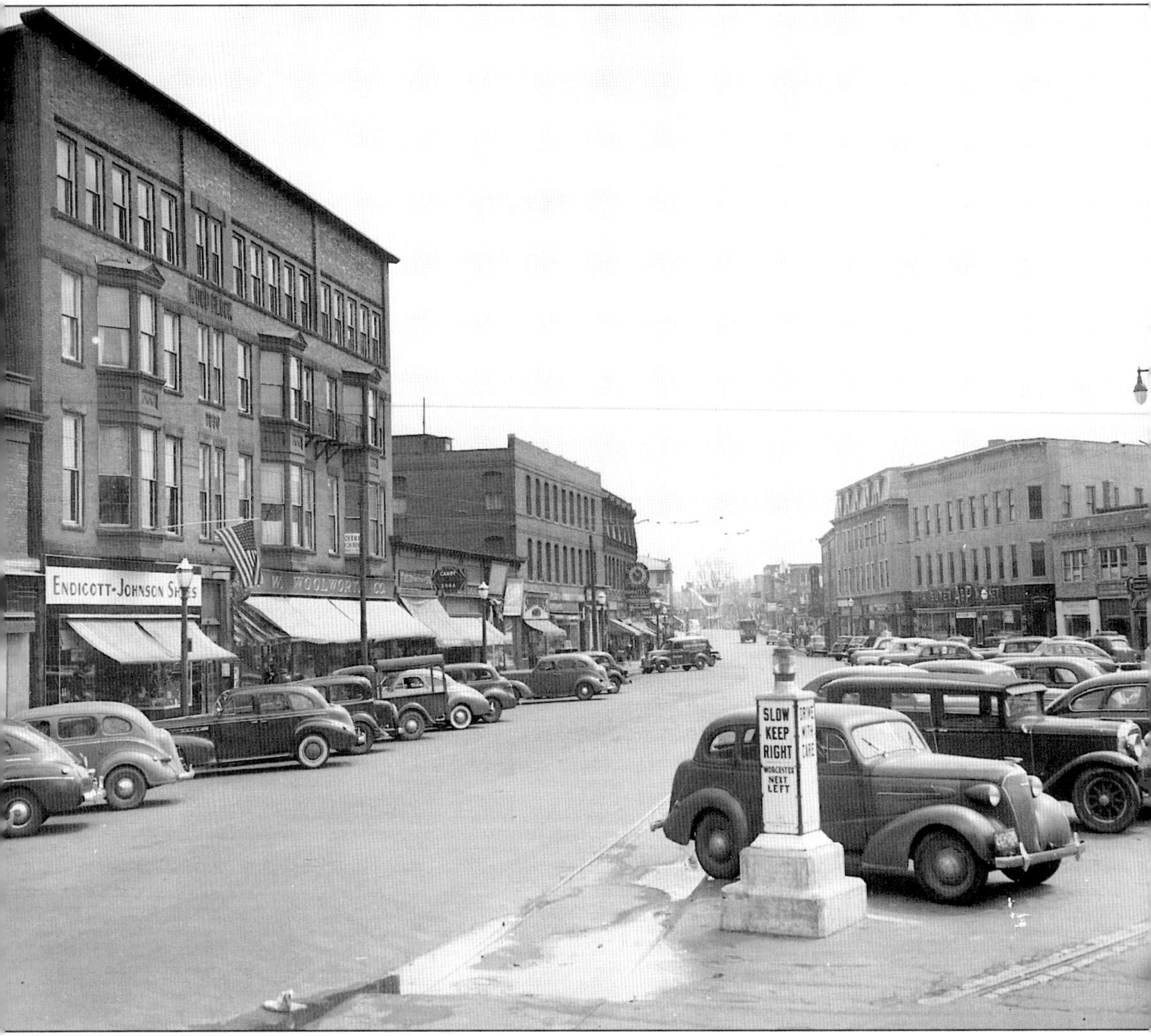

In this 1944 picture of Monument Square you can still see the old trolley tracks and the traffic divider light, pointing the way to Worcester via Route 12. Looking closely to the left, the edge of the sign for the Super A&P Market is visible. Downtown parking is sufficient at this time, due to less automobile traffic.

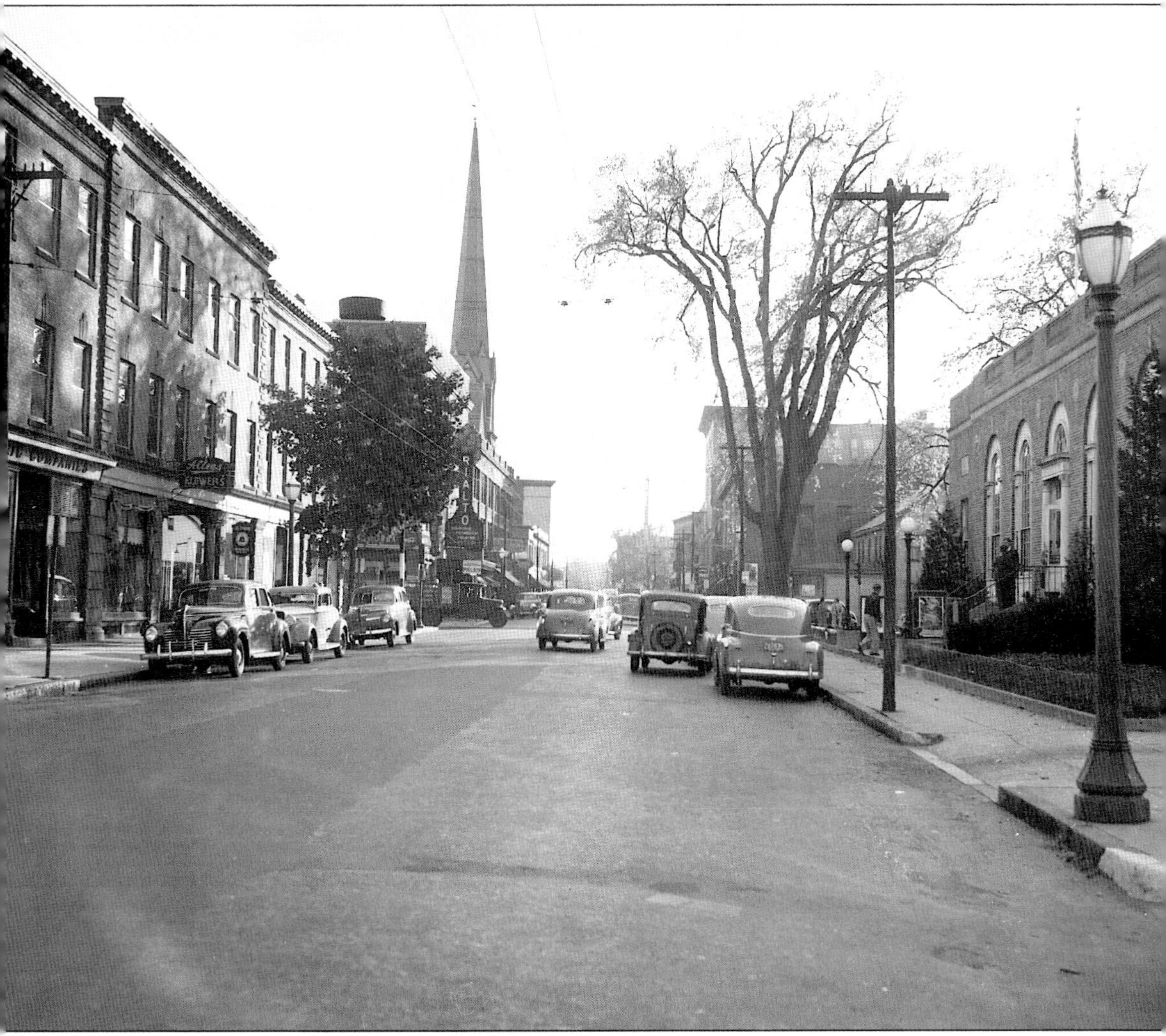

This photograph, looking south down Main Street, was taken in October of 1944. The post office is on the right, across from the Columbia Block; the steeple of the Methodist church dominates the skyline. Just past the post office on the right was a house that was also home to a millinery store; it was torn down to make room for the new Grant's Department Store in 1949. The Rialto Theatre marquee urges customers to "Visit our Plymouth Theater!"

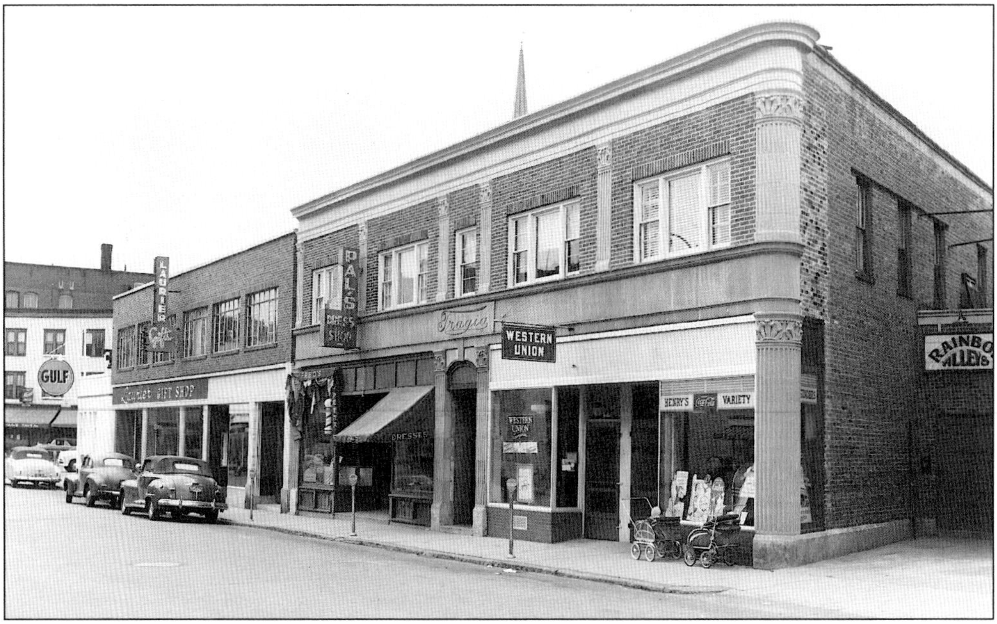

This picture looks up Mechanic Street towards Water Street, c. 1940. Across from the Gulf Station (which was later a taxi stand) was the Captain's Tavern, located on the site of today's BankBoston parking lot. The Tragia Building and the Goguen Block were destroyed in the Sport Mart Fire in 1973.

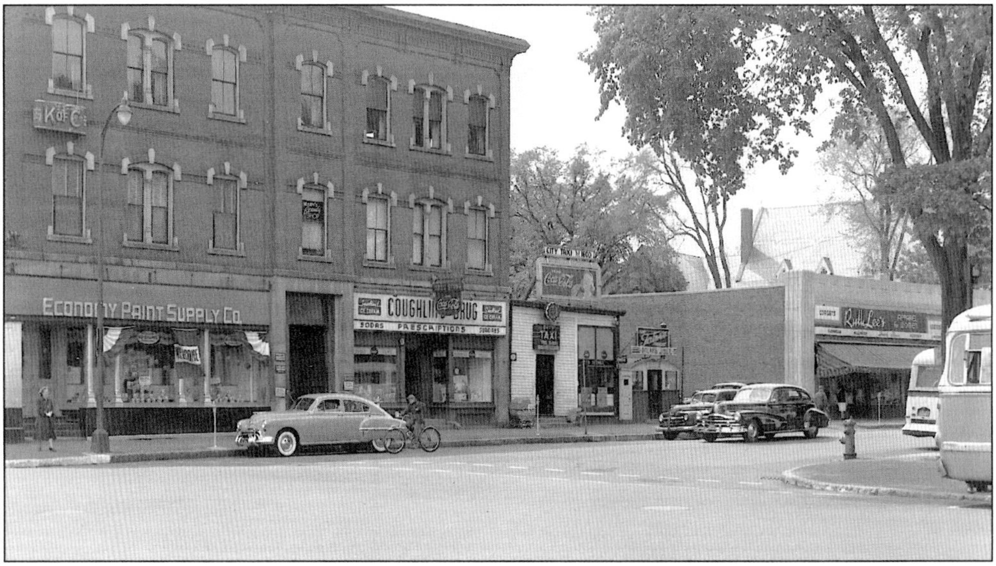

This view of Park Street, c. 1950, shows several retail landmarks. Ruth Lee's is still well known for fine women's clothing and has been doing business at 7 Park Street for 57 years. Economy Paint Supply opened in 1941 and moved to North Main Street in 1980. You'll still find Mae Epstein behind the counter, and chances are she still remembers your home's exact paint colors and wallpaper styles! Beyond Ruth Lee's was the First National Grocery Store. Dolan's "Rolling" Diner and the office of City Taxi were torn down in 1957.

In 1851, Leominster's fourth town hall was built on what is now the parking lot between the Unitarian and Baptist churches. Town offices were located here until the city hall opened in 1915; the police department, the American Legion, and the Spanish-American War Veterans then moved in. The "Old Town Hall" served as police headquarters until a new station was built in 1959. Despite efforts to save it as a unique town treasure, the building was torn down in 1966.

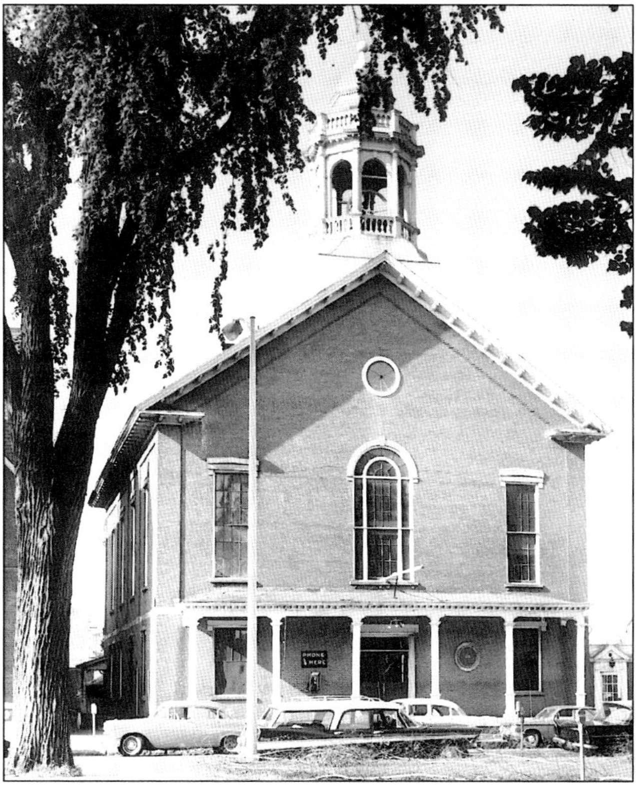

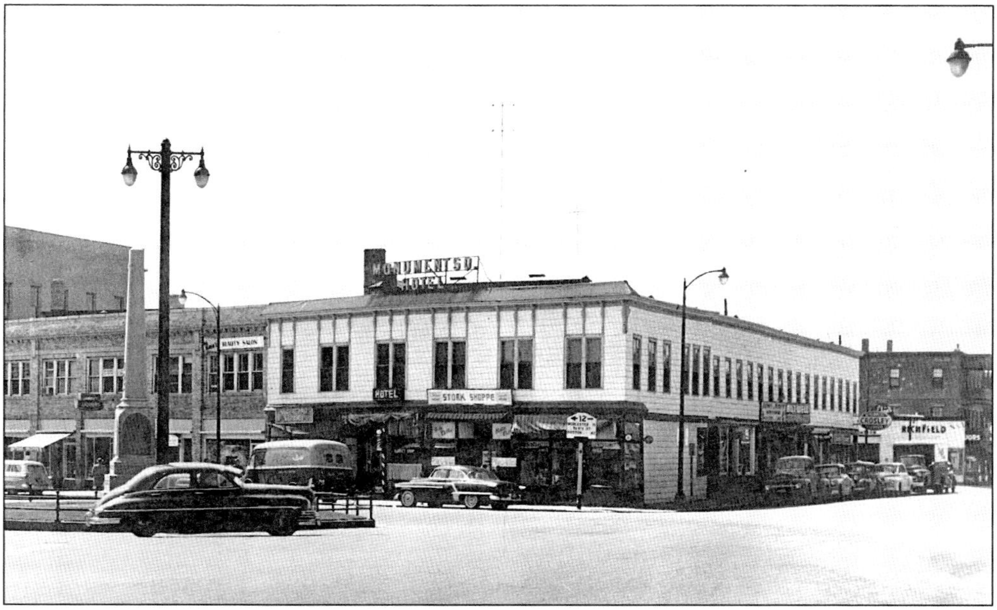

To the right of the hotel, there is a glimpse of the many small businesses that were located on Pleasant Street before various banks and Wyman's Liquors came on the scene. The Stork Shoppe was a popular infant and children's clothing store.

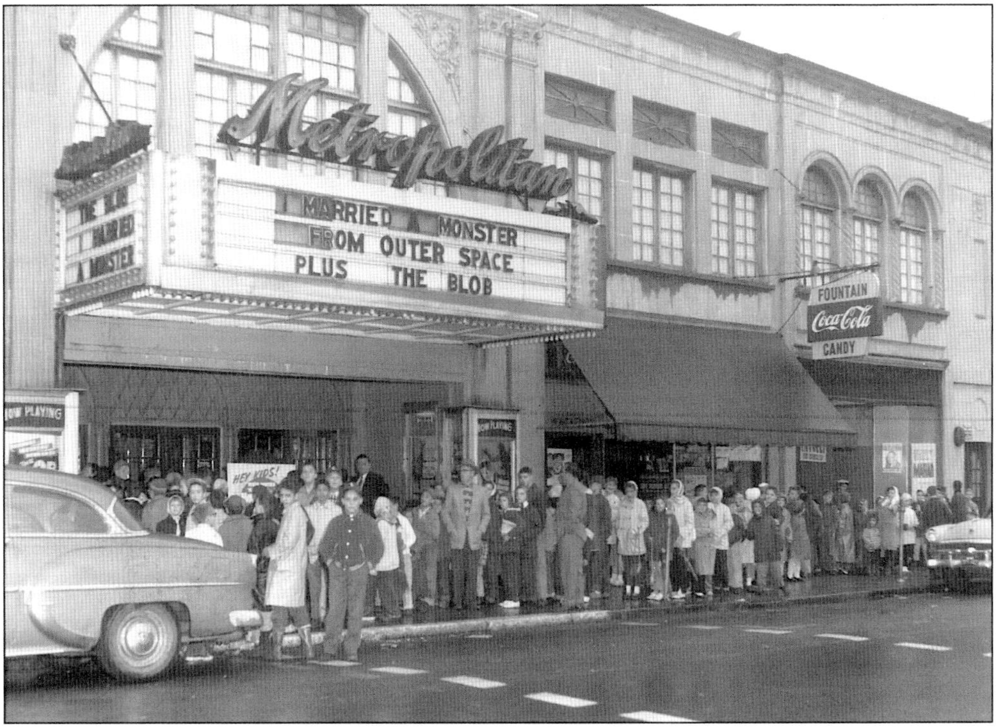

The Metropolitan Theater, opened in the 1920s, still attracted a crowd in this 1950s photograph. Many great memories came from going to movies at the "Met" or the Plymouth, where a mere quarter bought a ticket. Moviegoers were treated to a short serial, a cartoon, and two features. Theater owners often used gimmicks and giveaways to increase business.

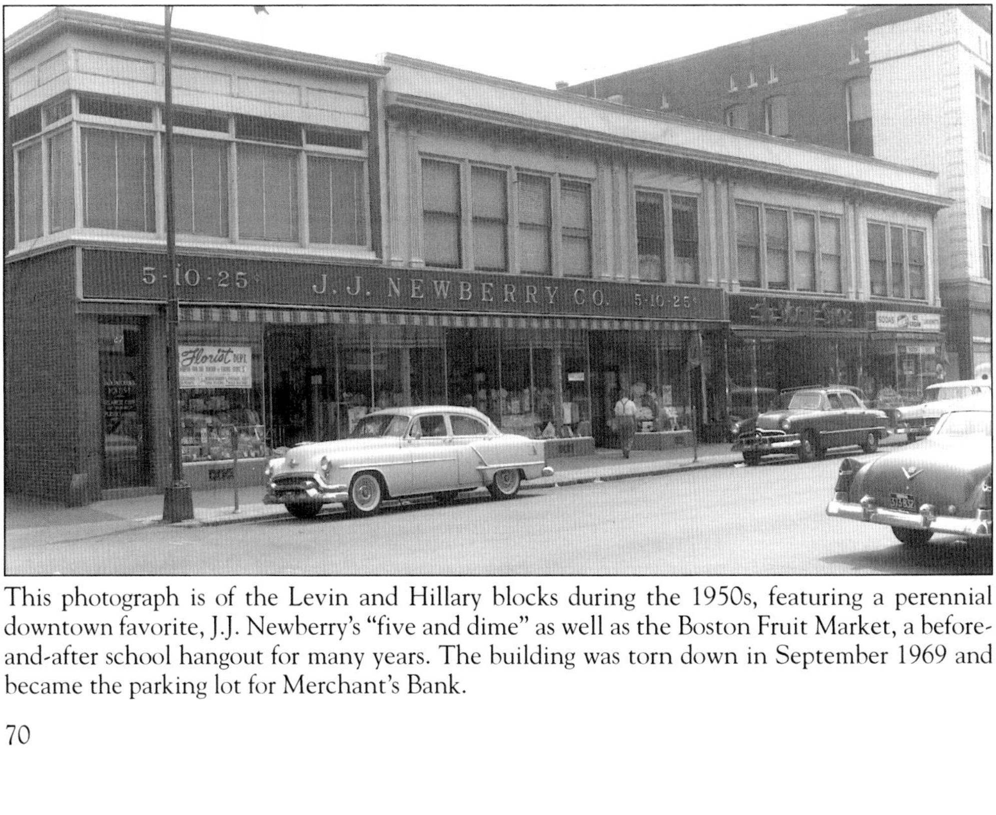

This photograph is of the Levin and Hillary blocks during the 1950s, featuring a perennial downtown favorite, J.J. Newberry's "five and dime" as well as the Boston Fruit Market, a before-and-after school hangout for many years. The building was torn down in September 1969 and became the parking lot for Merchant's Bank.

Joseph and Norah Goodhue founded Goodhue's Restaurant and Bakery in 1931 at 46 Main Street. They operated here until moving to a new, air-conditioned location at 22 Main Street, where they offered specialties like Norah's Oatmeal Bread and a Thursday night "Shopper's Supper" for 99¢. The window display advertises their famous, fresh frozen pie varieties. The business closed in 1959.

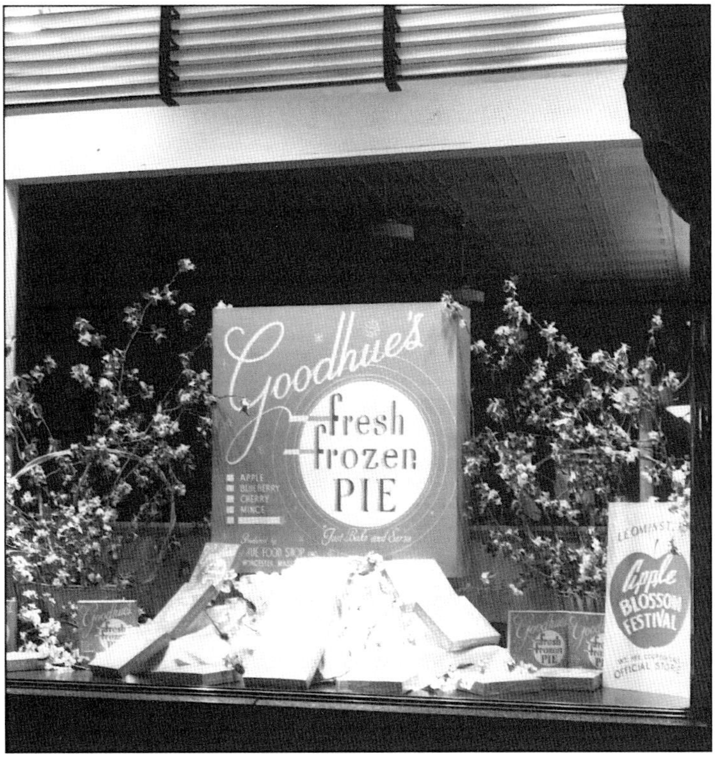

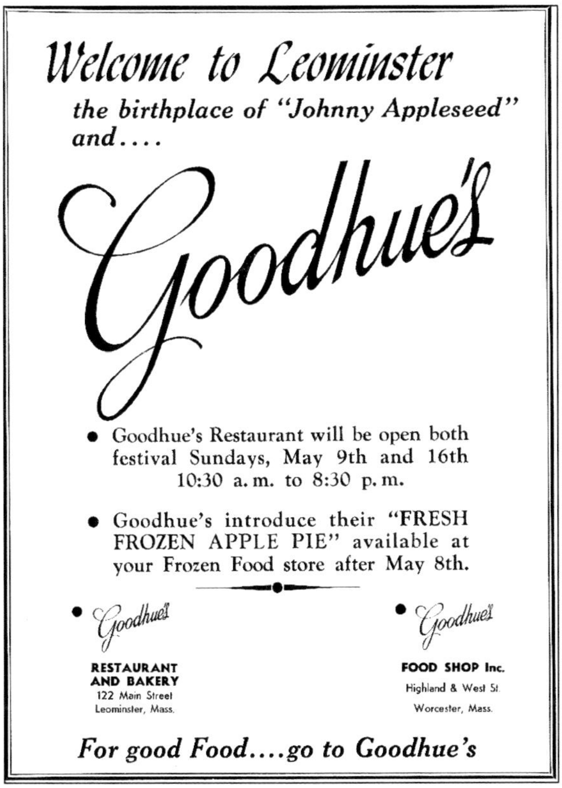

Leominster folks knew that "for good food, go to Goodhue's." This advertisement for Goodhue's is from the 1948 Apple Blossom Festival program booklet. The festival, begun in 1940, was a tremendous celebration spotlighting products and services in the Nashoba Valley region. Many area communities participated, including Leominster.

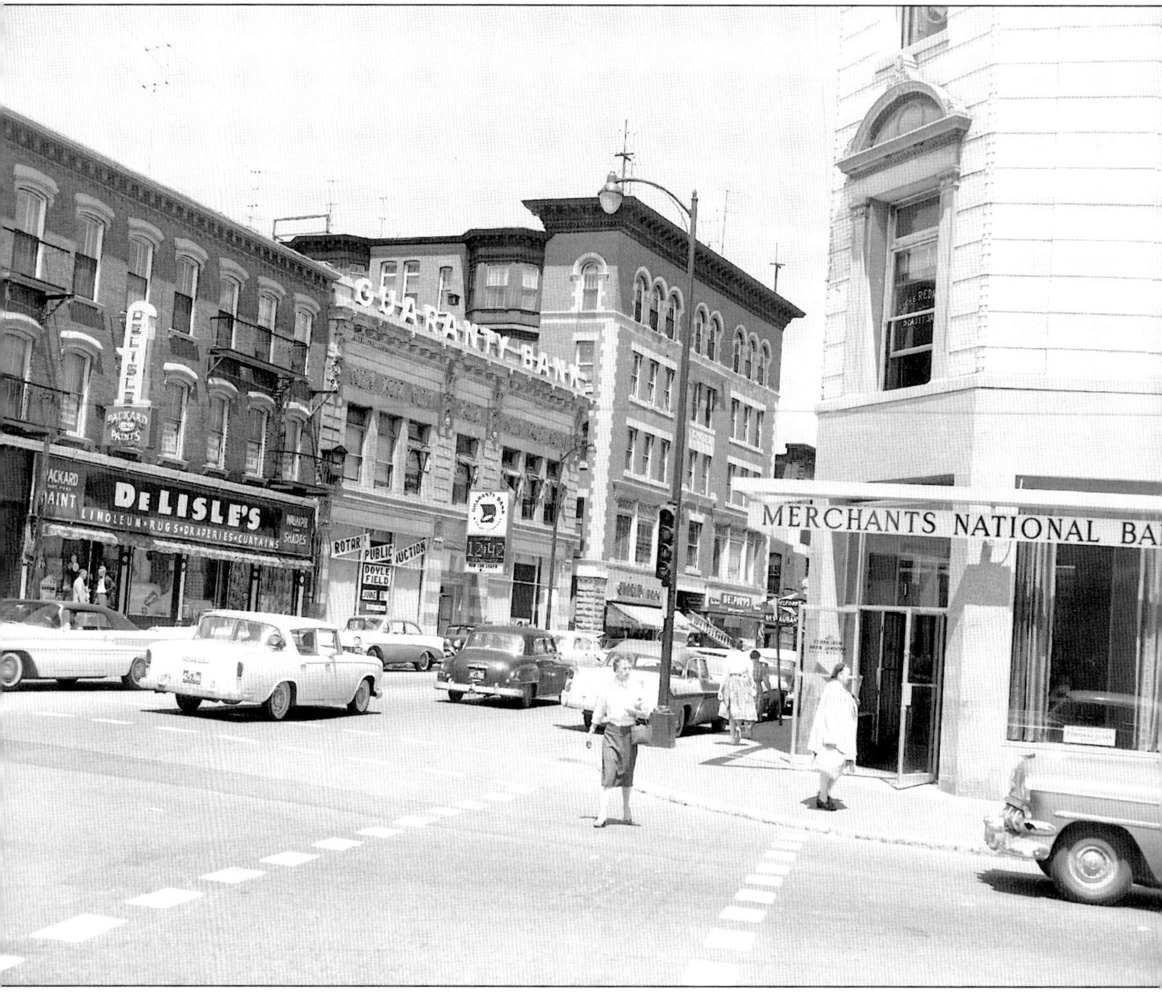

Merchants National Bank, located in the second McGrath Building is, on the right in this c. 1950 photograph. On the left are the Foster, Bank, and Richardson Blocks. Note the Guaranty Bank clock, a downtown mainstay to check time and temperature.

The Civil War Monument was moved in June 1984 as part of the urban renewal project, designed to improve traffic flow and promote the downtown area. The monument was originally dedicated in 1867; the names of major battles involving Leominster men and names of soldiers who died are inscribed on the monument. It was relocated on the Common in Monument Square.

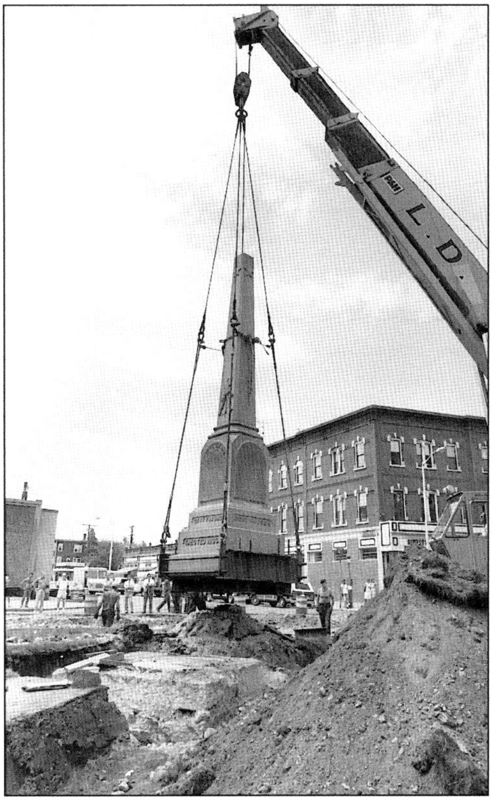

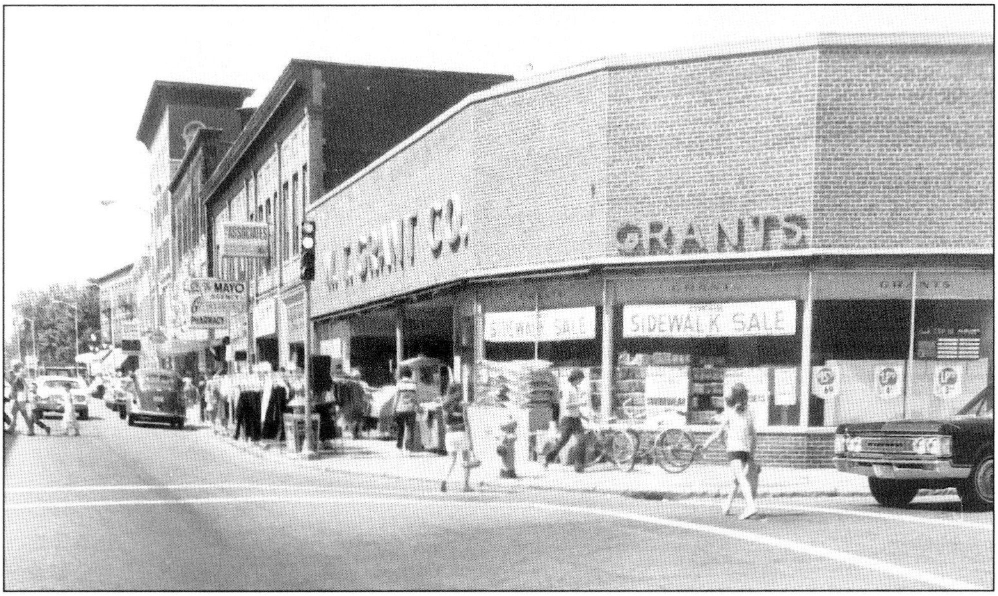

In November 1949, the W.T. Grant Company opened its Leominster store at the corner of Main Street and Merriam Avenue. It was one of the largest stores in actual floor space in this part of the country, and it employed over 100 people when it opened. "Sidewalk sales" were popular with many downtown stores at this time. The building is presently used for business and legal offices.

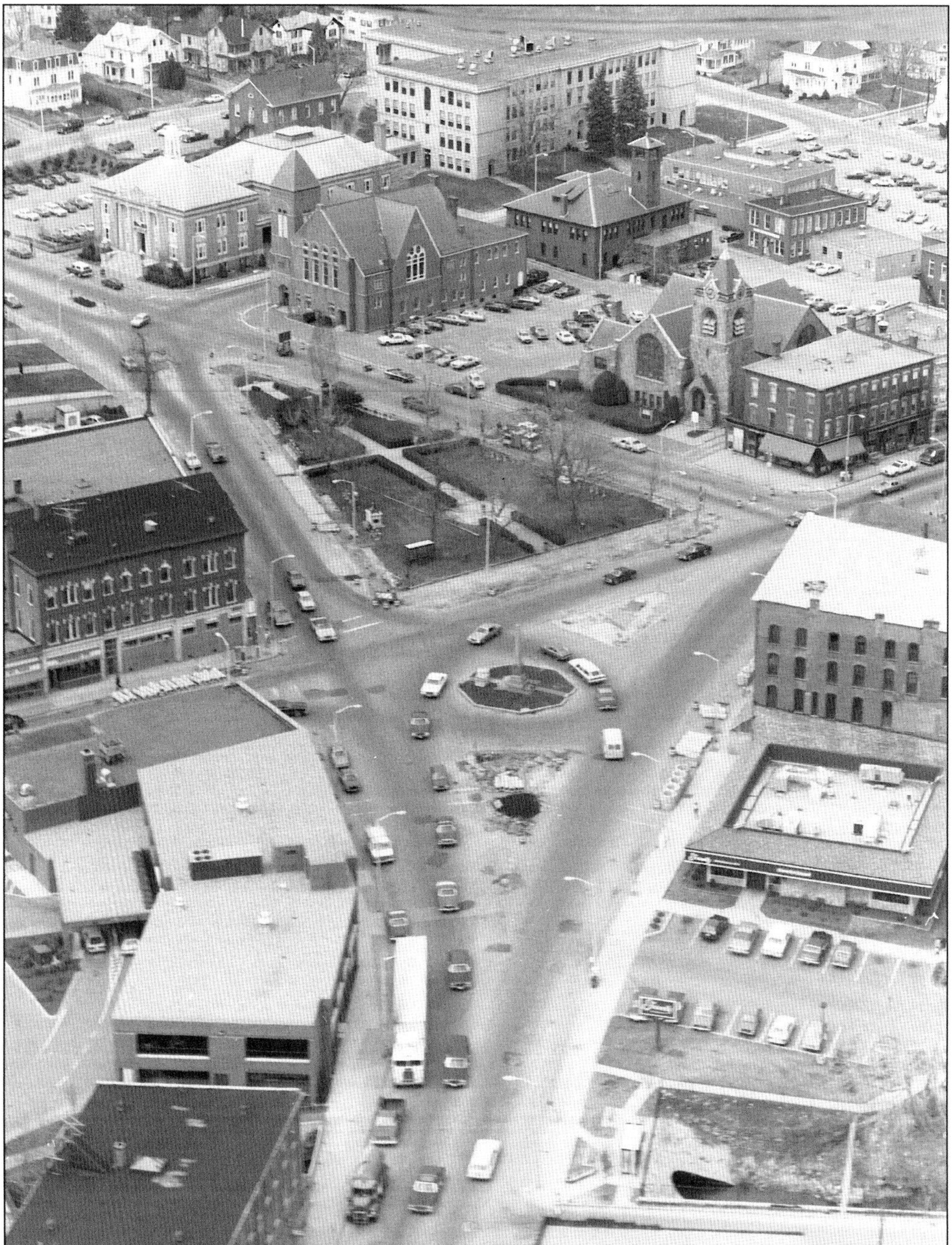

This fine, aerial perspective of the Common and central downtown area was taken in May 1984. This was just before the Civil War monument was moved and the traffic pattern was changed; note the buildings that are gone and have been replaced by parking areas.

Four

LEOMINSTER PEOPLE

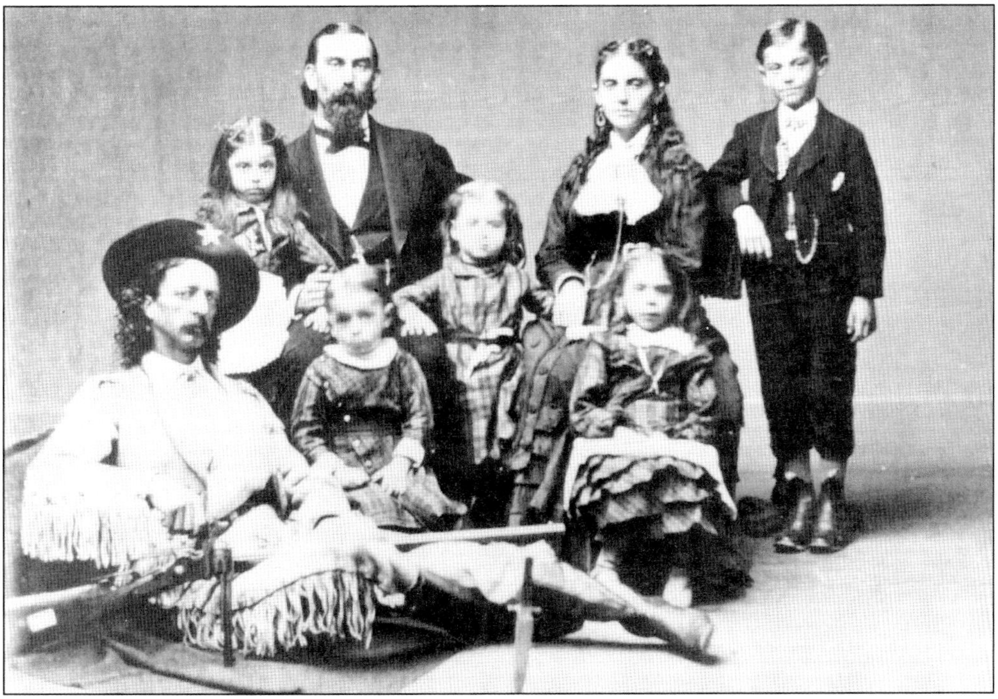

Leominster's Major Samuel Stone Hall "rode at about 125 pounds, and fought at four or five tons," according to his obituary in the *Boston Sunday Herald* of February 15, 1886. Known to his readers as "Buckskin Sam," Hall was a Texas Ranger, a spy for the North during the Civil War, and the author of over 50 "dime novel" thrillers published between 1877 and 1899. Here he is posed with the Dutcher family with whom he lived.

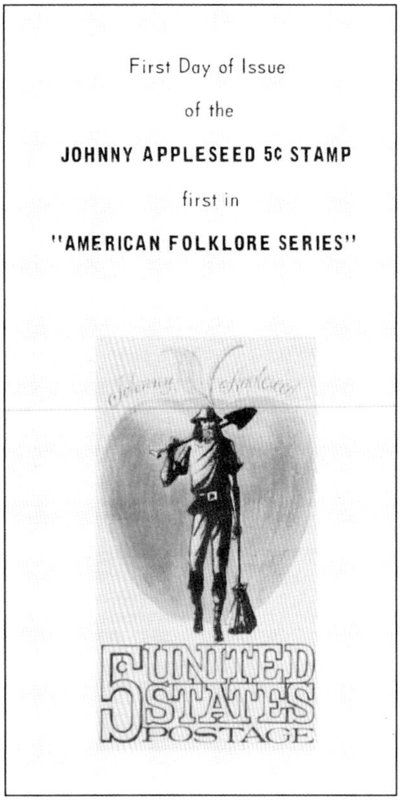

This brochure commemorates the first day of issue for the "Johnny Appleseed 5-cent Stamp" at Leominster Post Office in 1966. Beloved folk hero John Chapman was born in Leominster on September 26, 1774. A memorial marker and garden stands near the site where his family lived on what is now Johnny Appleseed Lane. Chapman is believed to have begun his westward pilgrimage at about the age of 23; he died in Fort Wayne, Indiana, in 1845.

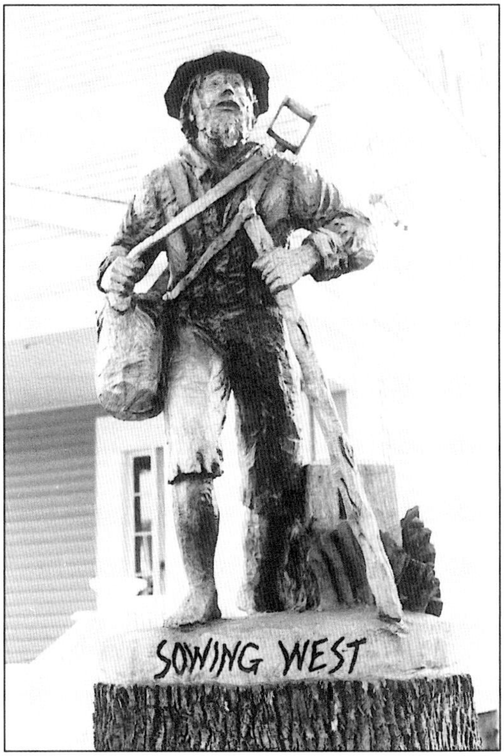

Thousands watched during the five days it took artist Clayton Coss of Oklahoma to create this carving of John Chapman at 50 West Street; it was done entirely by chain saw. Coss captured the spirit of this deeply religious nurseryman who planted seeds, set out orchards, and sold or gave trees to pioneers. "Sowing West" was completed on the Saturday of Leominster's Johnny Appleseed Festival in September 1998. (Courtesy David Mattos.)

Joseph Palmer, born in Notown in 1789, made the mistake of appearing in public after a long winter with a full beard. At that time most men were clean-shaven. Palmer was denounced from the pulpit and was eventually jailed for assault when he slashed two men who were attempting to shave him. Palmer was imprisoned for a year, refusing to leave without an official statement that he had a right to wear a beard. He had to be carried out, tied to a chair. Palmer is buried in Evergreen Cemetery.

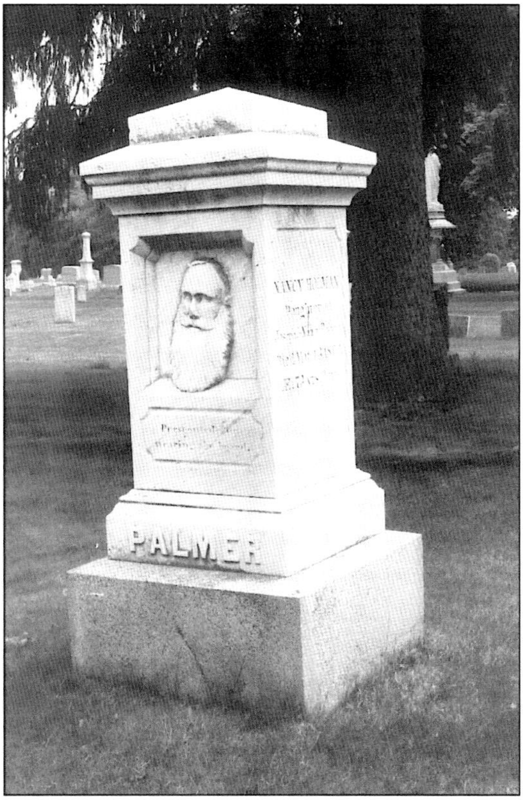

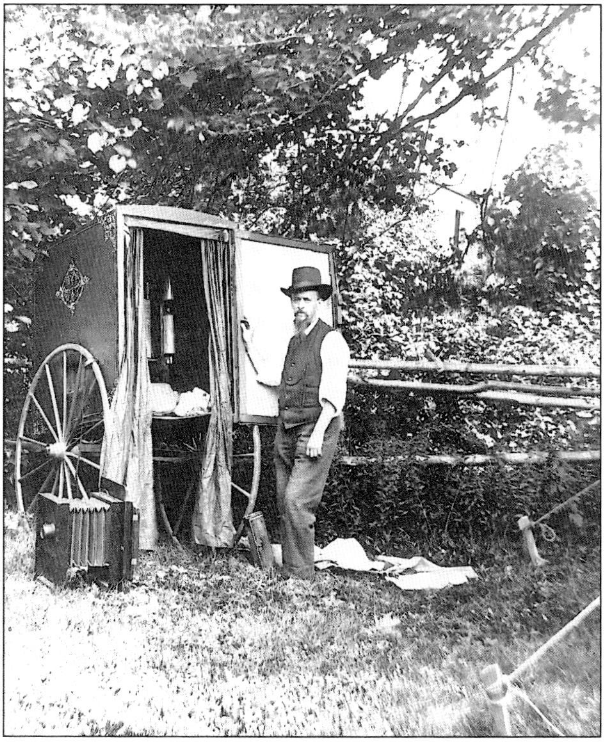

This self-portrait of photographer Edmund G. Davis was taken at Carter Park, where he began his career in the 1860s. The traveling cart served as his darkroom. Davis took many of the images in the historical society's glass negative collection, which provides a valuable source of information about Leominster. Davis was a descendant of Gershom and Tamar Houghton, the town's first settlers; he was also curator of the town's first museum. As a photographer, he was ahead of his time, taking innovative "stereoscopic" views 30 years before any of his peers.

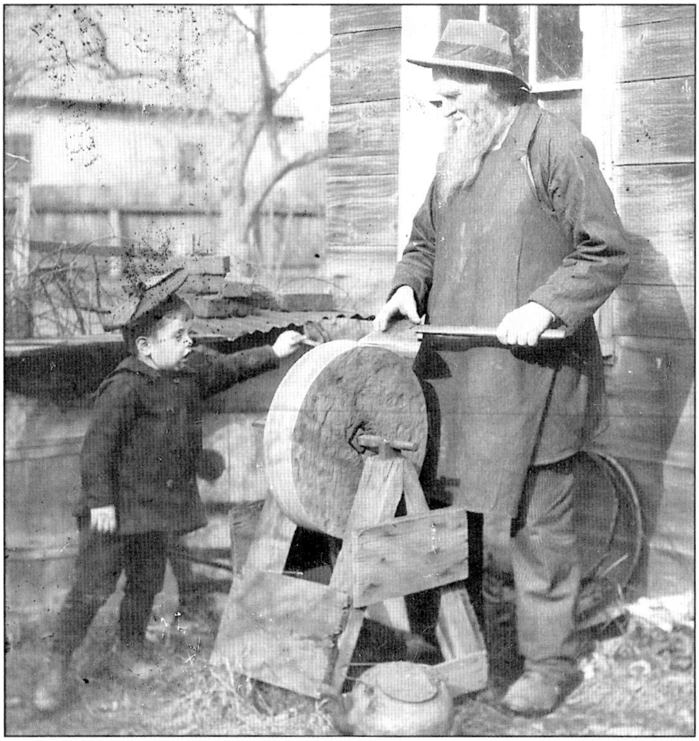

This c. 1850 Davis photograph shows Whiting Gates using a grinding wheel to sharpen a small object, perhaps a stick or pen-knife, for a young boy. Gates's house on Johnny Appleseed Lane still stands today. The farmhouse was built in 1801 by John Divoll, Gates's grandfather.

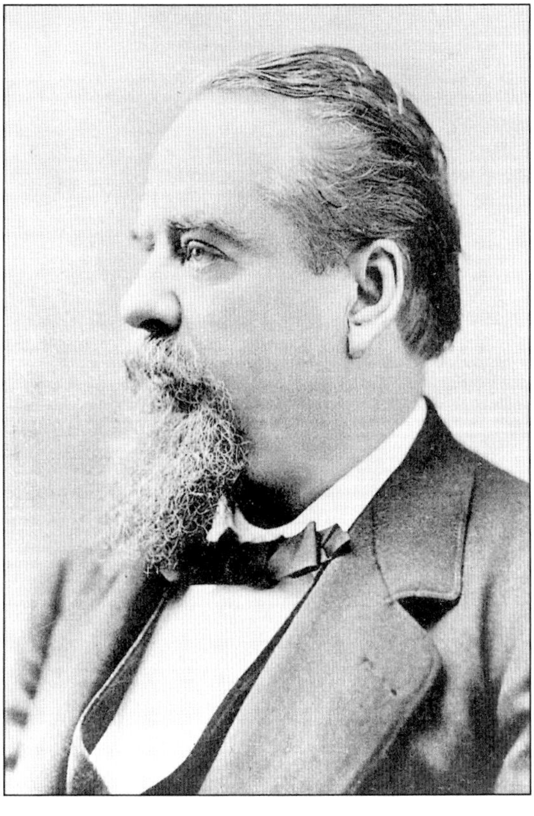

Leominster native Samuel Gardner Wilder found fame and fortune in Hawaii in the mid-1850s. He sailed by clipper ship from California, landing in Honolulu in 1857; he soon established several sugar cane plantations, built a railroad, and founded the Wilder Steamship Line. When Hawaii was still a kingdom, he was named Minister of the Interior and President of the Legislature, holding the position until his death in 1888.

Bernard W. Doyle, born in 1873, founded the hugely successful Viscoloid Company. At one time, Doyle employed 60% of Leominster's workforce! He donated his money, land, and time to improve life in Leominster. Doyle's contributions included the Leominster Hospital, Doyle Field, St. Leo's Cemetery and Church, the Veterans' Center, the recreation center, and the Notown Reservoir. He served as mayor and was active on many boards. Each day, something Bernard Doyle accomplished or gave to Leominster influences its citizens; his daughter Louise continues this tradition of generosity and community support.

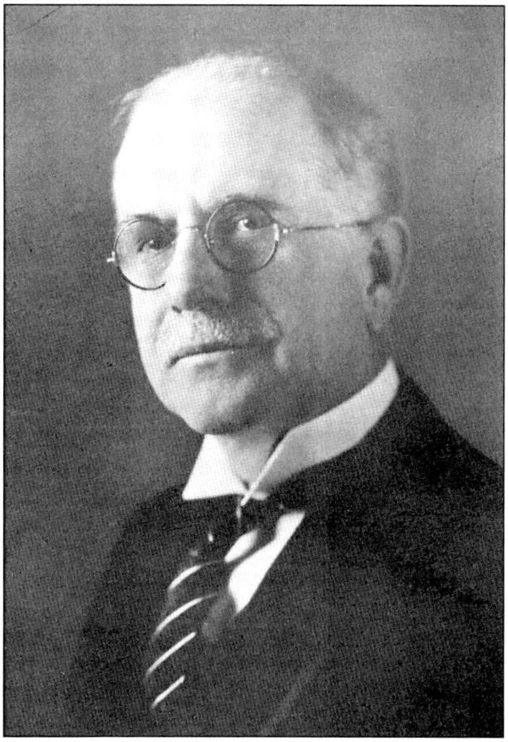

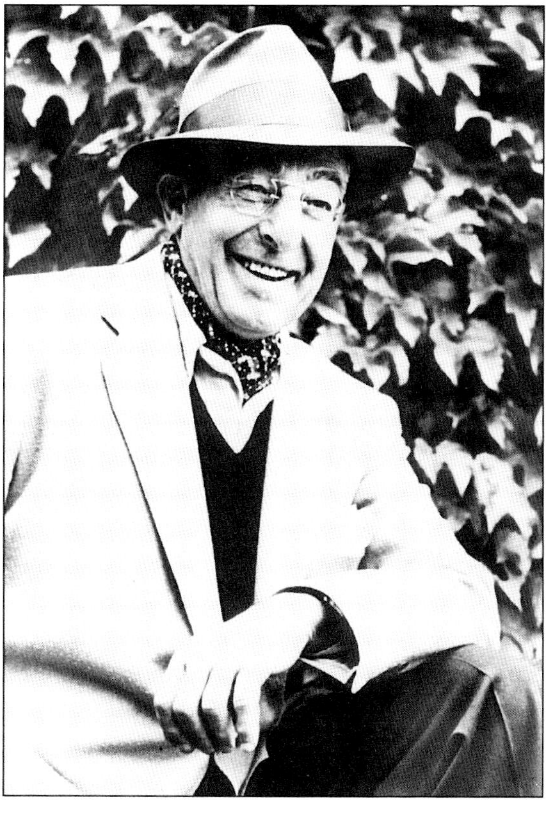

"Hello you back there in Leominster!" The speaker was Hall of Fame football coach Lou Little on national radio from Pasadena, California, where his "hopelessly outclassed" Columbia team had just defeated powerhouse Stanford University in the 1934 Rose Bowl. Sixteen days later, on January 17, 1934, the coach was greeted by one of the biggest celebrations in Leominster history. "Coach of the Era" in 1955 and a personal friend of President Eisenhower, Lou Little never forgot his hometown.

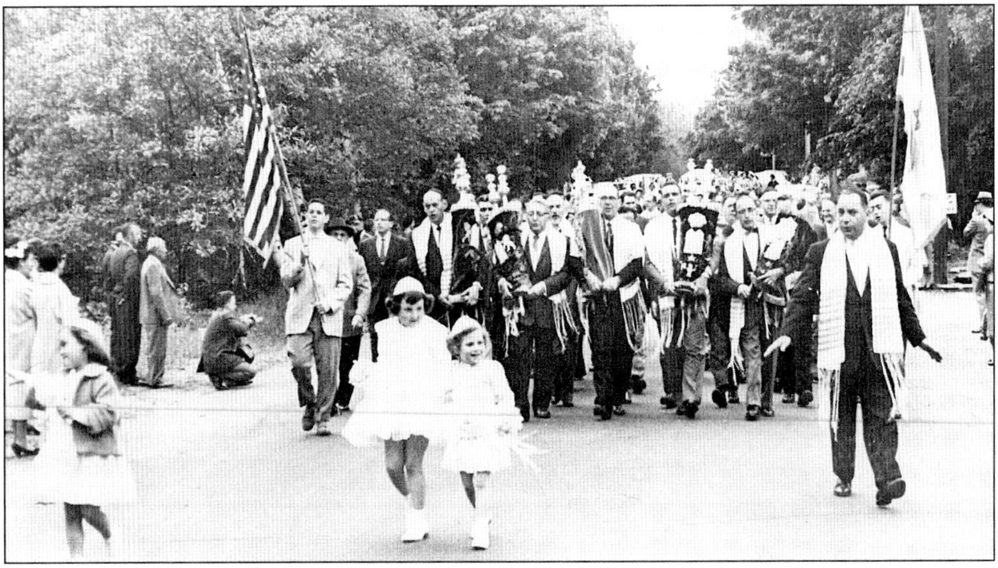

Leominster's first synagogue, dedicated in 1924, was located at Pleasant Street and Morse Place. Congregation Agudas Achim was then led by Rabbi Morris Taubes. In 1952, congregation president Joseph C. Foster began plans to construct a new synagogue, which was completed in 1959. Thousands of people lined the streets as the Torah scrolls were removed from the ark on Pleasant Street and a procession marched to the new synagogue on Washington Street. This photograph captures that proud day.

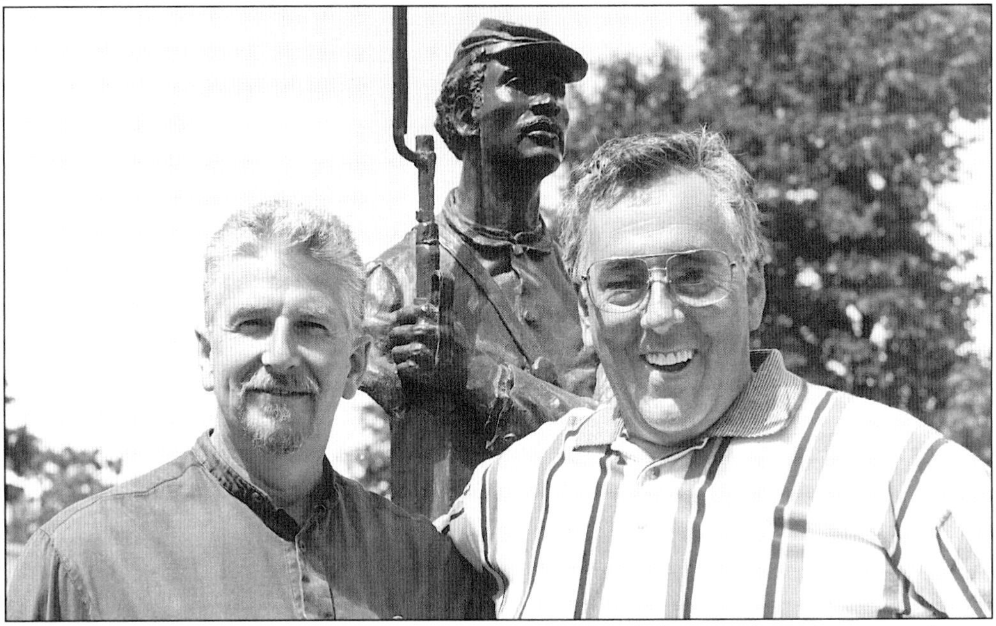

The rededication of Carter Park in July 1998 was crowned with the unveiling of a statue in honor of Leominster's Oliver Hazard, a member of the all-black 54th Massachusetts Volunteers. Seen here, from left to right in front of the statue, are Leominster native and nationally acclaimed sculptor Phil Cote and president of the Leominster Historical Society Thomas "Tucker" Hazzard. The Society, along with the Vietnam Veterans of America Post 116, were major sponsors of the statue and the park rededication effort.

When Florence Wheeler reported to work at the Leominster Public Library on October 1, 1900, she began a career that would span almost 50 years! Miss Wheeler, librarian, historian, and preservationist, literally put Leominster "on the map" when her meticulous research in the 1930s established the city as the true birthplace of American folk hero Johnny Appleseed. Miss Wheeler is shown here with trustee Herman Nelson Curtis c. 1949.

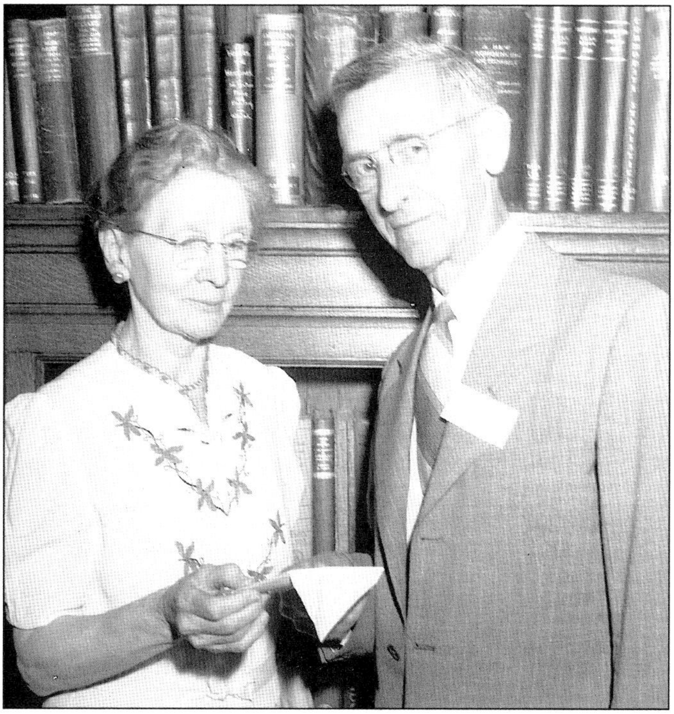

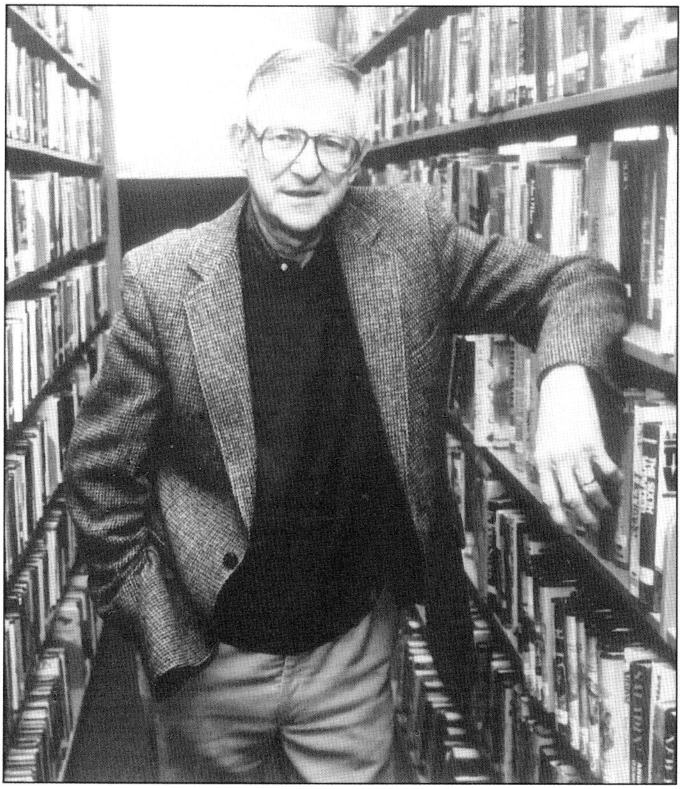

Robert Cormier remembers the moment he knew what his life's work would be. In seventh grade, after he presented his teacher Sister Catherine with a poem, she announced, "Robert, you are a writer!" His first novel, *Now and at the Hour*, was published in 1960. In addition to his award-winning newspaper career, he has written 17 internationally acclaimed books, three of which have been made into movies. Born in Leominster's "French Hill" section in 1925, Cormier evokes this time and place in many of his novels. He is shown here in the stacks of the Leominster Public Library.

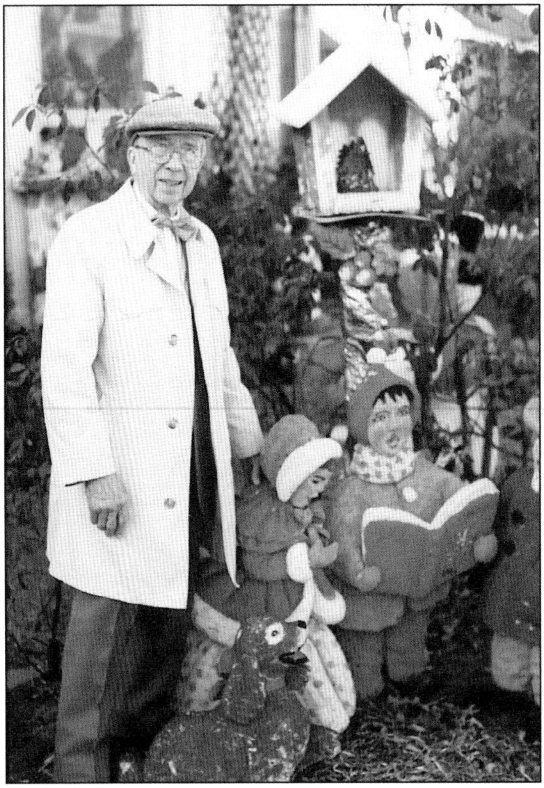

Celebrated carver Louis Charpentier came to Leominster from Canada with his family in 1932 at the age of 12. He worked as a designer at Paragon Plastics for 47 years; after retiring, he began volunteering in city elementary schools, teaching carving to children. Louis has represented Massachusetts artists and craftspeople at the Smithsonian Institution and, in 1982, was named Leominster's Citizen of the Year. He is shown here with several of the carvings of his legendary Christmas lawn display, begun in 1950.

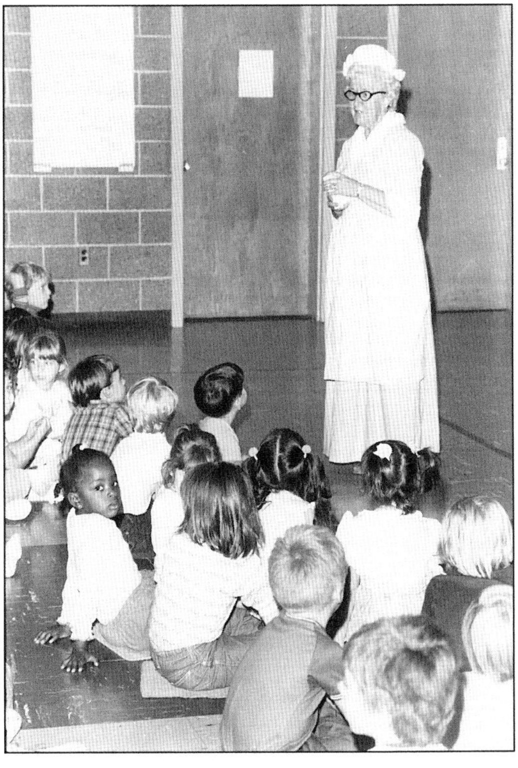

Mayor Richard Girouard once called her "the Heart of the City." For decades, Evelyn Hachey has dedicated herself to preserving and communicating the history of Leominster in general and Johnny Appleseed in particular. She has won numerous awards for her work, including the prestigious Daughters of the American Revolution (DAR) History Award, and has been a contributing author of several books and pamphlets about Leominster's history. Here she brings Johnny Appleseed's story to life for students at Johnny Appleseed School.

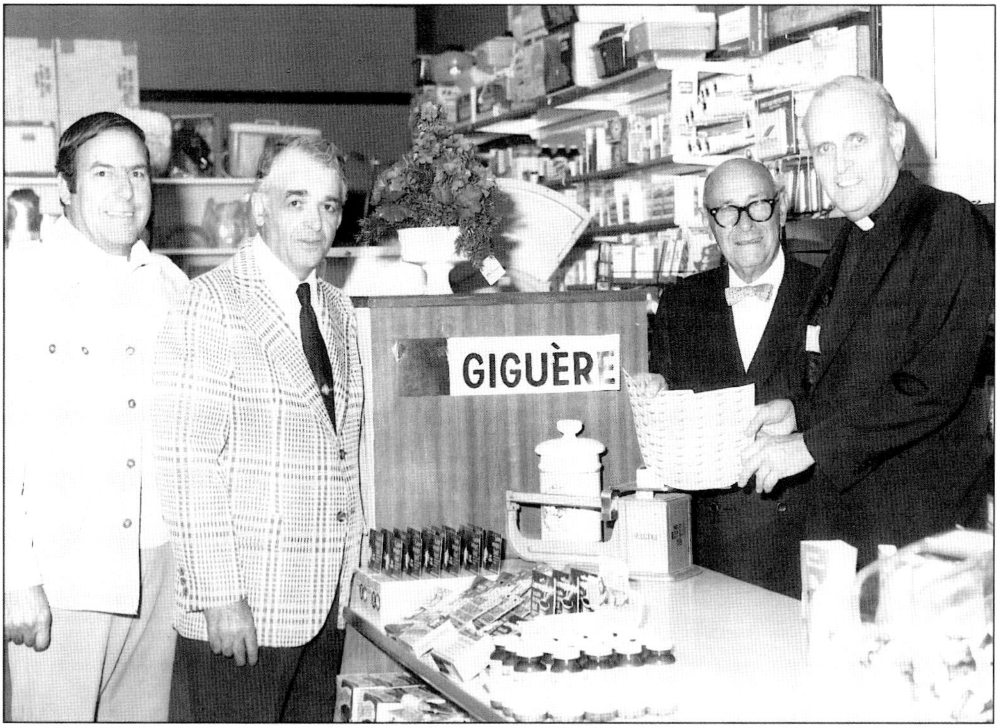

When Giguere Drug opened its Central Street store, a satellite post office was added to better serve the area's customers. Shown in this 1971 photograph, from left to right, are building owner Nunzio Lattanzio, beloved State Representative Angelo Picucci, store owner Ignazzio Carluccio, and Father Drinan, U.S. Congressman from our then Third District.

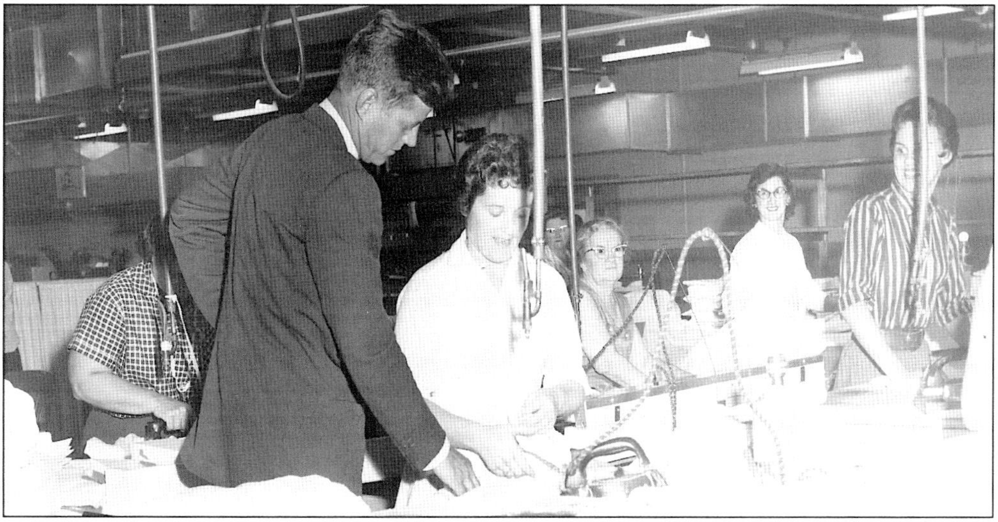

John F. Kennedy visits the Cluett Peabody & Company shirt factory in 1959 during his campaign for president. Established in August 1899, the company was located on First Street, between Spruce and Water Streets. Over 600 employees manufactured Arrow shirts, collars, handkerchiefs, and underwear until the plant closed in June 1971. Leominster's shirt-making industry, which included F.A. Whitney's Wachusett Shirt Company, was even the subject of a poem, "Song for a Leominster Shirt."

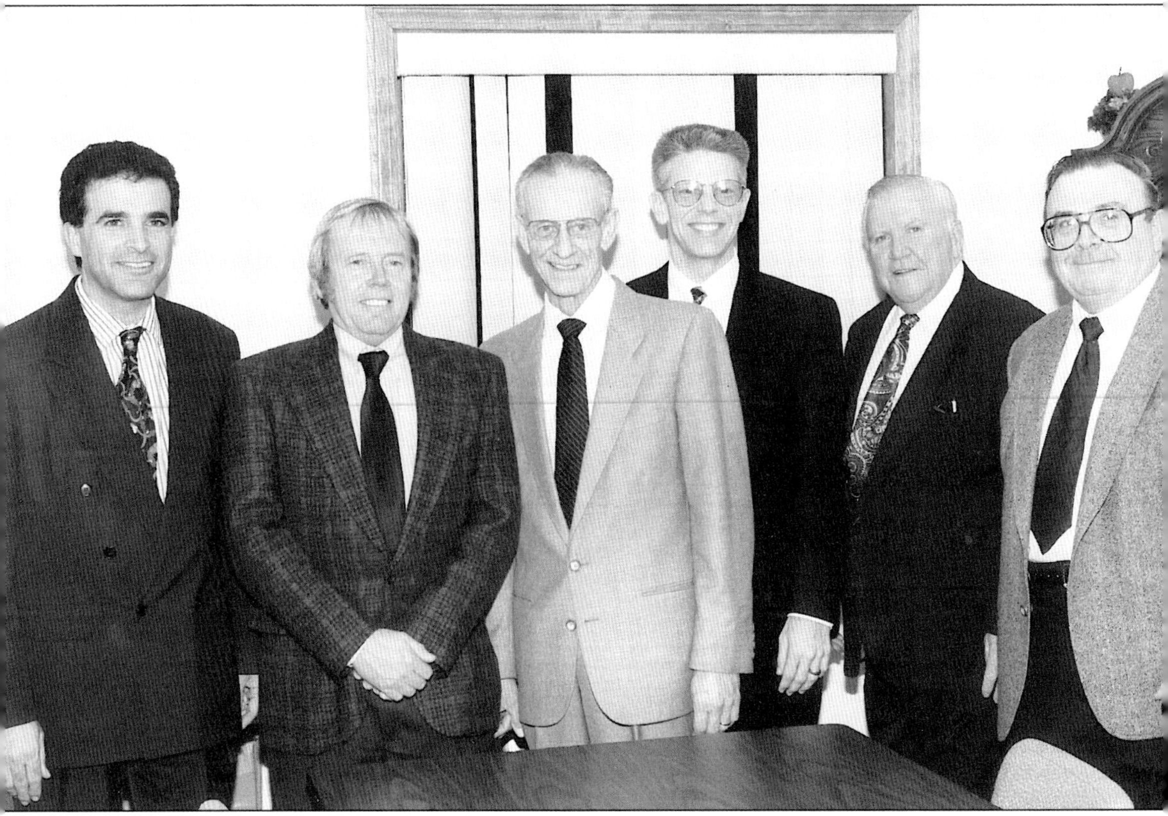

All of Leominster's living mayors gathered to dedicate the new Leominster Senior Citizens Center on Pond Street to Mayor Richard Girouard, who was instrumental in securing many donations of money, materials, and labor to build the center. Missing in the photograph is John B. McLaughlin, mayor of the city from 1974 to 1977. Mayors present, from left to right, are Dean J. Mazzarella, 1994 to present; Raymond D. Harper, 1980-1981; Richard J. Girouard, 1982-1988; Stephen A. Perla, 1988-1992; John P. Mahan, 1992-1993; and Joseph T. Moriarty, 1978-1979. A total of 28 years of service to the city of Leominster is represented in this picture.

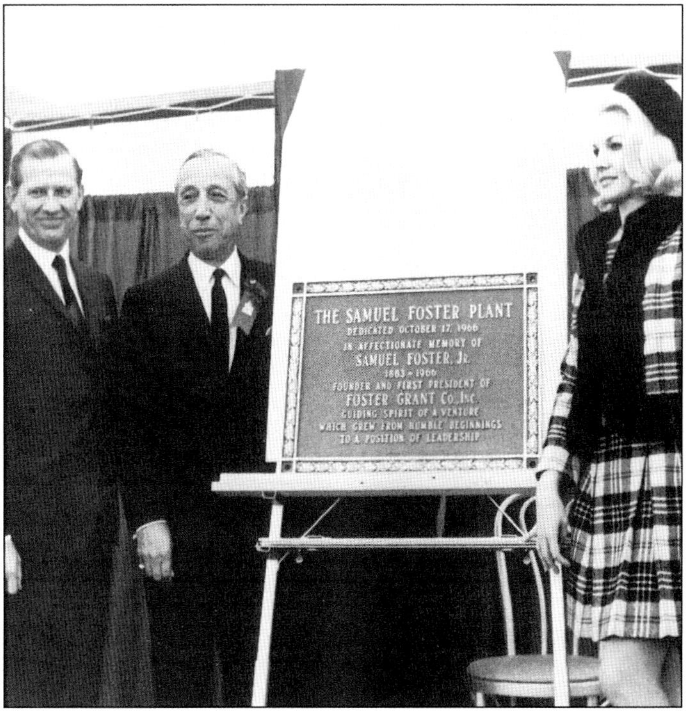

Massachusetts Governor John Volpe and screen star Carroll Baker join Joseph Foster at the 1966 dedication of the Samuel Foster Sunglass Plant in Leominster, the most modern production facility in the sunglass industry. Miss Baker was then starring in Foster Grant's "Sunglasses of the Stars" advertising campaign.

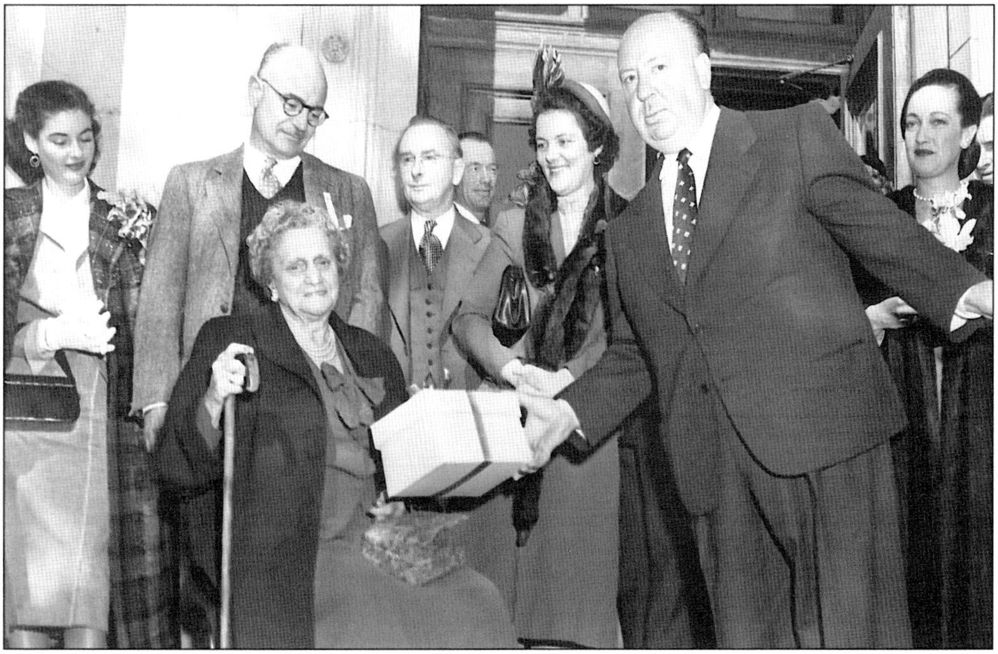

On the steps of City Hall in 1951, legendary movie director Alfred Hitchcock presents a corsage to Rosina McEvoy, owner of the Rialto and Plymouth Theaters. Actress Dorothy Lamour (far right) looks on. The entourage that accompanied Hitchcock also included film stars James Whitmore, Deborah Paget, Tom Breen, and Margaret Sheridan. The movie industry representatives, most likely here as part of a promotional tour, received Foster Grant sunglasses and a carton of native apples during the welcoming ceremony.

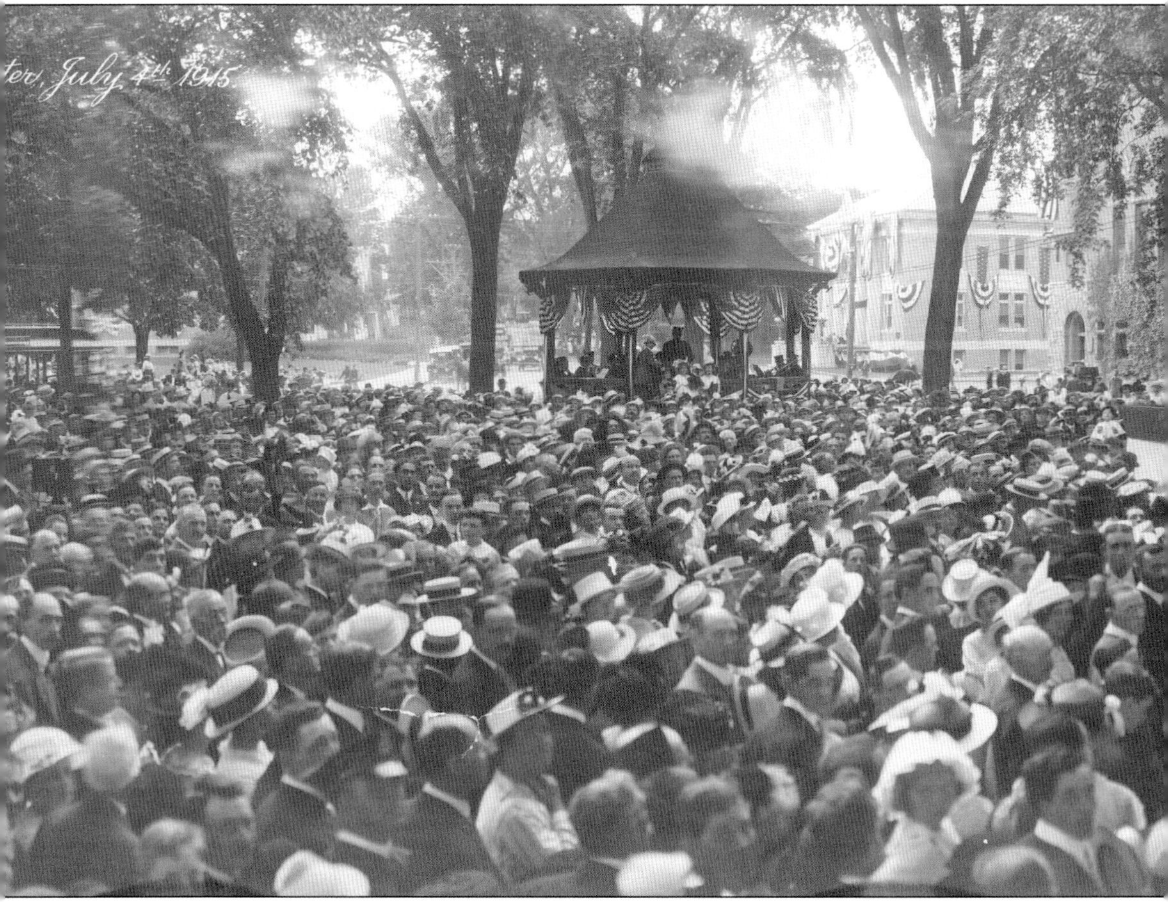

This panoramic photograph, taken July 4, 1915, shows Leominster citizens celebrating the 175th anniversary of the founding of the town in 1740. The huge crowd is being addressed by Mayor Henry Sawtelle; the impressive sea of hats on both men and women reveal the popularity of straw hats for men at this time. This picture is an interesting blend of old and new; the Old Town Hall, the new municipal building, the new library building, the second Unitarian church,

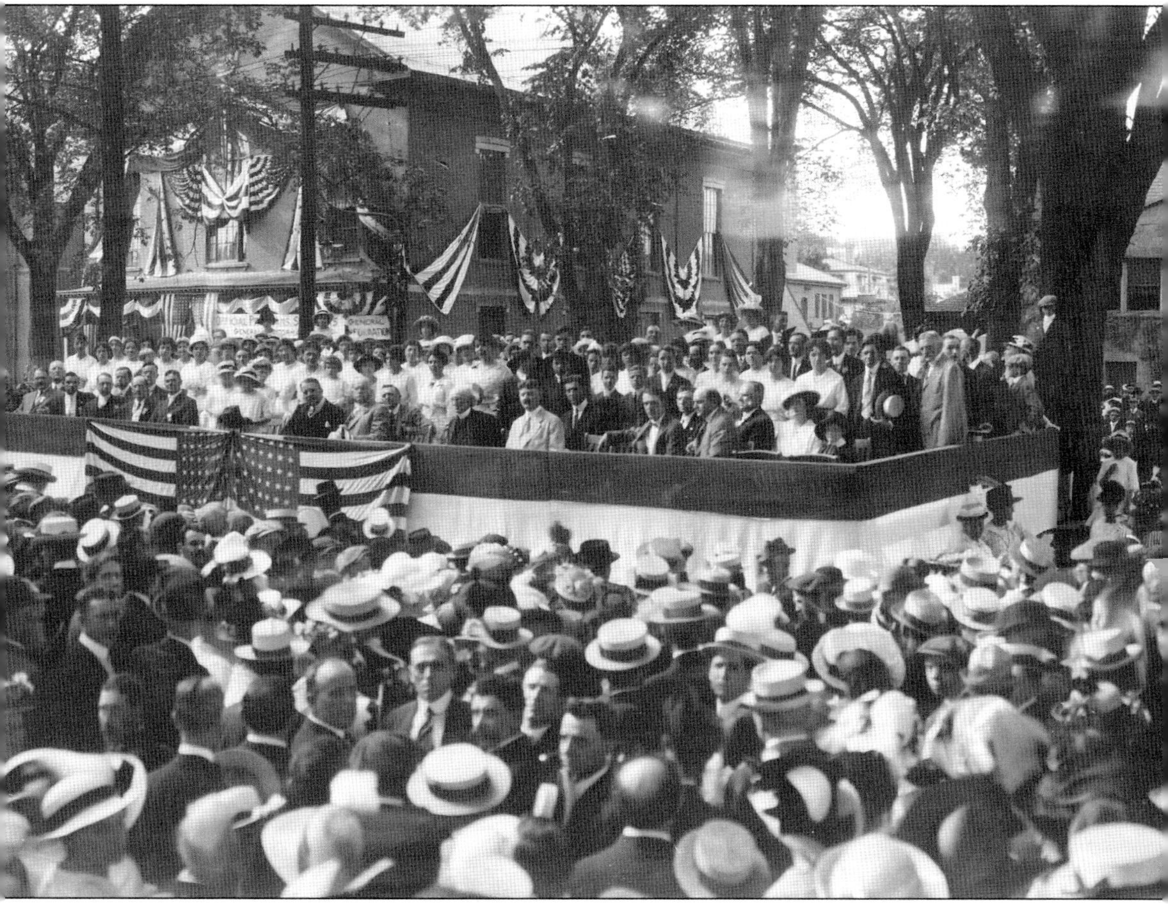

and the old bandstand are all visible; many are even decked out in spectacular bunting. This photograph shows Leominster at a turning point; it has become a city, with excitement and opportunity ahead. But the Great War had begun, and the world was now a more complex and dangerous place.

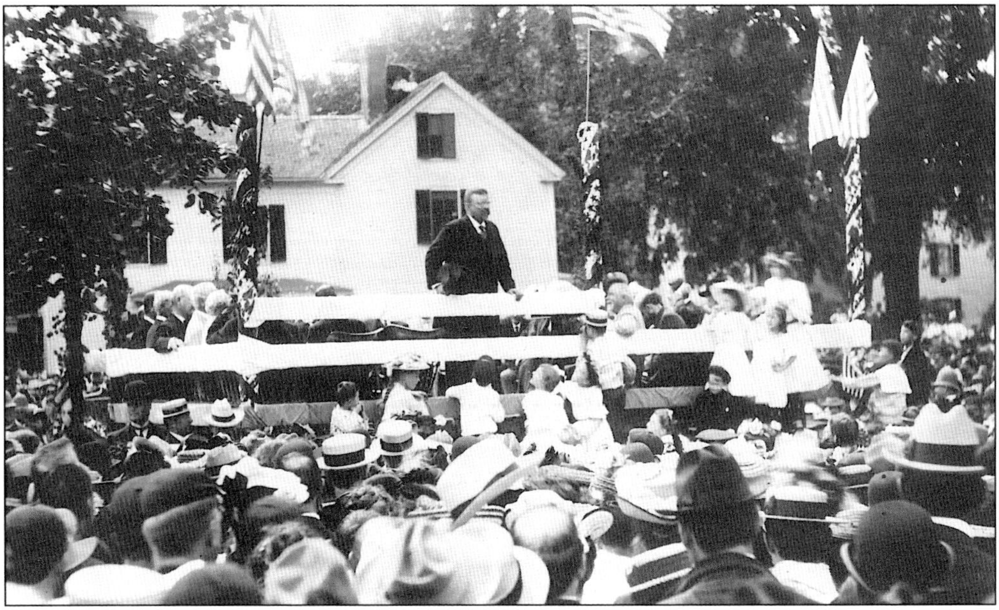

One of Carter Park's most historic moments occurred on September 2, 1902, when President Theodore Roosevelt stopped at the park to make a brief address. The 4-acre park was jammed with a crowd of over 5,000 people who came to see and hear the popular president. Roosevelt spoke for only three or four minutes and honored the Civil War veterans assembled on the train platform with other city officials.

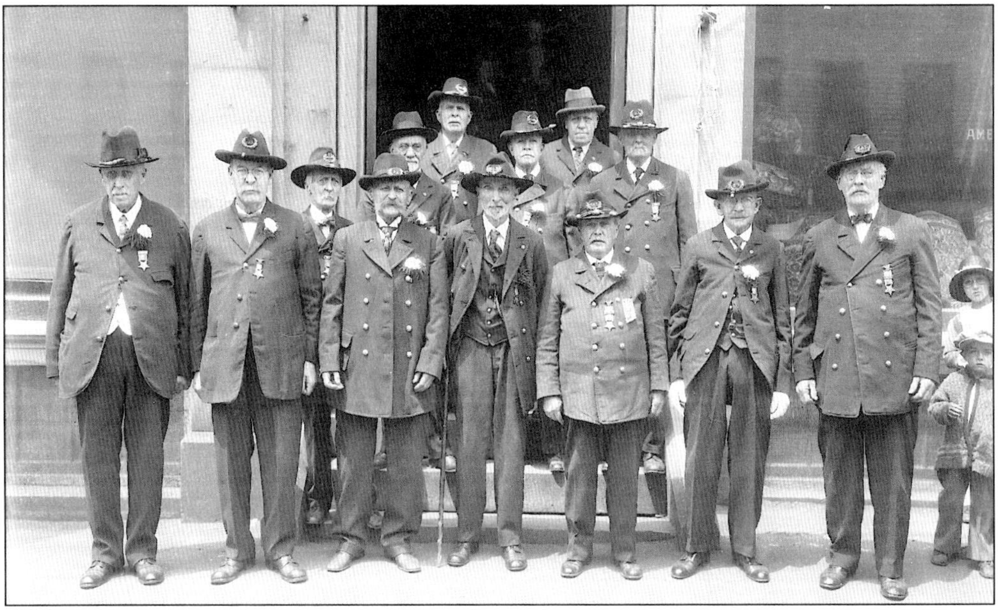

This is one of the last known photographs of Leominster's Civil War veterans, taken in the early 1900s in front of their headquarters at the Bank Block on Main Street. The Charles H. Stevens Post 53, organized in 1868, was named to honor Captain Stevens, the highest-ranking Leominster officer killed in the Civil War. The post's last surviving member was Charles F. Staples, who died shortly before his 97th birthday in June 1944. Seen above, he is in the second row, second from the left.

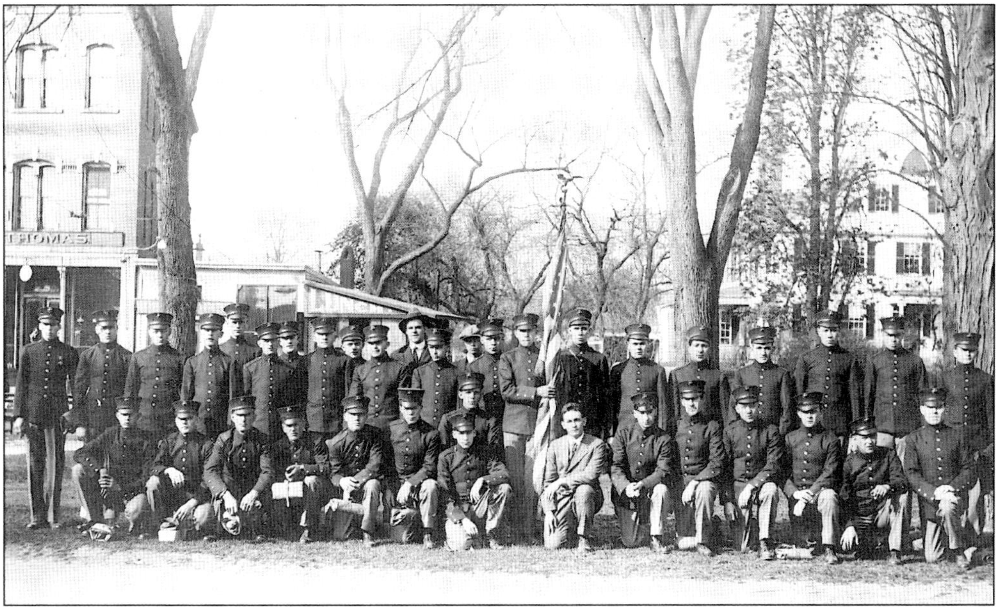

This photograph of the Second Marine Corps of Massachusetts was taken on the Common on May 19, 1917. This picture is unusual because these young men are already in uniform before they have even reported for duty. Fund-raising efforts by Capt. J.H. Johnston allowed loved ones to see their sons in uniform even as they led the farewell parade through town. The Allen home on Park Street can be seen in the upper right of the photograph.

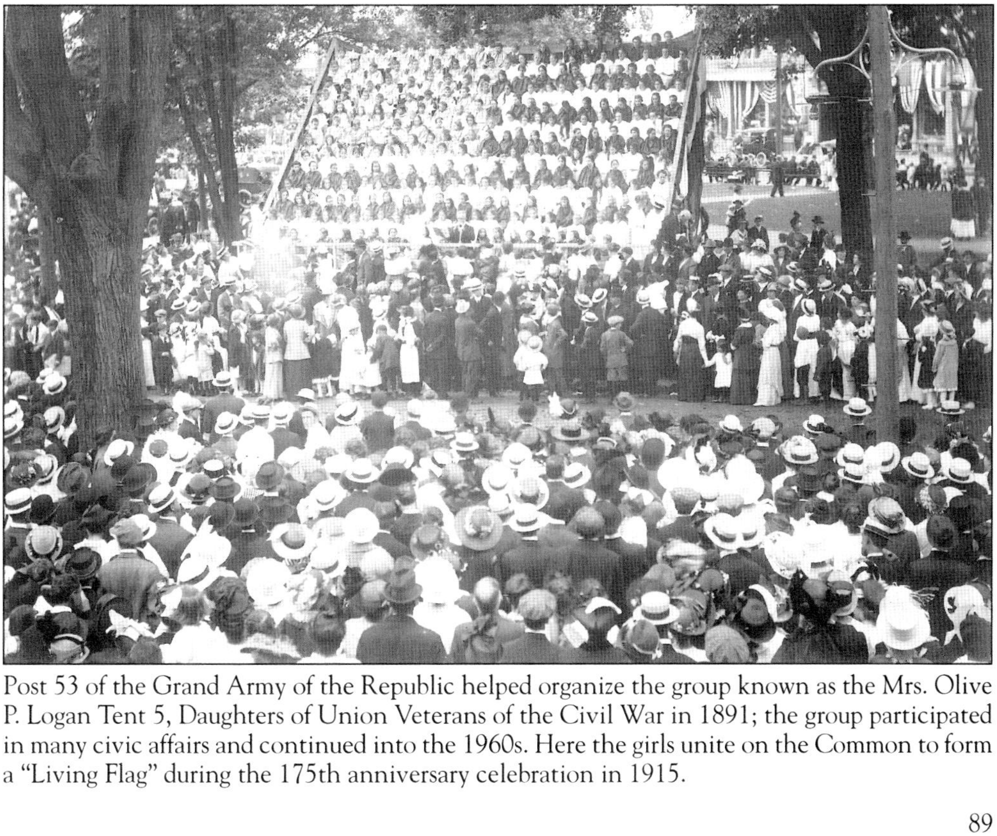

Post 53 of the Grand Army of the Republic helped organize the group known as the Mrs. Olive P. Logan Tent 5, Daughters of Union Veterans of the Civil War in 1891; the group participated in many civic affairs and continued into the 1960s. Here the girls unite on the Common to form a "Living Flag" during the 175th anniversary celebration in 1915.

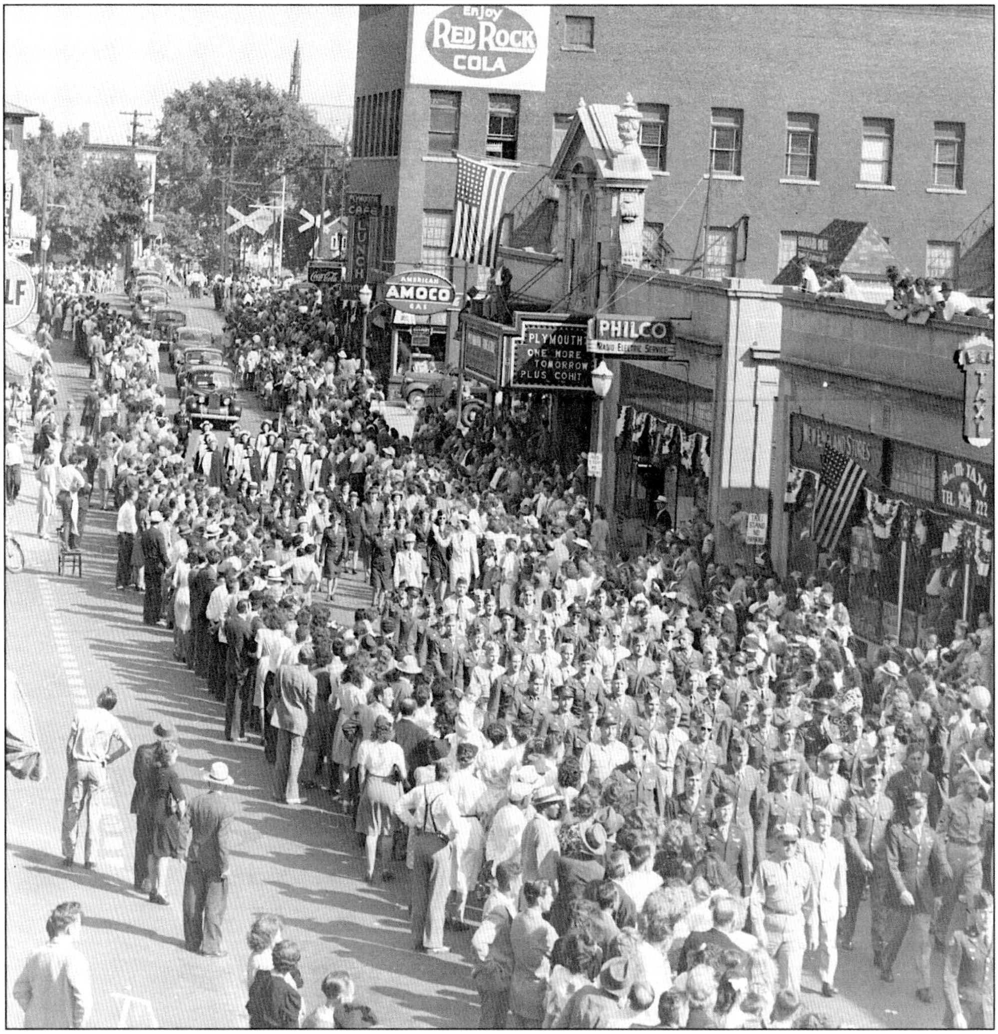

The "Welcome Home Parade" began at 2:30 p.m. on September 1, 1946. It contained nine divisions and was one of the largest parades in Leominster history. Dr. Charles Cronin was the parade's chief marshal; official guests included U.S. Senators David Walsh and Leverett Saltonstall, Gov. Maurice Tobin, and many other state and local leaders. The parade was part of a three-day celebration hosted by Leominster citizens to show their appreciation for the sacrifices of the 2,800 veterans of WW II. Absent from this parade were the 104 Leominster servicemen who lost their lives defending freedom.

This 1944 photograph shows 18-year-old Pete Bracani receiving an admiring salute from his brother Jake, age 3. After WW II, Pete went on to establish a popular coffee shop in North Leominster at the corner of Main and Prospect Streets, where he continued to "serve" the citizens of Leominster. Pete's wit and humor were matched only by his generosity and willingness to help those less fortunate.

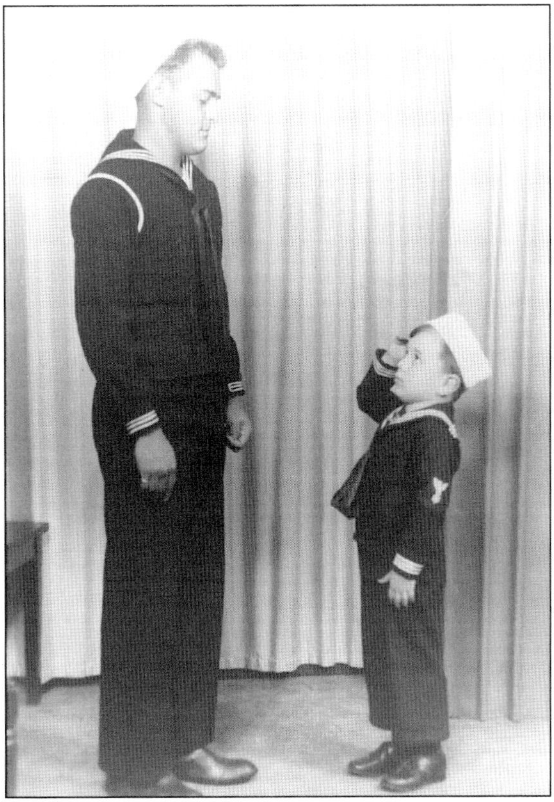

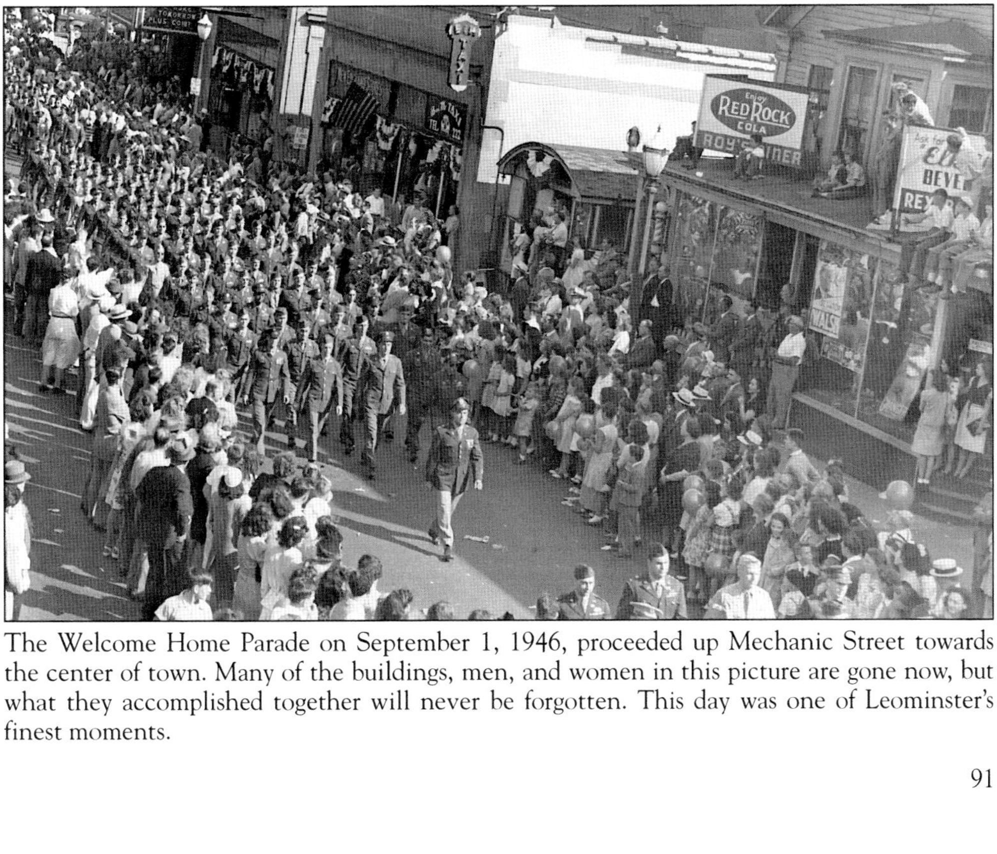

The Welcome Home Parade on September 1, 1946, proceeded up Mechanic Street towards the center of town. Many of the buildings, men, and women in this picture are gone now, but what they accomplished together will never be forgotten. This day was one of Leominster's finest moments.

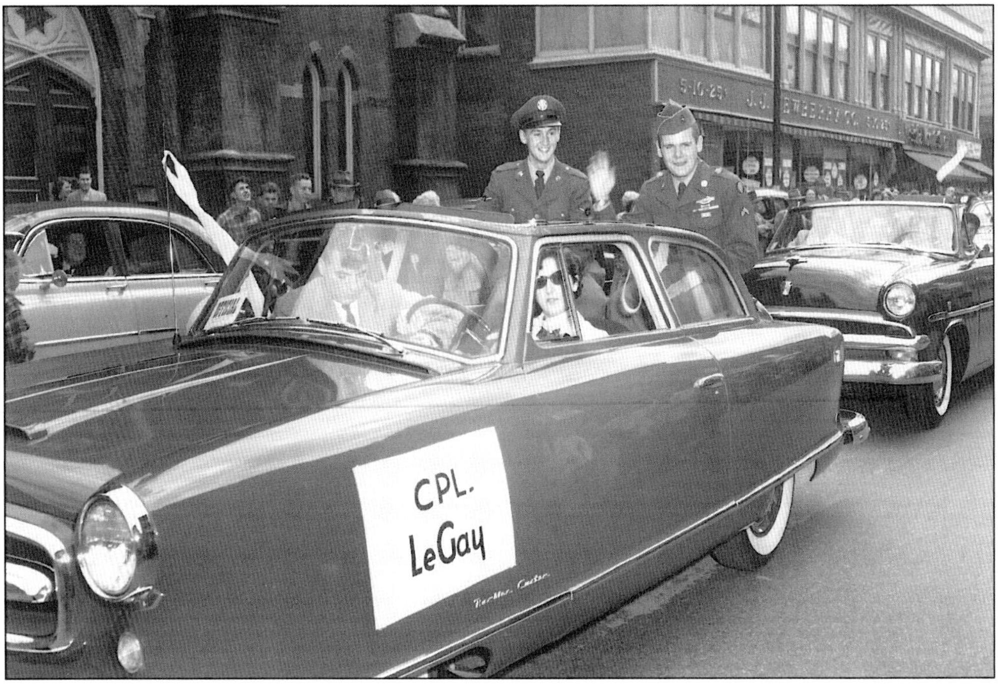

A huge Welcome Home Parade for U.S. Army Corporal Donald K. Legay was held in May 1953. Corporel LeGay had been wounded in the Korean War and endured 29 months in a Red Chinese prison camp. He was the first New England P.O.W. to be released. He was met at Logan Airport by his family and a delegation from Leominster. Dave Goodell, a local Ford dealer, donated the convertible Corporel LeGay is riding in; it was presented by Mayor Crossman as a gift from a grateful city.

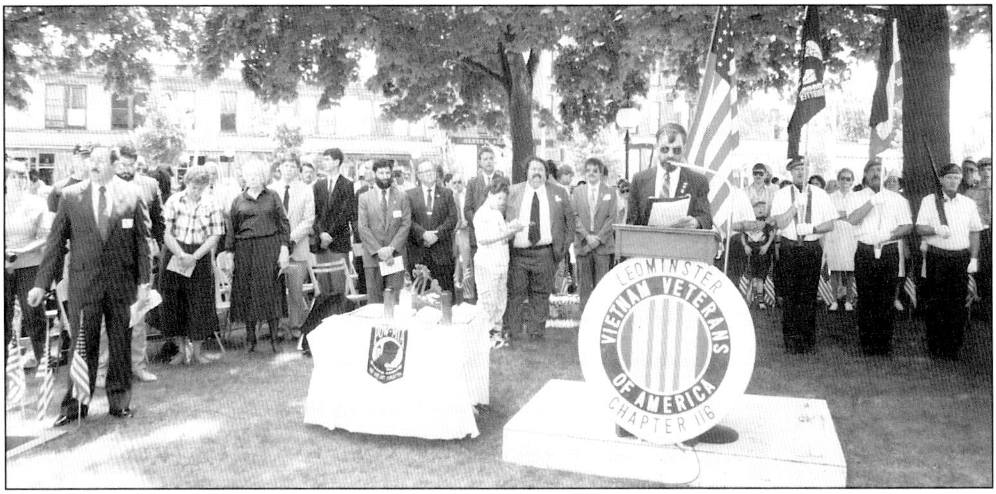

On Saturday, June 16, 1990, a moving ceremony marked the dedication of the Vietnam Veterans Memorial on Monument Square. Hundreds of city residents joined families who had lost loved ones "to honor with dignity the sacred memory of the war dead." Tucker Hazzard and Don Wakefield unveiled the monument; it was presented to the City of Leominster by Dan Joseph and Ron Freda. Pictured at the podium is Vietnam Veterans Pres. Richard Early, now the Leominster Director of Veterans' Services.

Five

RECREATION AND COMMUNITY LIFE

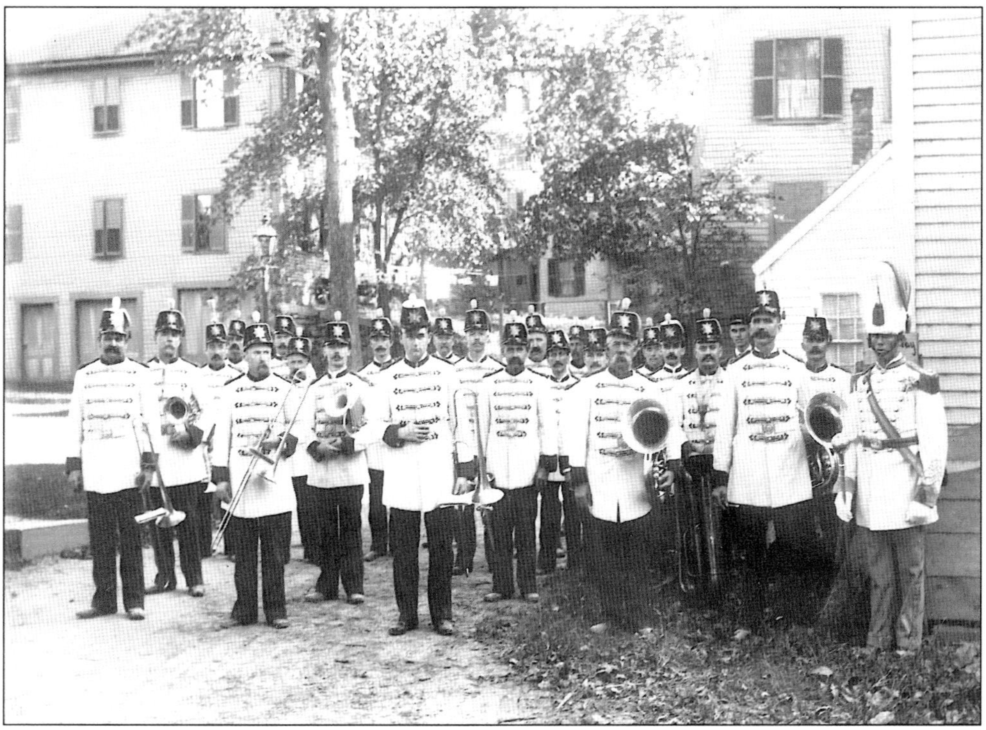

Military bands in Leominster have a rich history dating back to the Revolutionary War. Some members of the band pictured here were among those who enlisted in the Union Army in 1861. This band was known as the First Regiment Massachusetts Volunteers; they served 15 months before being discharged. Several members of the band then enlisted in the regular service. Brass marching bands such as this one remained popular into the early 1900s.

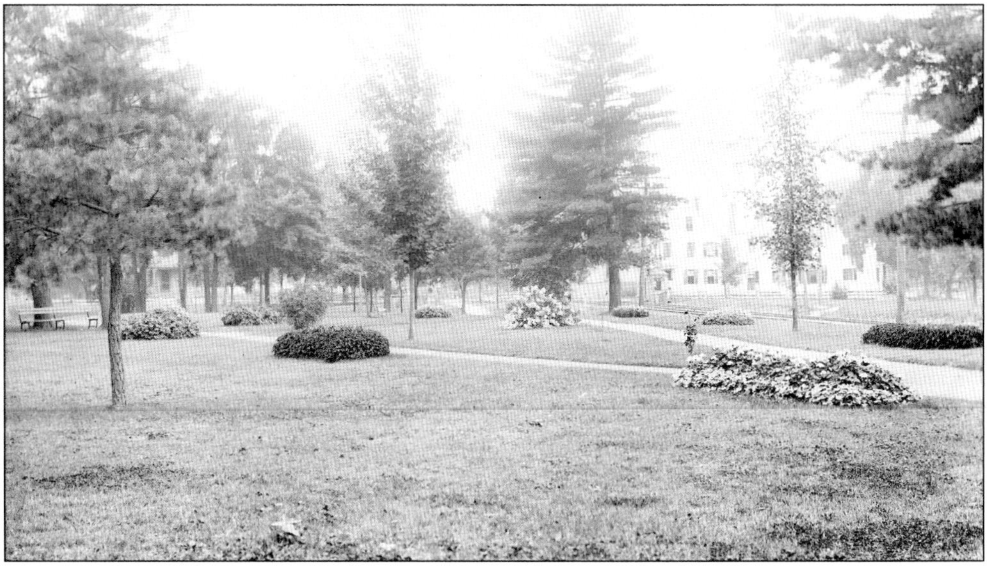

A late 1890s view of Carter Park shows its natural beauty. Oliver Carter, a town founder, donated the land in 1754 to be used "as a training field or perpetual common." Soldiers mustered out here for the French and Indian War, the Revolutionary War, the War of 1812, and the Civil War.

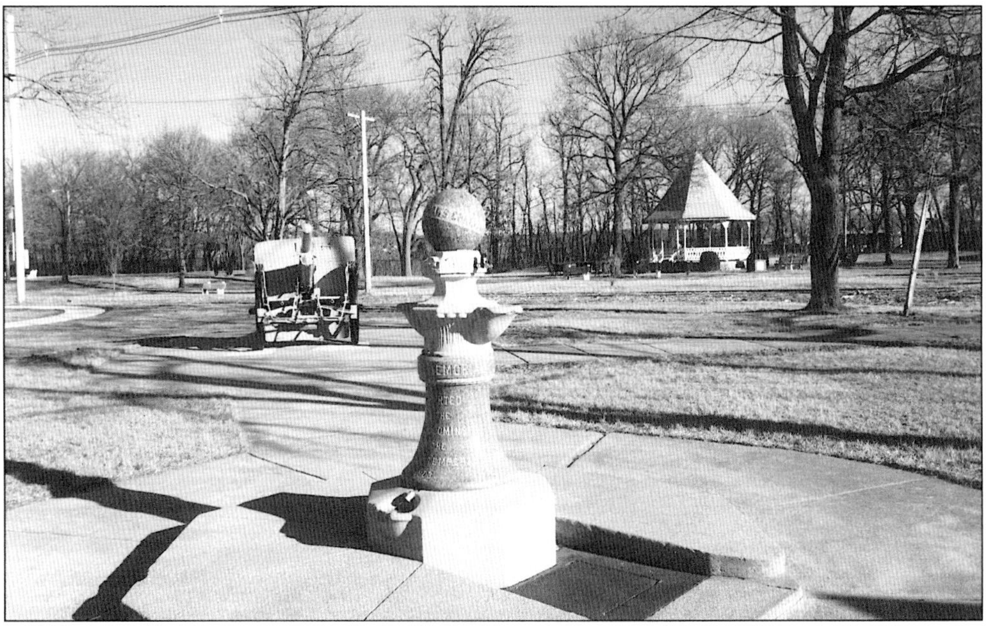

The 1998 renovation of Carter Park included restoration of historic artifacts located in the park. The 1903 Willard fountain and 1917 WW I cannon are pictured here. Also restored were an 1803 cannon and the DAR monument to Oliver Carter. A flagpole donated by the Landing/Ship/Tank (LST) Association was also installed.

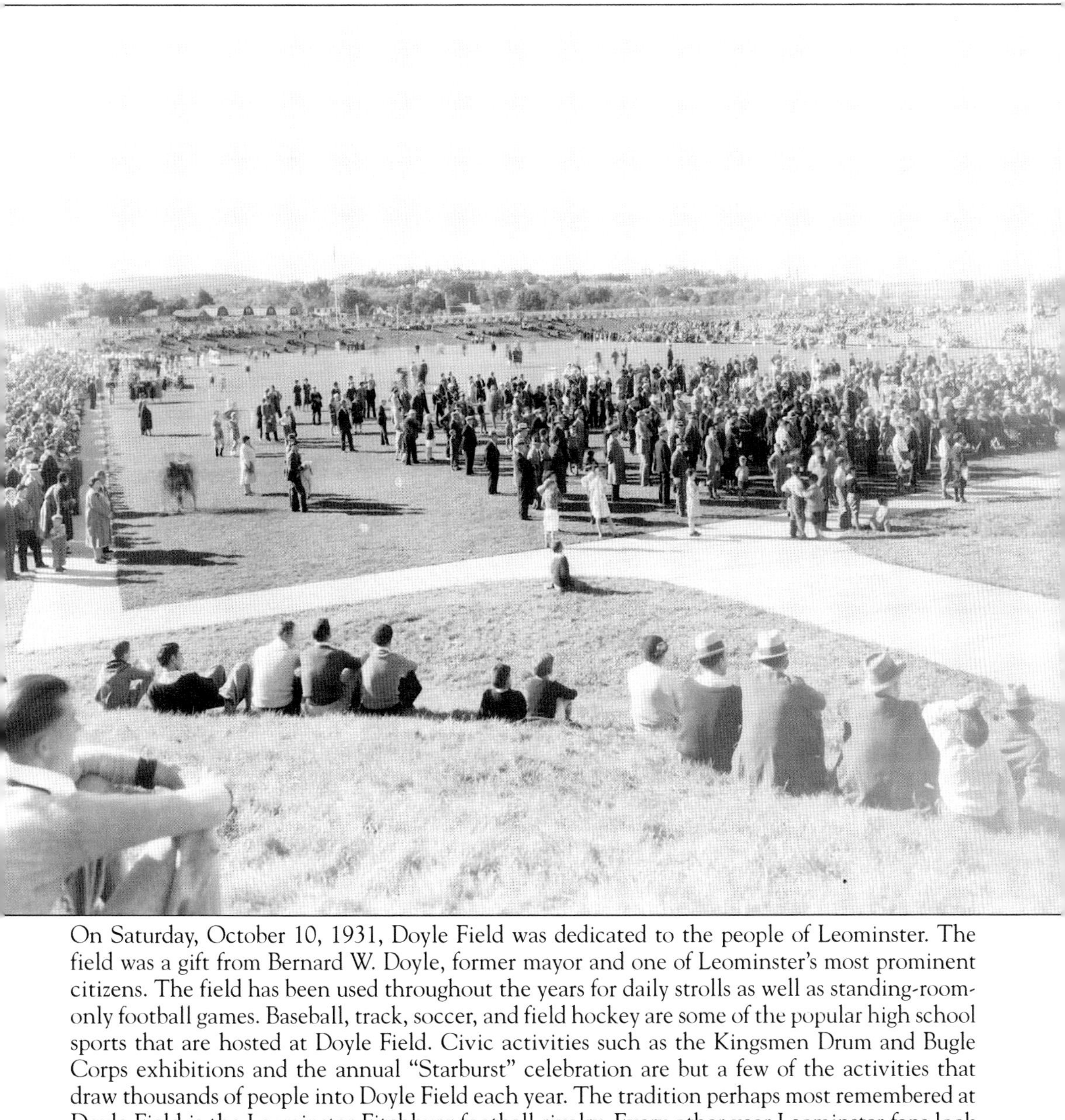

On Saturday, October 10, 1931, Doyle Field was dedicated to the people of Leominster. The field was a gift from Bernard W. Doyle, former mayor and one of Leominster's most prominent citizens. The field has been used throughout the years for daily strolls as well as standing-room-only football games. Baseball, track, soccer, and field hockey are some of the popular high school sports that are hosted at Doyle Field. Civic activities such as the Kingsmen Drum and Bugle Corps exhibitions and the annual "Starburst" celebration are but a few of the activities that draw thousands of people into Doyle Field each year. The tradition perhaps most remembered at Doyle Field is the Leominster-Fitchburg football rivalry. Every other year Leominster fans look forward to home field advantage as Fitchburg is hosted in another Thanksgiving Day classic. This picture, taken at the dedication, shows hundreds of people gathering to welcome Doyle Field into the Leominster community.

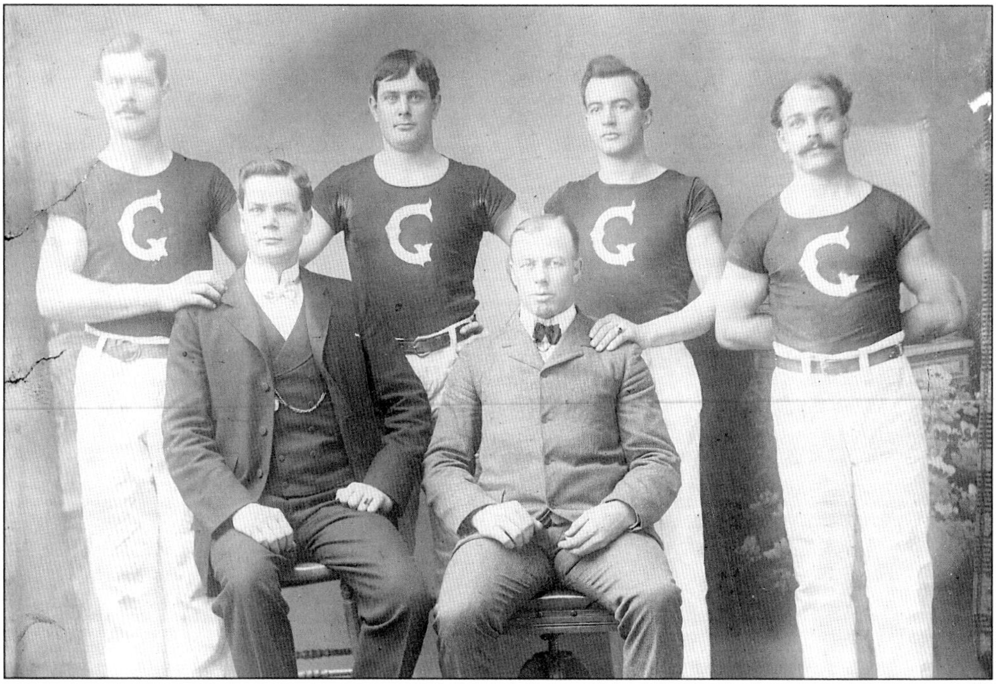

The G.A. Gane Shirt Company of Leominster was the world's-largest manufacturer of men's white dress shirts and the sponsor of this "Tug of War" team, considered one of the top teams in this part of the country. The team was organized in 1899 and remained undefeated in 20 consecutive pulls.

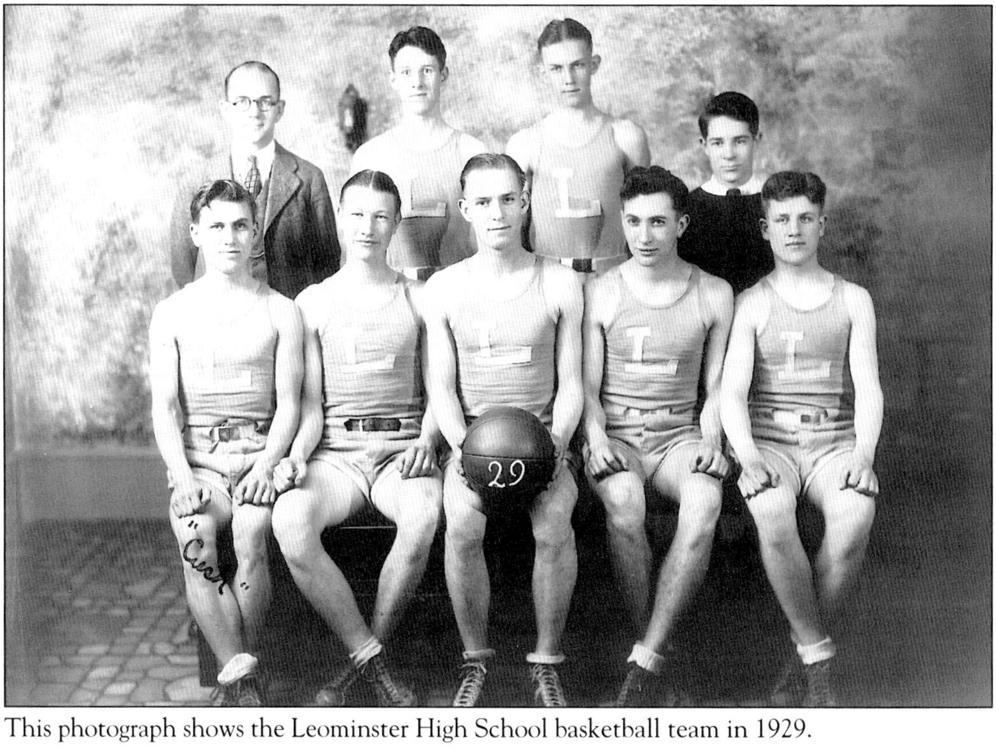

This photograph shows the Leominster High School basketball team in 1929.

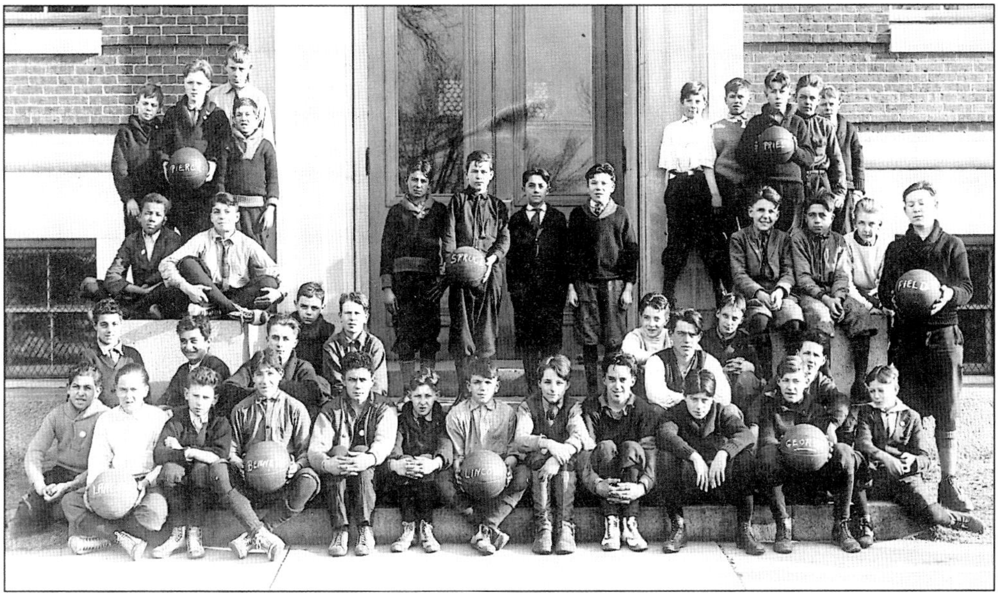

One of the highlights of the grammar school year was the city-wide basketball championship; teams competed at the "big kids' school" (Leominster High School on West Street), hoping to win a silver cup for their school. In this 1924 photograph, eight grammar schools were represented: Pierce, Lancaster, Bennett, Lincoln, George, Field, Priest, and Spruce.

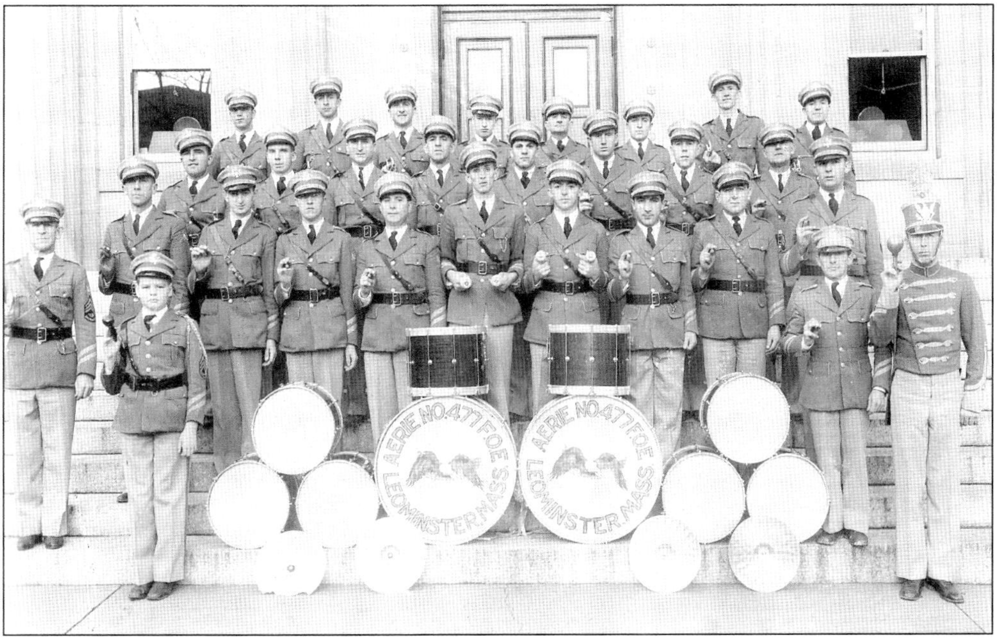

"Degree teams" were popular social activities among young men and women in the 1920s and 1930s; this photograph shows the Eagles degree team in front of the Leominster City Hall. These groups specialized in synchronized marching and used few instruments other than percussion and batons. When they performed in an auditorium, a piano was sometimes used. Candidates for membership received their "degree" after completing an initiation ritual. The Eagles degree team was the state champion from 1935 to 1938.

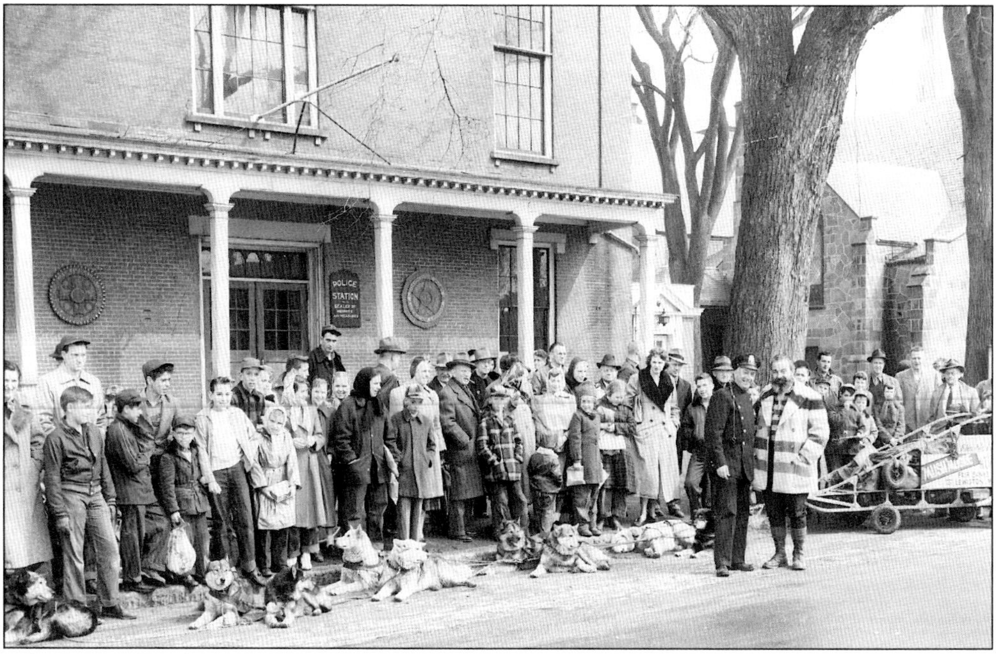

A large crowd gathered as Driver Cecil A. Moore and his nine-dog sled team arrive in Leominster on March 17, 1951, on the final leg of a trip to Lewiston, Maine. Moore set out from his home in Fairbanks, Alaska, in November 1949; he hoped to write a book about his experiences and use his trip as a fund-raiser for underprivileged children.

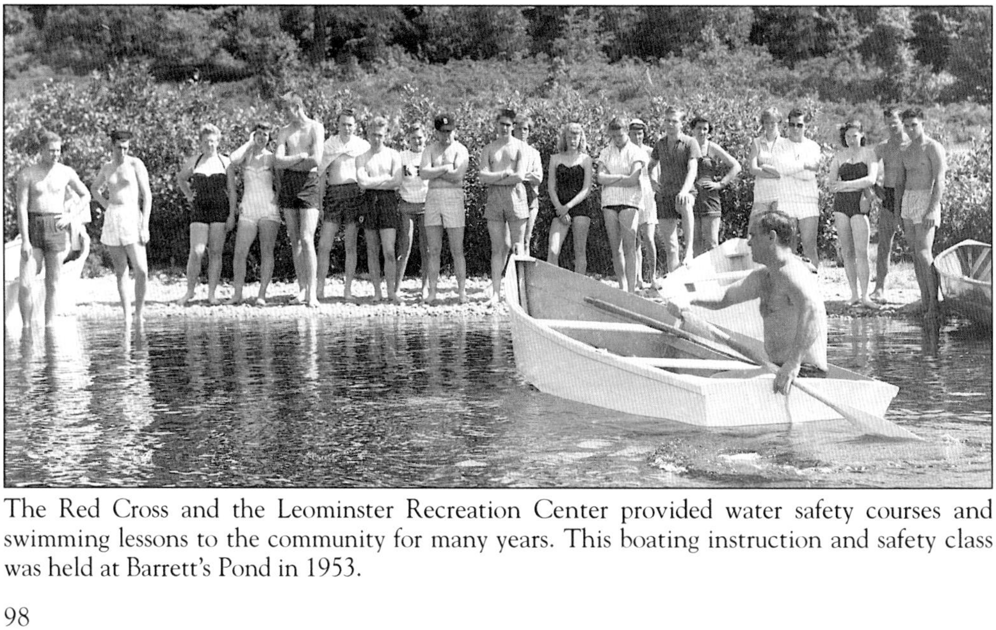

The Red Cross and the Leominster Recreation Center provided water safety courses and swimming lessons to the community for many years. This boating instruction and safety class was held at Barrett's Pond in 1953.

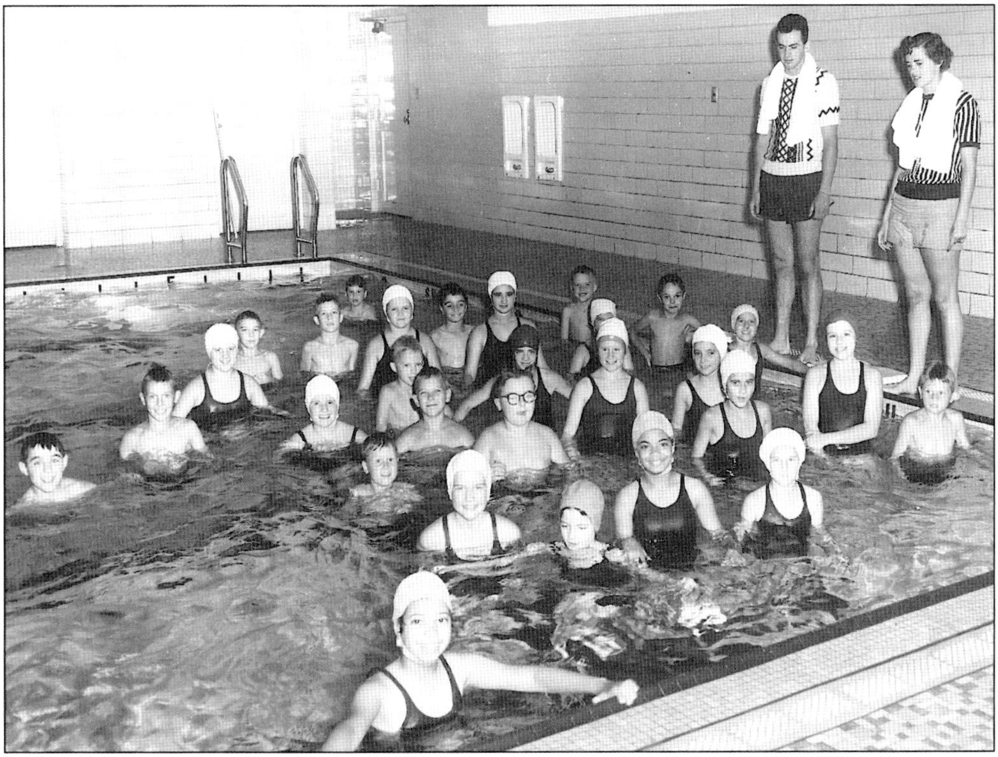

As seen in this photo, swimming lessons at the recreation center were an enjoyable activity for many Leominster youngsters.

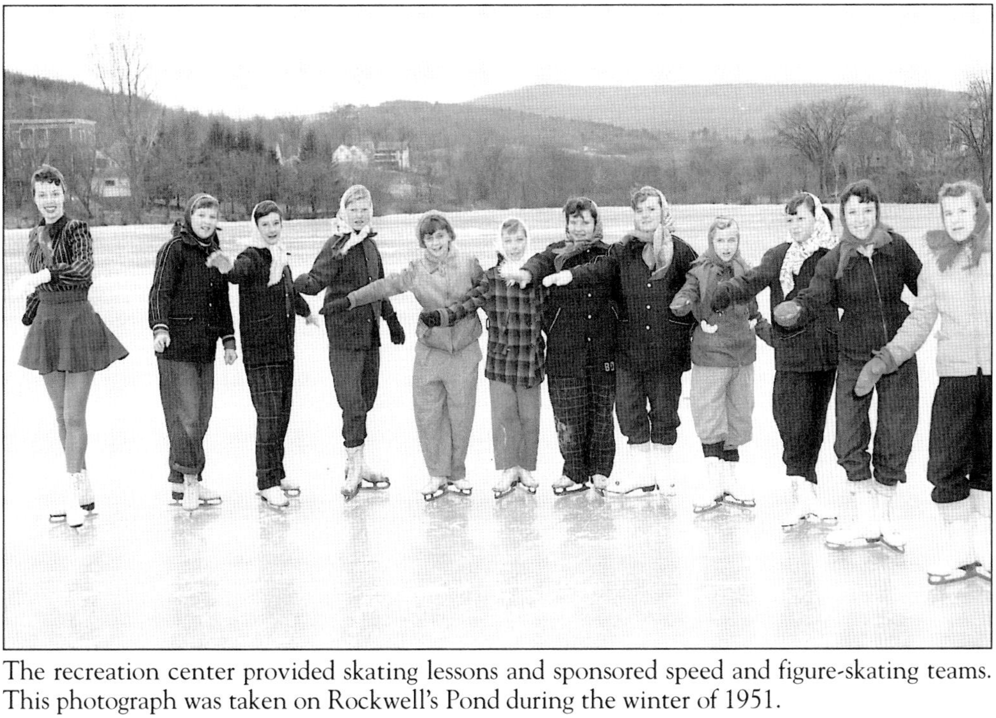

The recreation center provided skating lessons and sponsored speed and figure-skating teams. This photograph was taken on Rockwell's Pond during the winter of 1951.

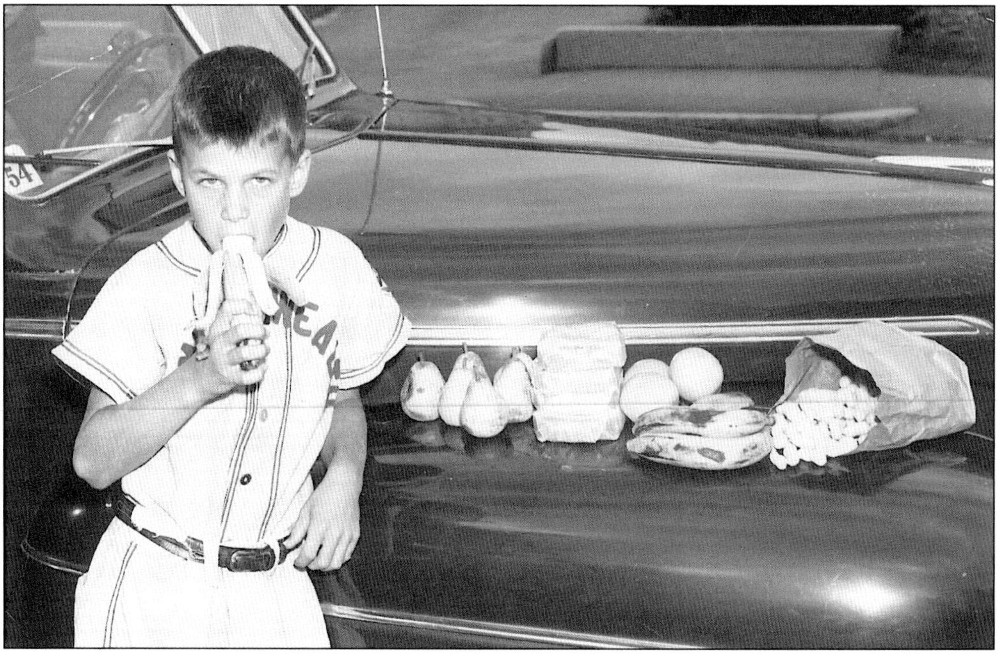

This Little Leaguer, enjoying a hearty lunch in this *c.* 1954 photo, probably played on a ballfield that no longer exists. Regan Field (Willow and Hall Streets), Haws Field (Leominster Armory), Solar Field (Solar Chemical Corporation on Marguerite Avenue), United Trans Field (United Trans Company at Cottage and Cotton), and Saxton Trade Field (Whitney Street) are fond memories now.

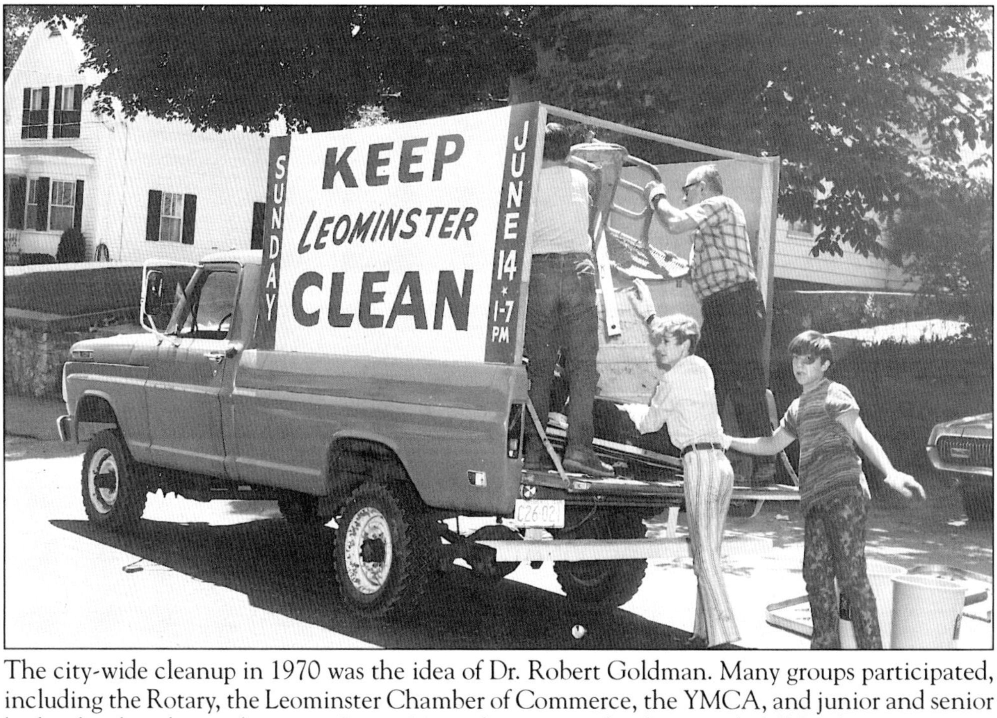

The city-wide cleanup in 1970 was the idea of Dr. Robert Goldman. Many groups participated, including the Rotary, the Leominster Chamber of Commerce, the YMCA, and junior and senior high school student volunteers. Over 100 trucks went to the dump with full loads!

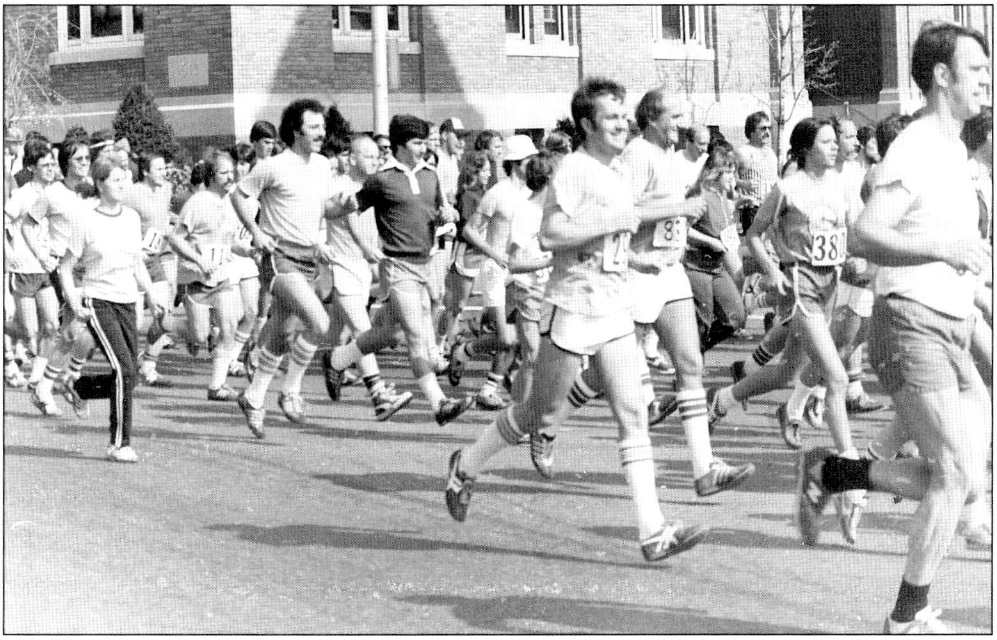

This photograph shows one of the first Leominster-Fitchburg road races of the 1970s. Leominster citizens enjoy a host of popular civic activities throughout the year, including many church fairs, the "Starburst" band concert and fireworks at Doyle Field, Searstown's "Kidsworld" fair, the Johnny Appleseed Festival and Parade, and the Twin Cities First Night Celebration.

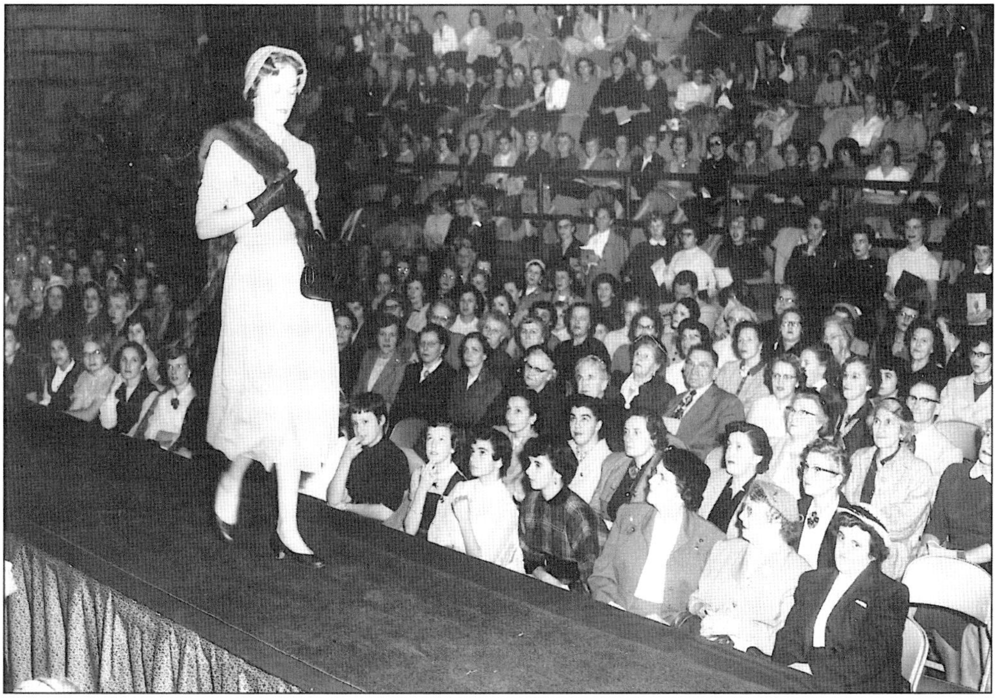

Fashion shows were held at the recreation center several times each year, with women's specialty shops like Ruth Lee's or the Vogue Shop supplying the outfits. Stores such as Rubin's, Lubin's, and Shapley Brothers were also sponsors of these well-attended events.

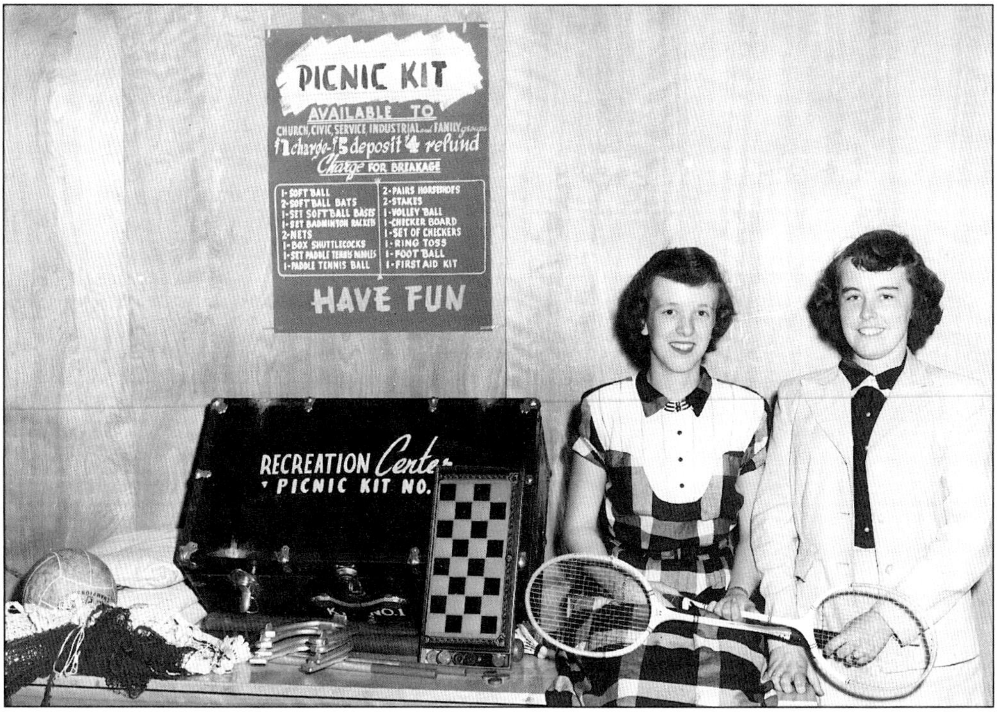

The recreation center advertises their complete "Picnic Kits" in this 1951 photograph. At a cost of only $1, the "price was right!"

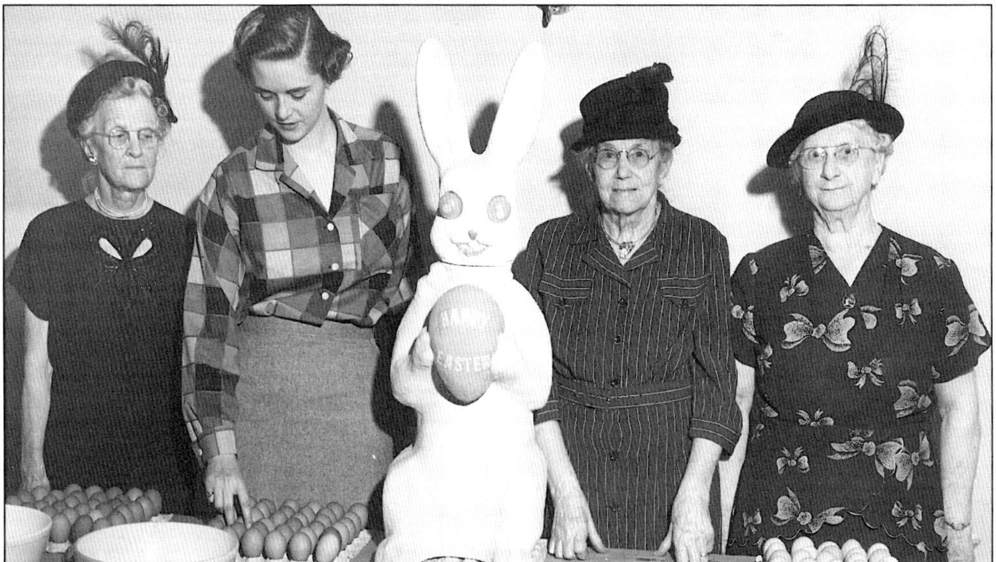

This group of ladies prepares Easter eggs at the recreation center, where there were always programs offered for very young children. Meeting the Easter Bunny was always one of the favorites.

In this photograph, young people dance the night away at a popular recreation center dance. City youth had received permission to use rooms in the basement for after-school dancing to the new "Rock-n-Roll" music. All of the materials and labor needed to redo the basement dance area were furnished by the center's youth. Later, the gym was used on weekends.

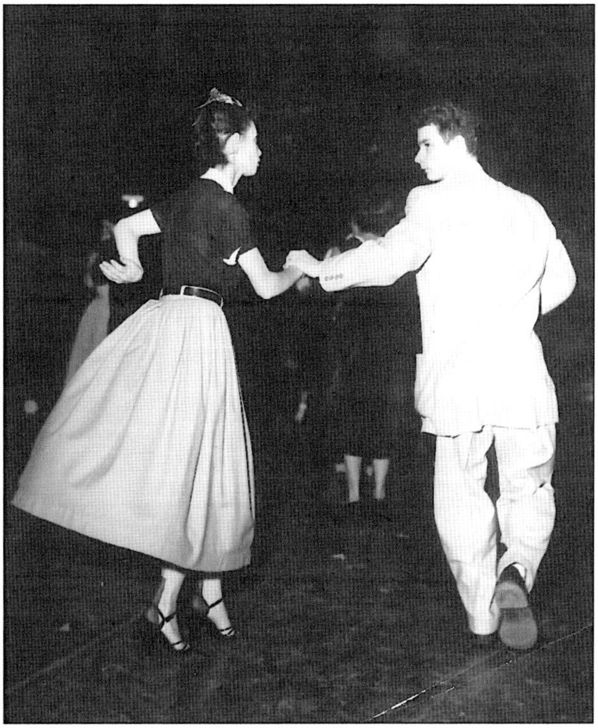

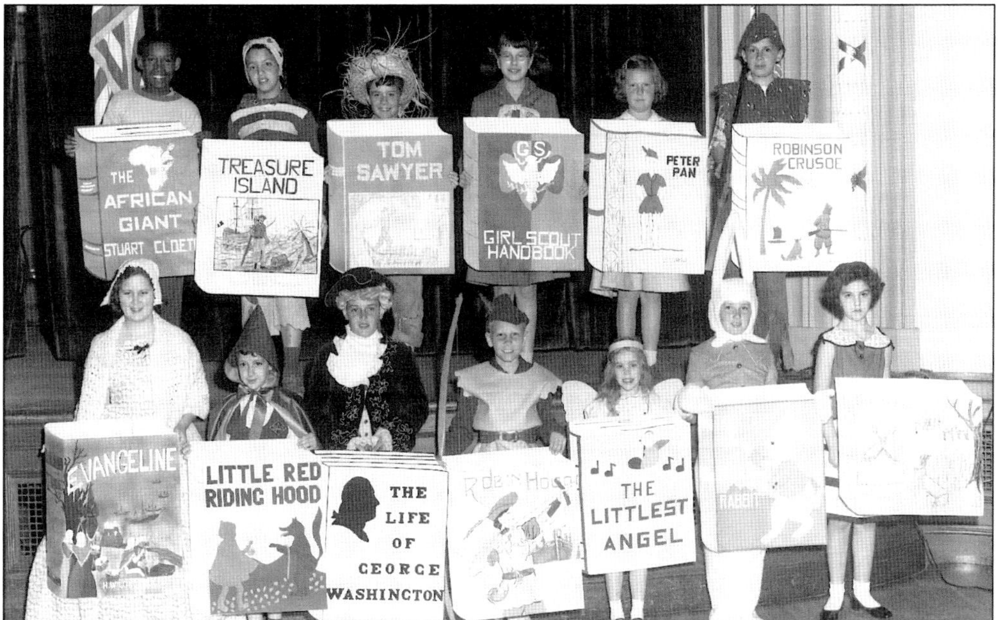

The Leominster Public Library centennial celebration was held Sunday afternoon, May 6, 1956, in the City Hall auditorium. Here, elementary school children dress as characters from favorite books in a pageant directed by Mrs. Harold Follansbee of George Street School. The production commemorated 100 years of library service and featured students from each of the Leominster public and parochial schools.

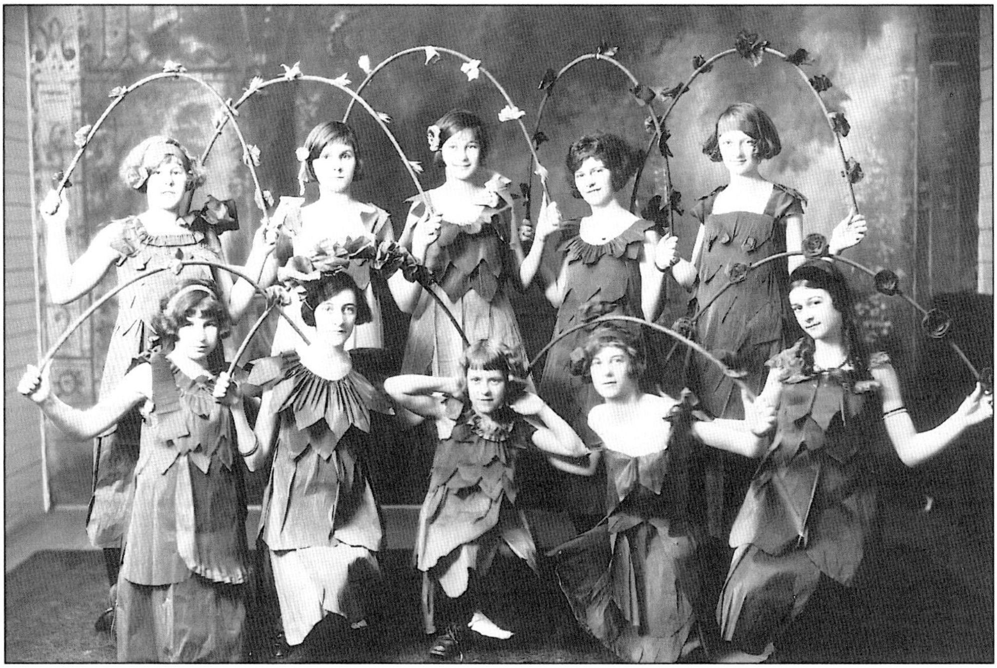

The young ladies of the "Flower Dance" were members of a production of *The Pirate's Daughter*, staged at the new town hall, *c.* 1900. The auditorium was constructed with a sloping floor and comfortable seating; many fine plays, comic operas, and diverse entertainments were offered. The auditorium could be converted to a dance hall by removing the chairs and lowering the floor until level for dancing.

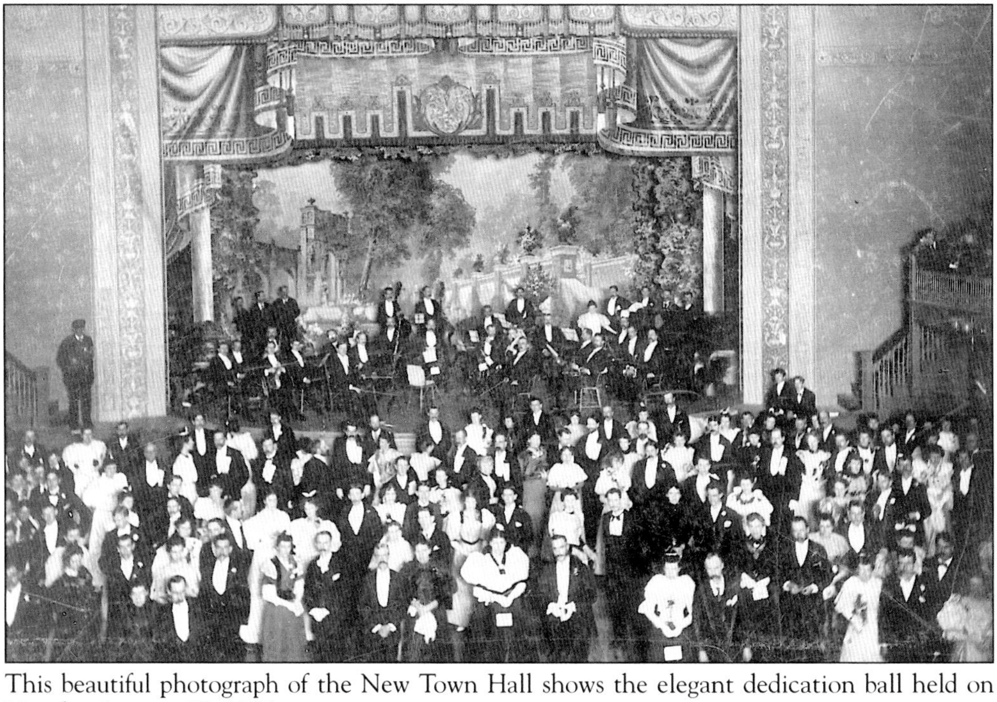

This beautiful photograph of the New Town Hall shows the elegant dedication ball held on Monday, January 28, 1895.

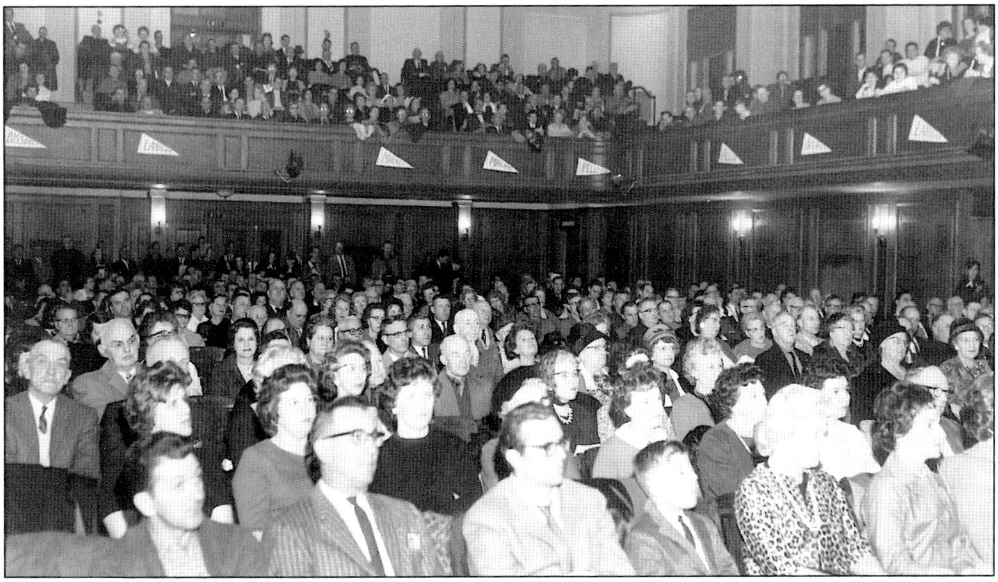

When Mayor Laurie Cormier officially resigned in January 1964 to take another position, a special mayoral election was held on March 3, 1964. This is a photograph of a Candidates' Night, sponsored by the League of Women Voters for this election. Note the standing-room-only attendance for this event, which is in real contrast to the low turn-out at many modern-day political forums.

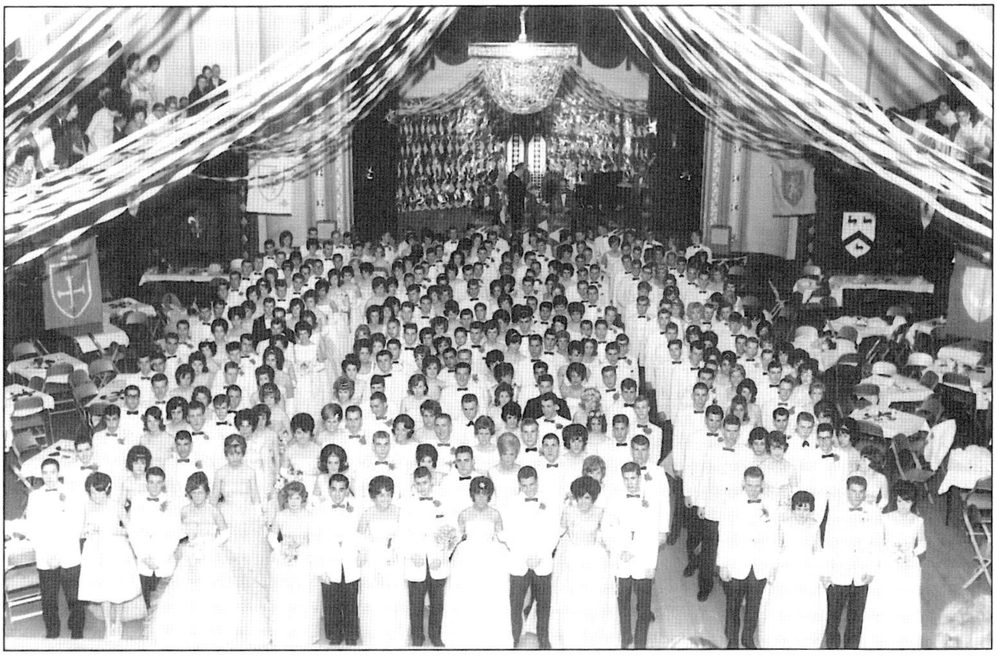

City Hall served as a social and cultural center for Leominster along with its municipal functions. This photograph brings back memories of "Happy Days" as the Leominster High School classes of 1963 and 1964 enjoy their junior-senior prom. Note the beautiful chandelier, which has not been accounted for in many years.

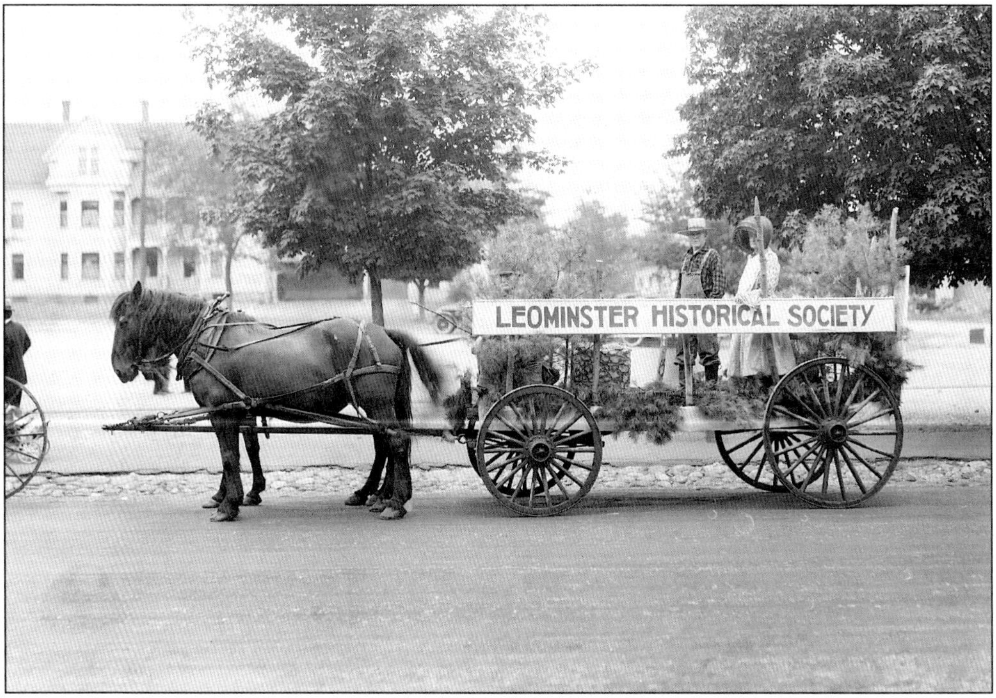

This Leominster Historical Society parade float was from the 1920s. The Society prides itself on participating in almost every city parade with an interesting float depicting an episode in Leominster's history.

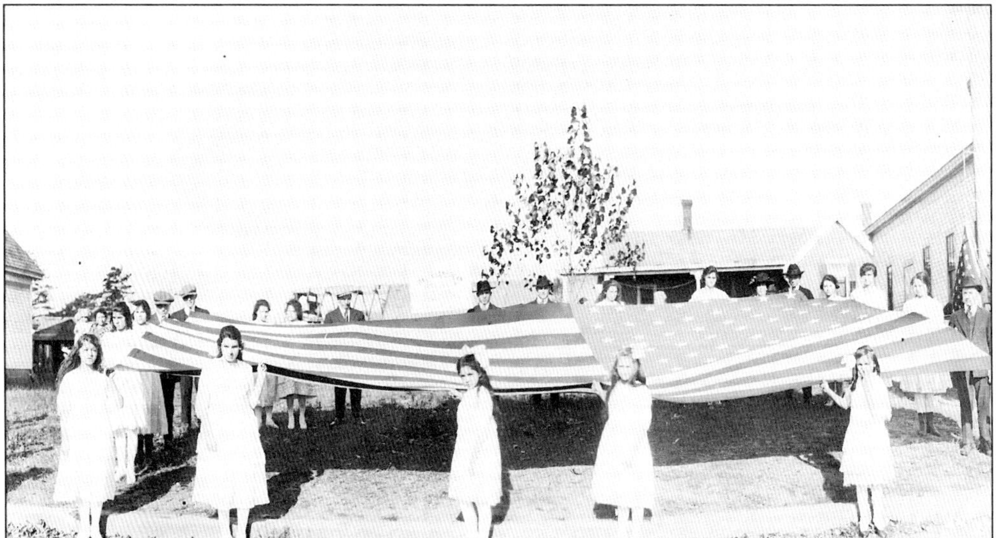

Columbus Day in 1919 is celebrated by the Italian-American Naturalization Club at Columbo Hall. The hall was located at the corner of Middle and Sixth Streets. Many of the Italian clubs chose names that reflected the districts they came from: Regioni D'Italia No. 185, Figlii D'Italia, Societa Saladino, and Societa Santa Maria Del Campo were but a few.

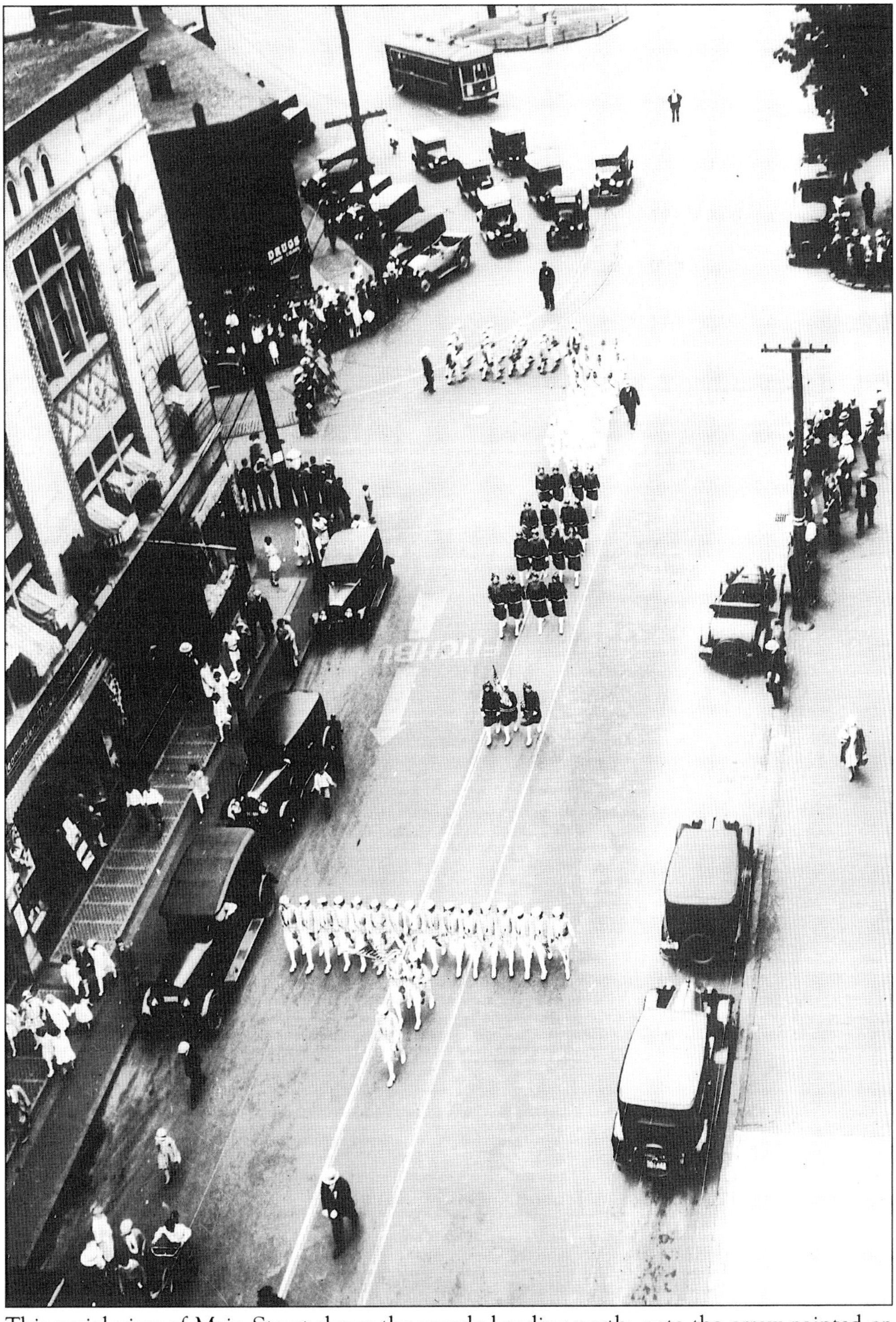

This aerial view of Main Street shows the parade heading north; note the arrow painted on the roadway pointing out the route to Fitchburg. This photograph, and most of the Leominster Historical Society's aerial photographs, were the work of Arthur Beaudoin.

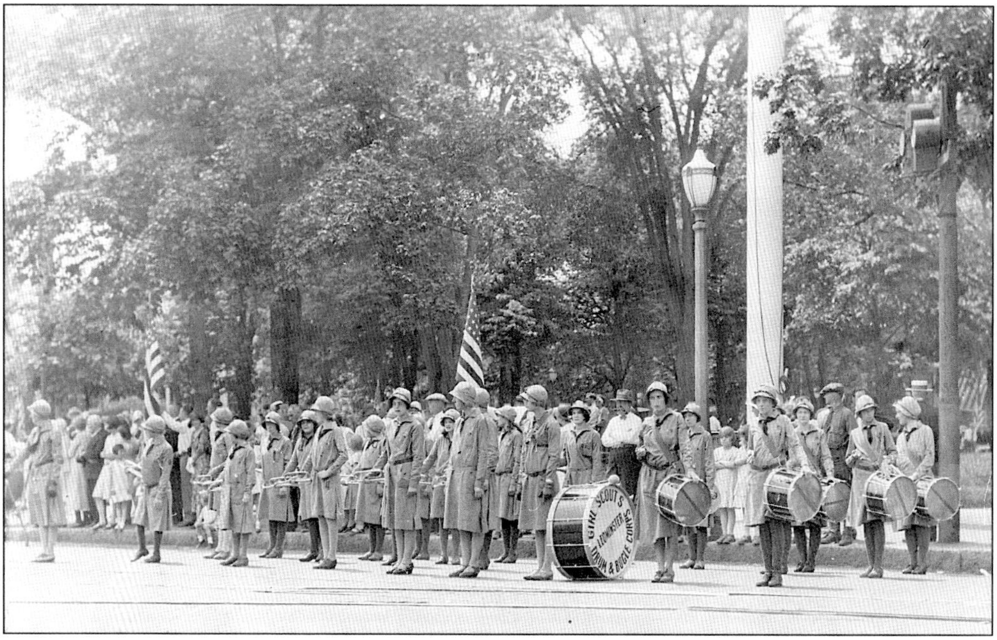

The Leominster Girl Scouts Drum and Bugle Corps was founded in 1929. This group of girls are at the corner of West and Main Streets; the old flag pole on the Common can be seen in this photograph. In 1943, Mr. Doyle gave the Girl Scouts the property at 100 West Street, buying extra land to provide passage and shore holdings at the pond. The parcel reverted back to the City when the scouts no longer used the building. It is now the Veteran's Center.

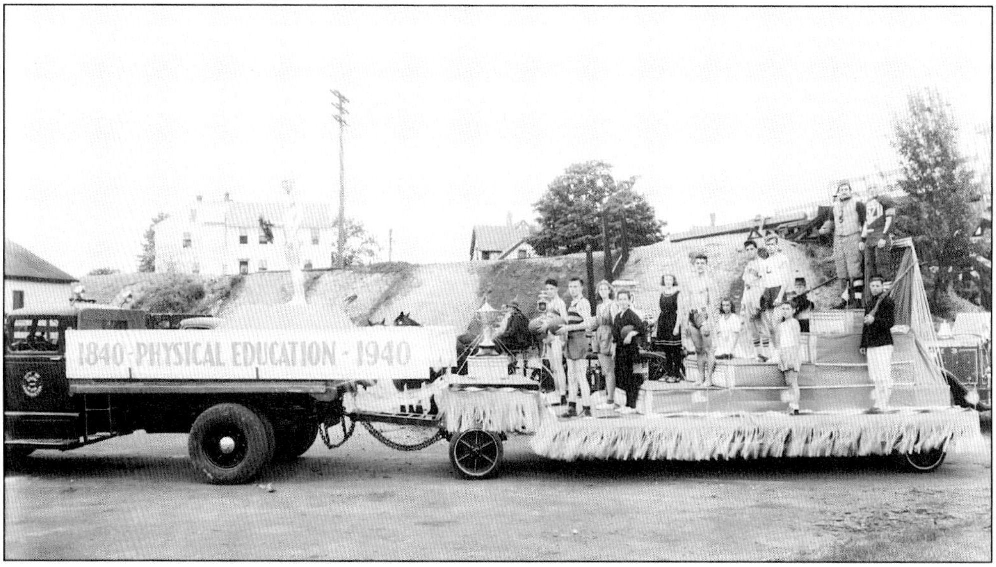

Pictured here is the "Physical Education" float, commemorating the centennial of physical education during the Bicentennial Parade in June 1940. The truck in the picture was from the street and sewer department; later in the day, Gunnard Reynolds would stand in the back of the truck, posed as a statue. On the float is the "Haldie Nicholson Trophy Cup," played for each year by Fitchburg and Leominster High Schools. This float won the prize for the best historical float.

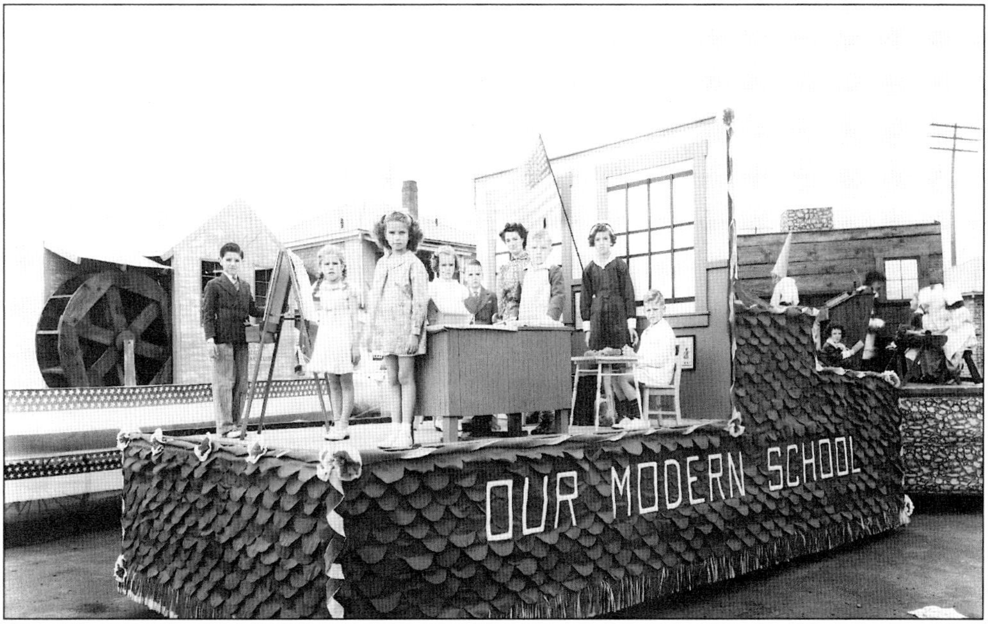

This photograph shows the parade float "Our Modern School" during the 1940 Bicentennial Parade. The float to the right, "Ye Olde School," depicted an old, one-room schoolhouse. The children wore old-fashioned costumes and sat on benches. These floats attracted wide attention as they passed along the parade route; "Ye Olde School" received honors as one of the most original floats in the parade.

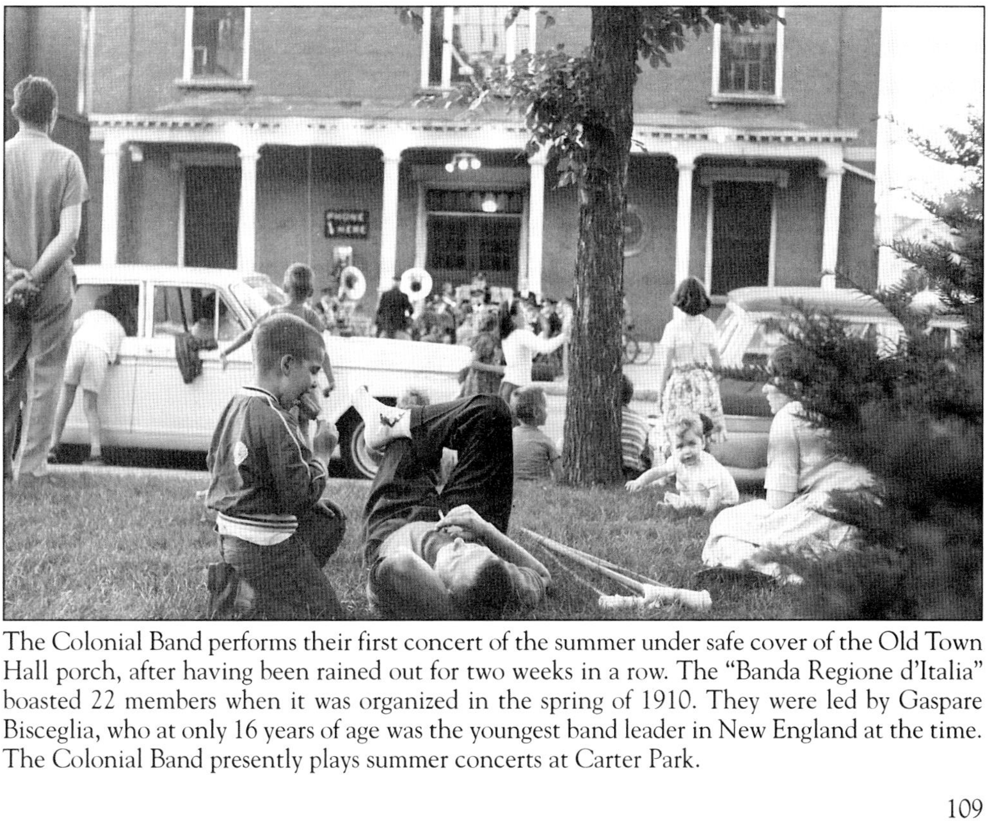

The Colonial Band performs their first concert of the summer under safe cover of the Old Town Hall porch, after having been rained out for two weeks in a row. The "Banda Regione d'Italia" boasted 22 members when it was organized in the spring of 1910. They were led by Gaspare Bisceglia, who at only 16 years of age was the youngest band leader in New England at the time. The Colonial Band presently plays summer concerts at Carter Park.

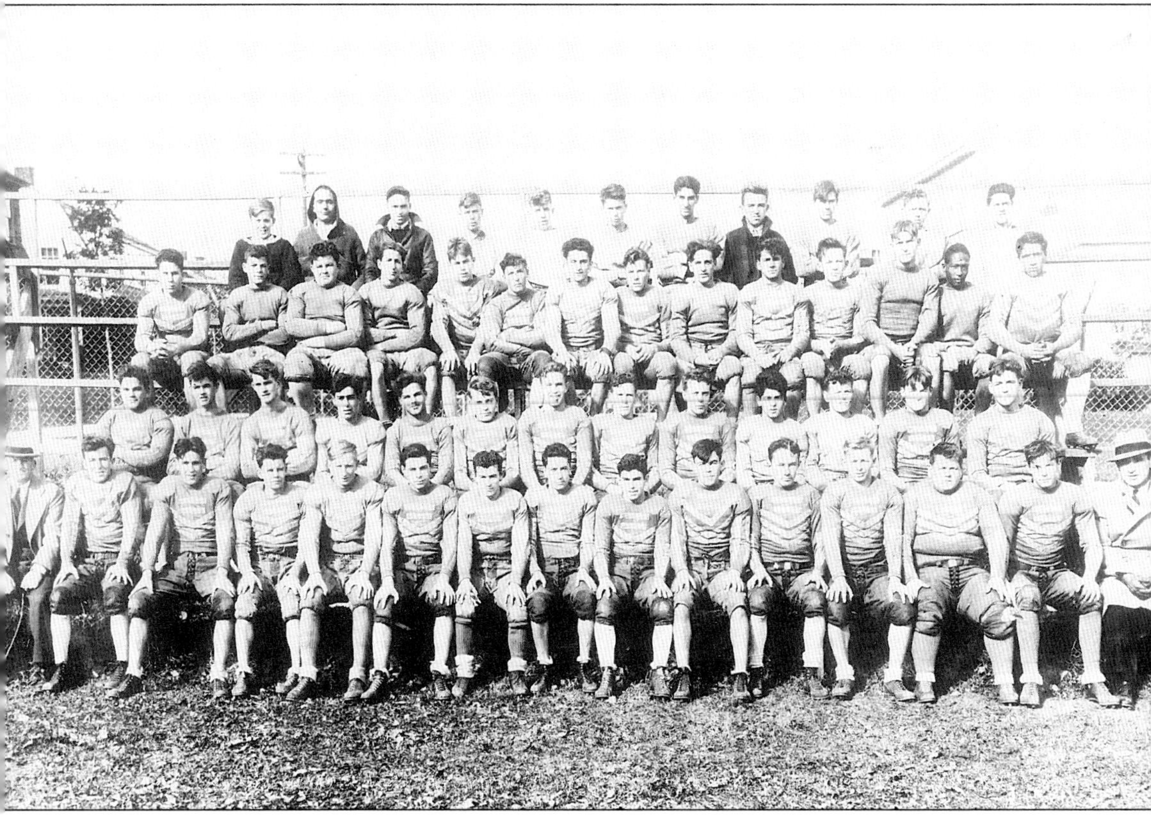

Leominster has a long, proud history concerning sports, especially football. This 1931 Leominster-Fitchburg team photograph is special because this is the first Leominster football team coached by the legendary Charley Broderick and was also the first team to play on the city's revered Doyle Field. The entire team reflects the caliber of the boys, who became the men, who would influence Leominster history. This team included Ron Cahill, who many feel is the greatest player in LHS history, and Angelo Piccucci, future community leader. Other players were Richard O'Toole, Malcom Johnson, George Beaulieu, Alfred Cocci, Dan Bell, Alexander Dupee, John Haverty, Arthur Beaudoin, Ricardo Cavolli, and Bernard Tata. Broderick's assistant coach was Ted Kucharski, who later became principal at Leominster High.

Six

Leominster Institutions

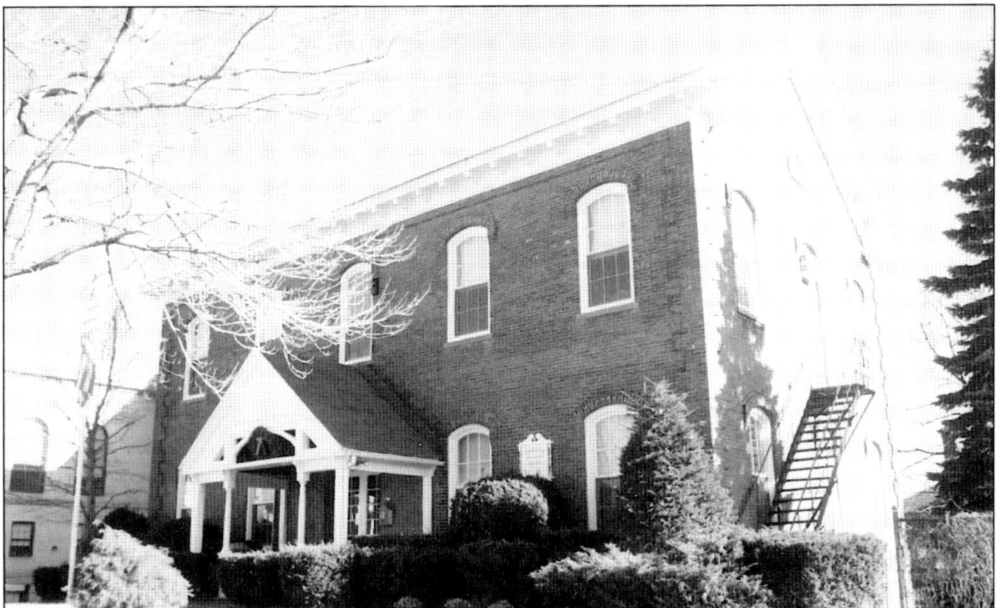

The Leominster Historical Society was established in January 1906 and is housed in the 1870 Field School building. It serves the community as an educational resource and maintains a museum, which preserves and displays articles of antiquarian, genealogical, and local historical interest. The society's collection includes artifacts, papers, letters, photographs, journals, and farm, home, and industrial implements, the majority of which are Leominster-related.

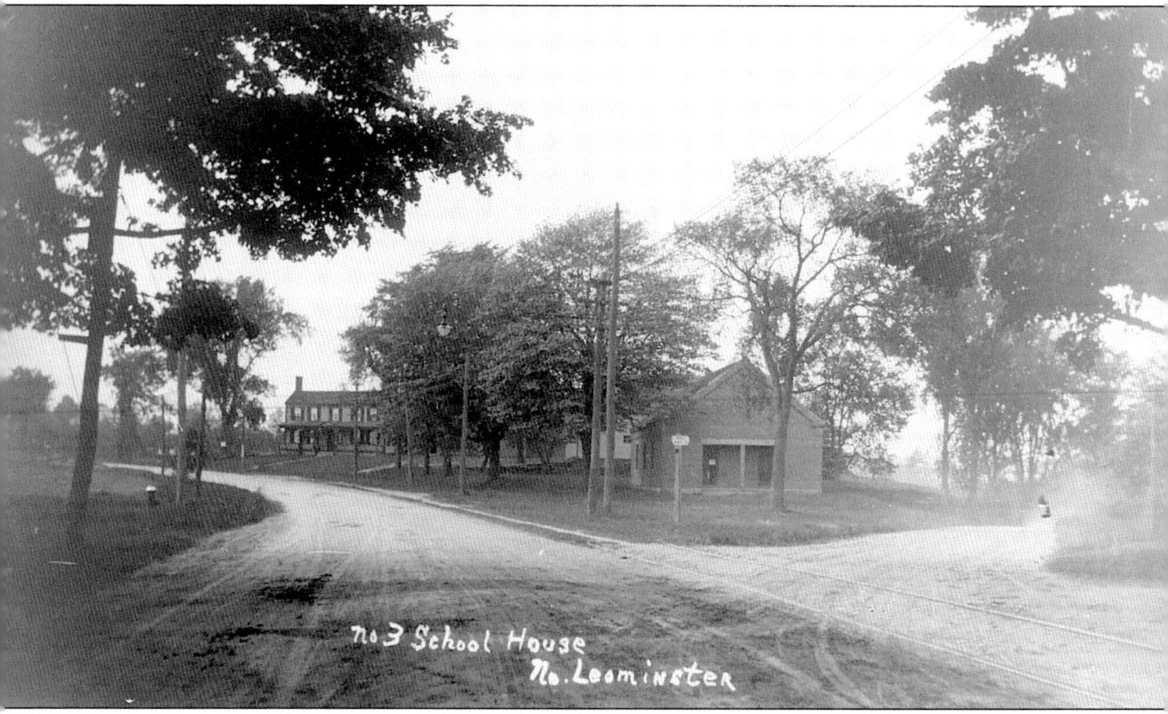

The No. 3 Schoolhouse at the corner of Main and Day Streets was built in 1767. It was moved much farther up Main Street and was later destroyed by fire. In 1849, the first brick schoolhouse was built on the same site and was used until 1888, when Pierce Street School was built. The Leominster Historical Society has erected a marker indicating that this is also near the site of the town's first burial grounds. A convenience store now stands there, with Johnny Appleseed School a short distance away.

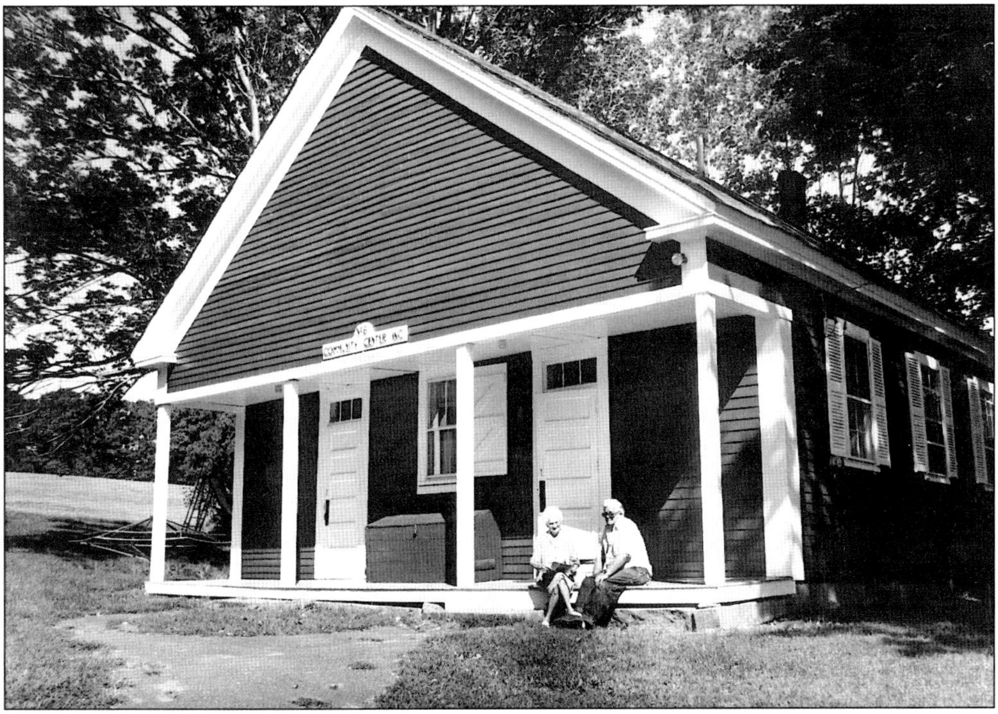

Number 6, "The Little Red Schoolhouse," is shown in 1989. Seated on the porch, from left to right, are L'Oretta Wass and Lester Prindle, longtime members of the "No. 6 Community Center" organization. The group formed in 1949 to preserve the 1851 schoolhouse, located at the corner of Pleasant and Wachusett Streets. Elsie (Powers) Fischer taught here for 32 years; she was known to prepare hot cocoa or tomato soup in the winter for students who carried cold lunches.

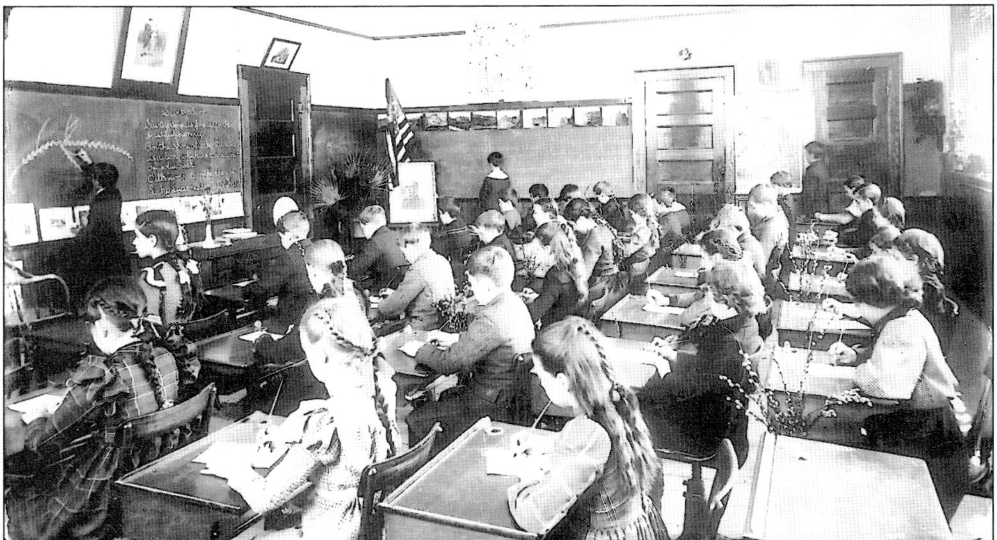

Miss Helen Pierce conducts this *c.* 1913 art class at George Street School. If you look closely, you see one boy at the chalkboard and another in the corner. A senior housing complex is now at this site. The school was built in 1896.

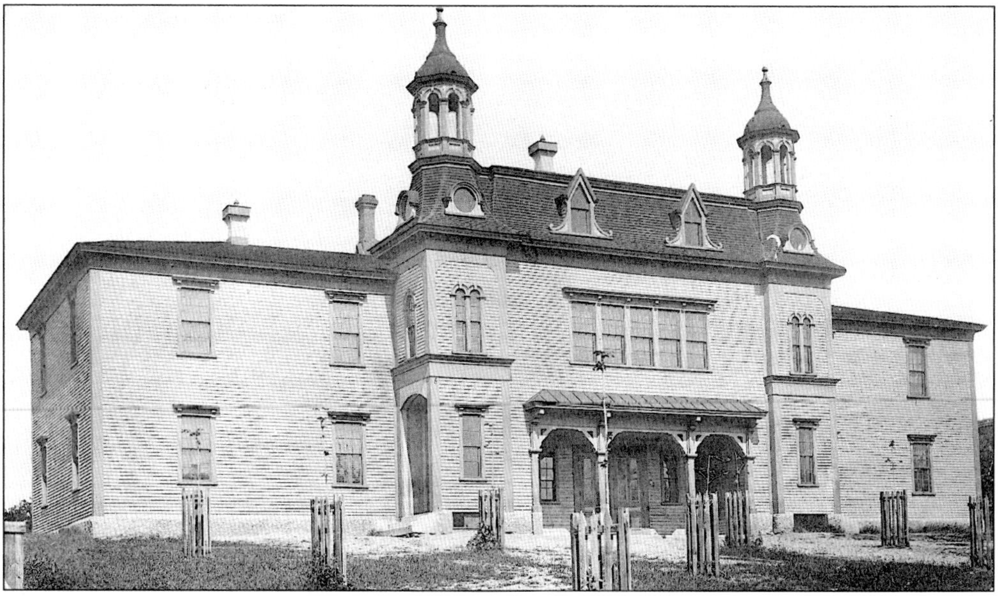

Leominster's first high school was located at 25 School Street, where the Gallagher Building now stands. Established in 1850, it was named after Dr. Caleb C. Field. The first class of 1868 graduated only six students; in 1871, Helen Burditt was the only graduate!

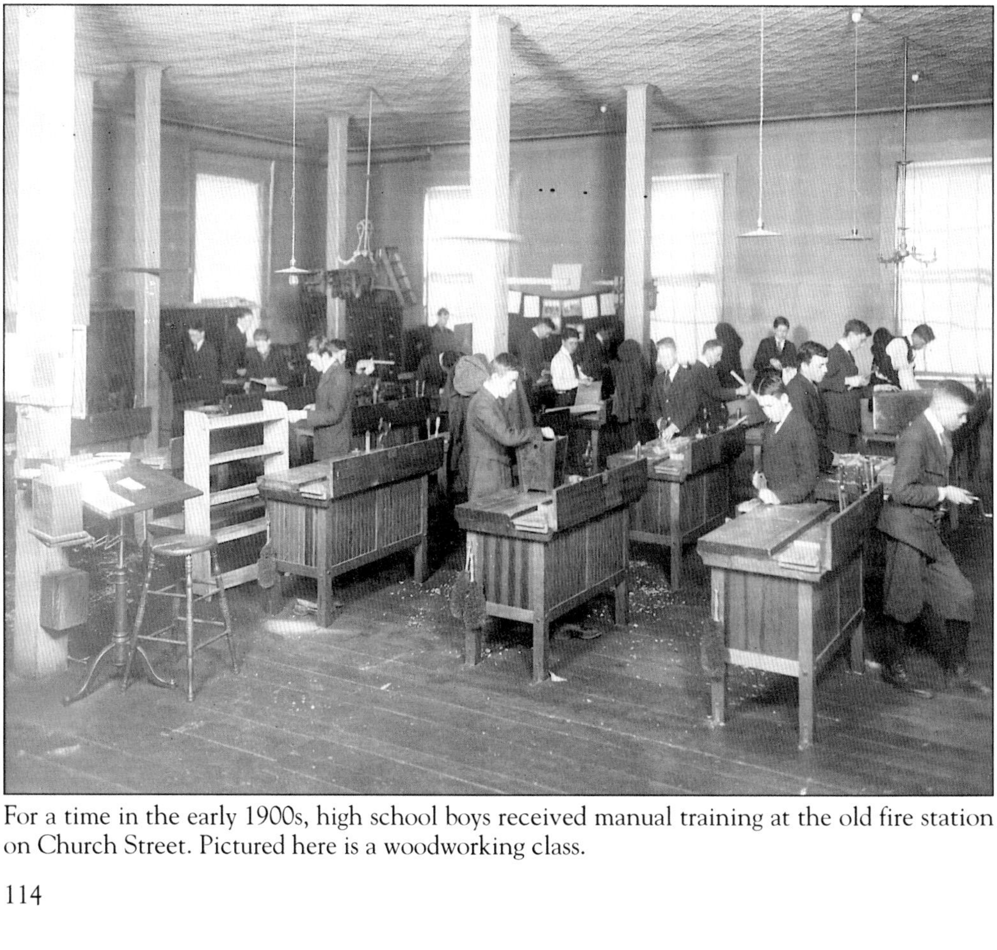

For a time in the early 1900s, high school boys received manual training at the old fire station on Church Street. Pictured here is a woodworking class.

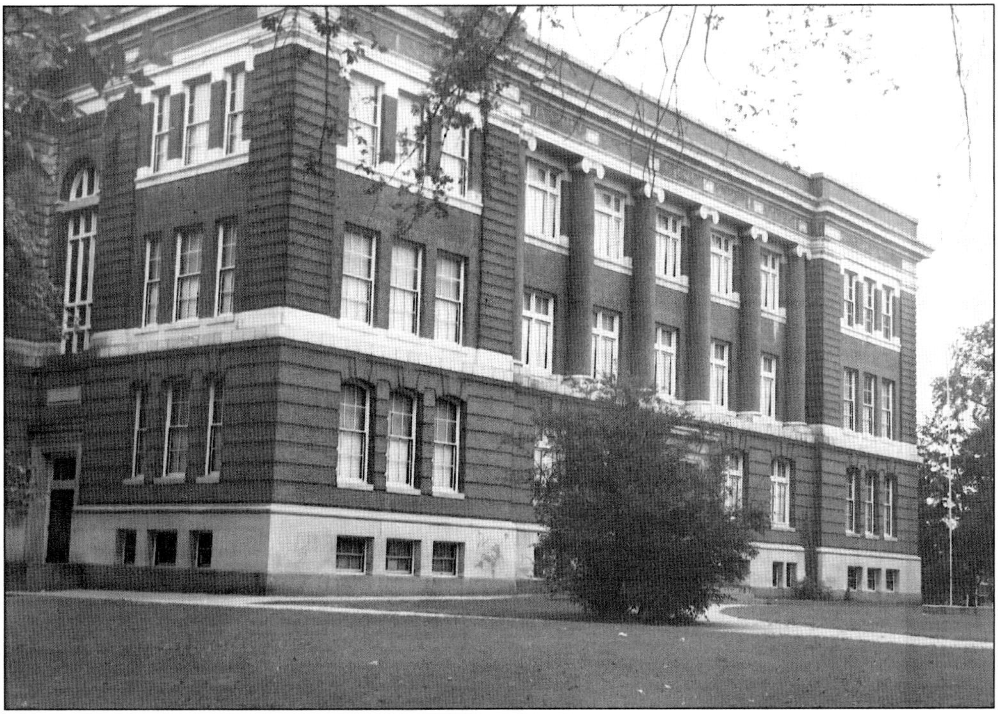

In 1906, the new high school on West Street opened, operating until 1963, when it became Carter Junior High School. The building has been vacant for many years now; it is scheduled to be converted into senior citizens' assisted-living space.

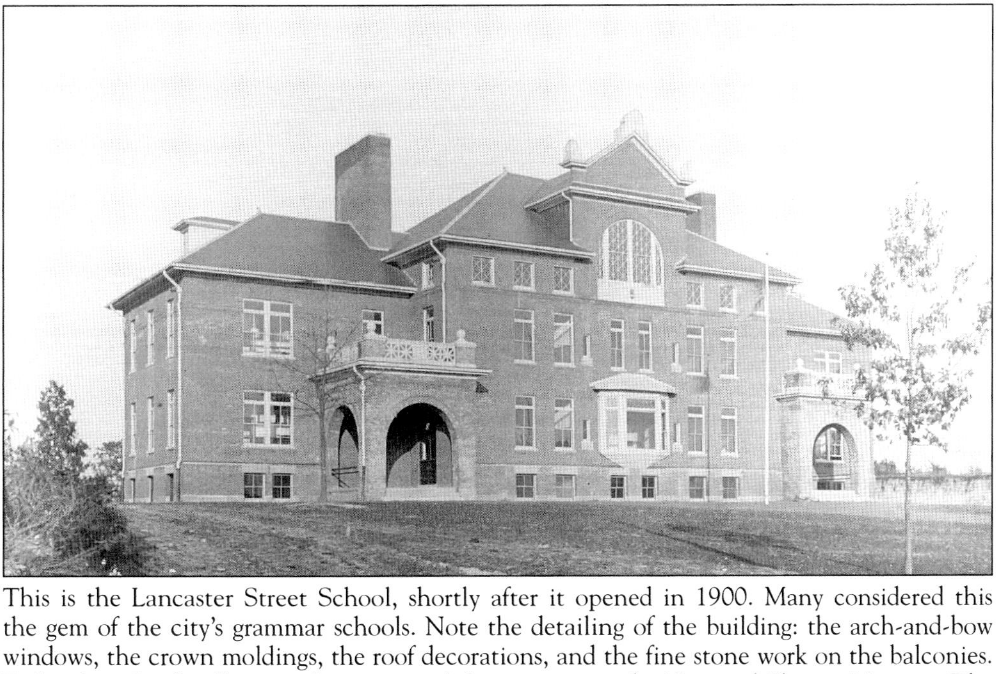

This is the Lancaster Street School, shortly after it opened in 1900. Many considered this the gem of the city's grammar schools. Note the detailing of the building: the arch-and-bow windows, the crown moldings, the roof decorations, and the fine stone work on the balconies. Today the school still serves the city—and the nation—as the National Plastics Museum. The building has been renovated and expanded, giving it a very different look.

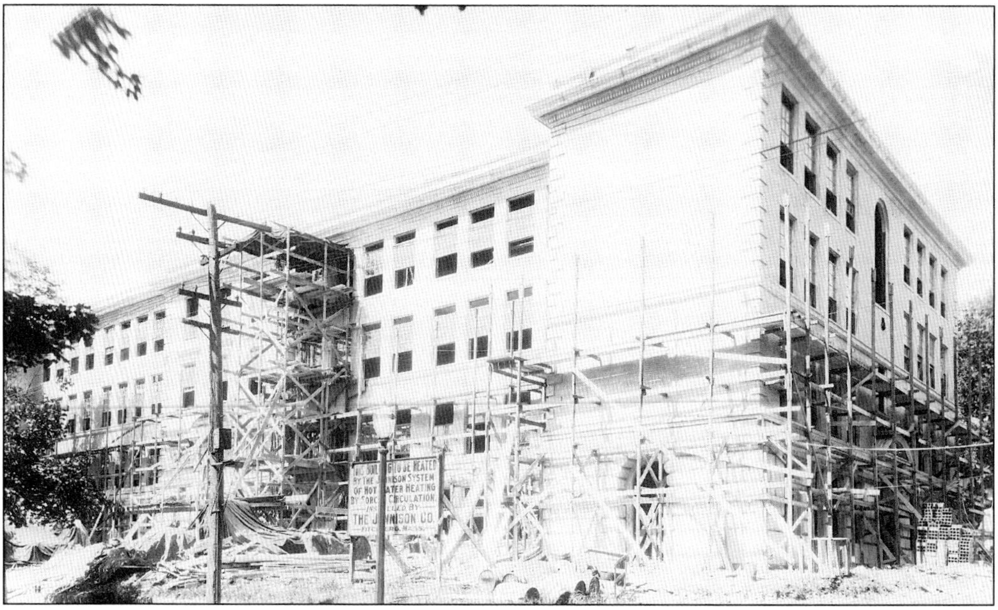

This photograph shows the Gallagher Junior High School under construction. A committee was organized in February 1926 to oversee the building of the school; Mayor Bernard Doyle was elected chairman. In April, the city borrowed $500,000 through a special act of the state legislature and ground was broken shortly thereafter. In February 1928, the new "fortress of education" was dedicated; it was named after legendary educator and longtime principal, May A. Gallagher.

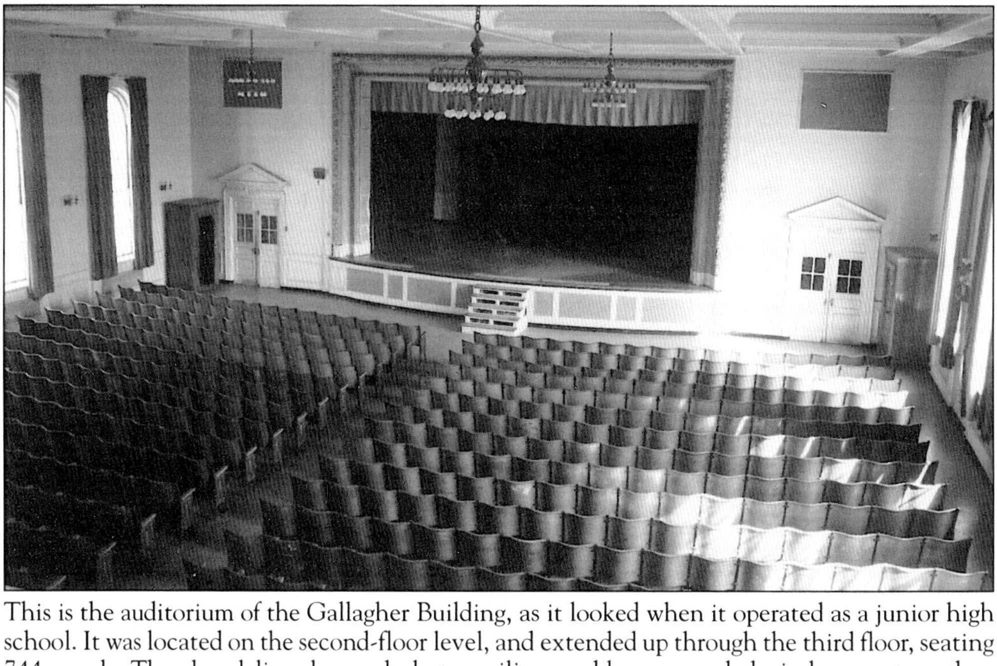

This is the auditorium of the Gallagher Building, as it looked when it operated as a junior high school. It was located on the second-floor level, and extended up through the third floor, seating 744 people. The chandeliers, beamed-plaster ceiling, and large, rounded windows portrayed an air of elegance. The building now houses the district court, the offices of the school department, and a credit union.

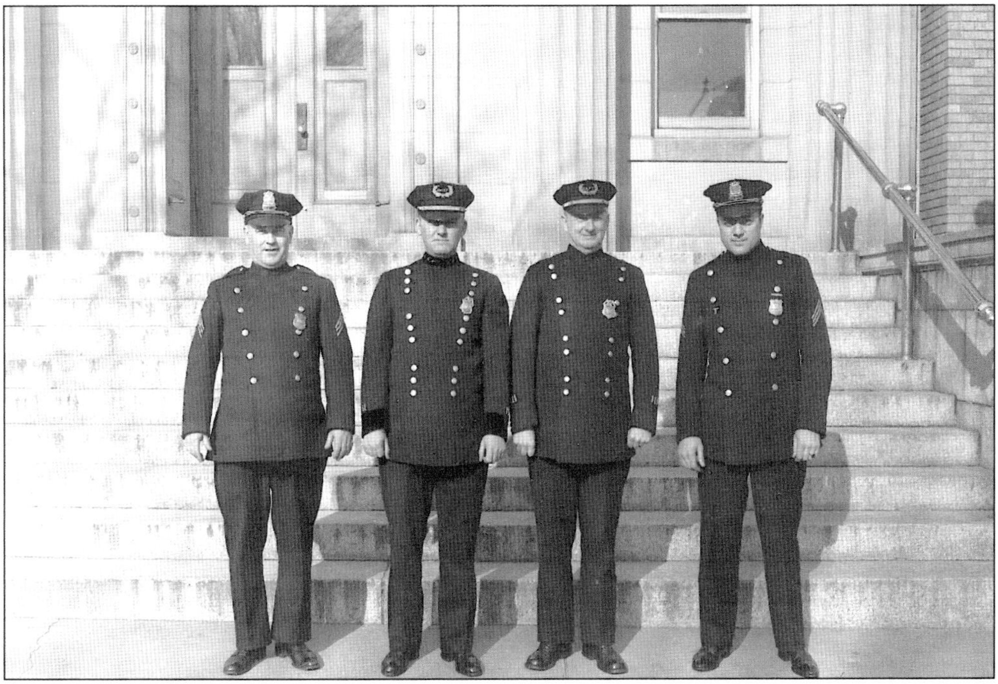

The officers of the Leominster Police Department are shown here, in front of City Hall, in 1942. From left to right are Sgt. Leo Comiskey, Chief George Smith, Capt. Francis Farwell, and Sgt. Henry O. St. Cyr. Sergeant St. Cyr was a police photographer for many years; several of his photographs appear in this book.

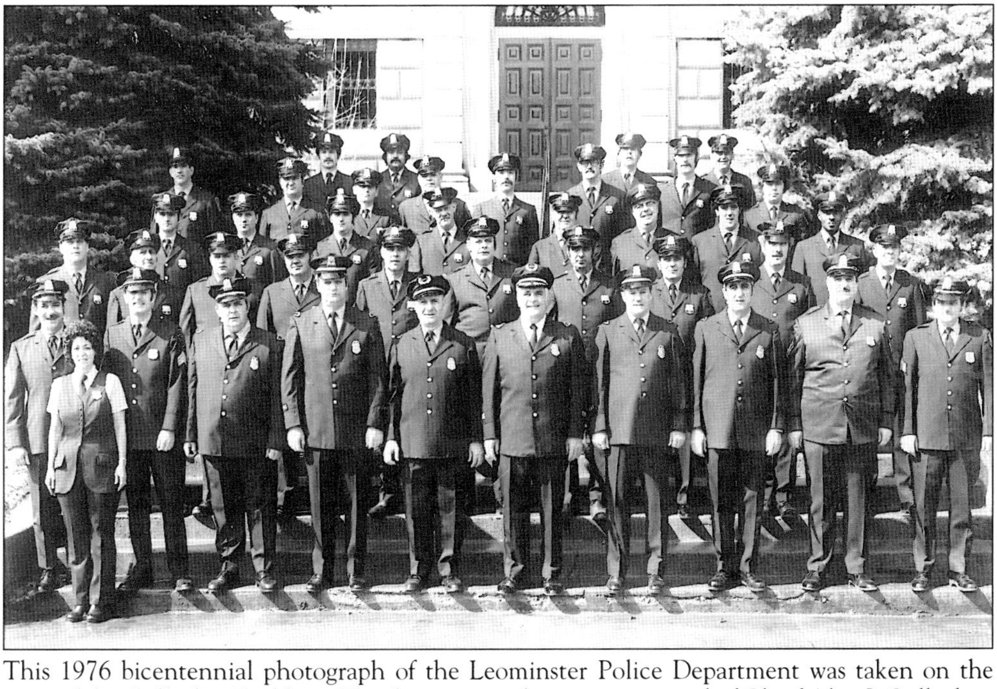

This 1976 bicentennial photograph of the Leominster Police Department was taken on the steps of the Gallagher Building. The department that year consisted of Chief Alan J. Gallagher, Capt. Lewis H. Cocci, five lieutenants, five sergeants, and 34 patrolmen.

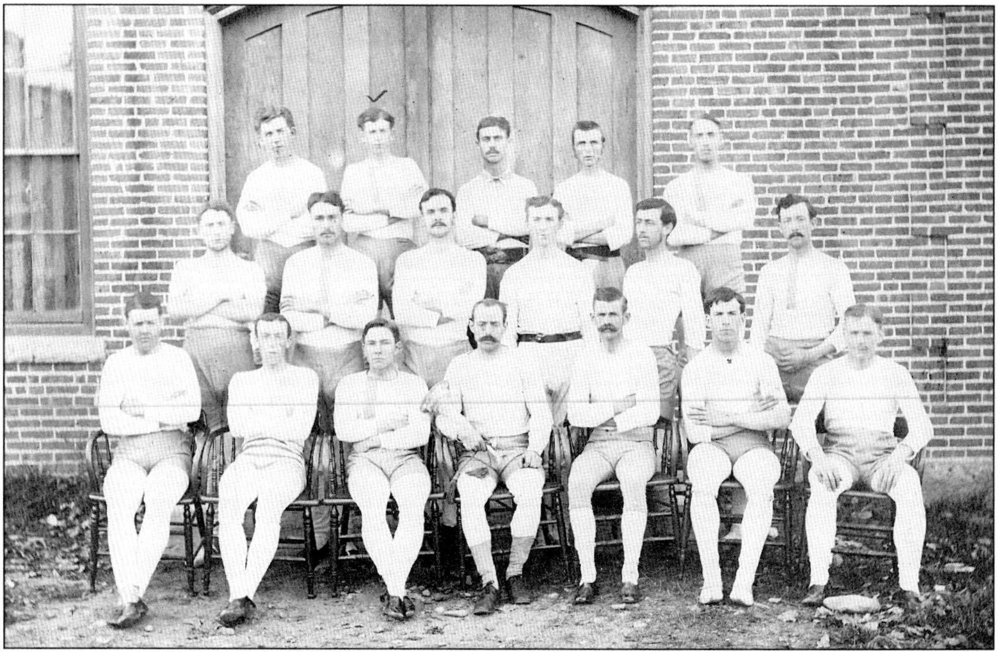

The members of the "Sprinter's Club" of the Hardscrabble Hook and Ladder Company #1 pose in front of the Church Street Fire Station *c.* 1877. Many athletic teams and muster organizations were sponsored by the various companies within the department.

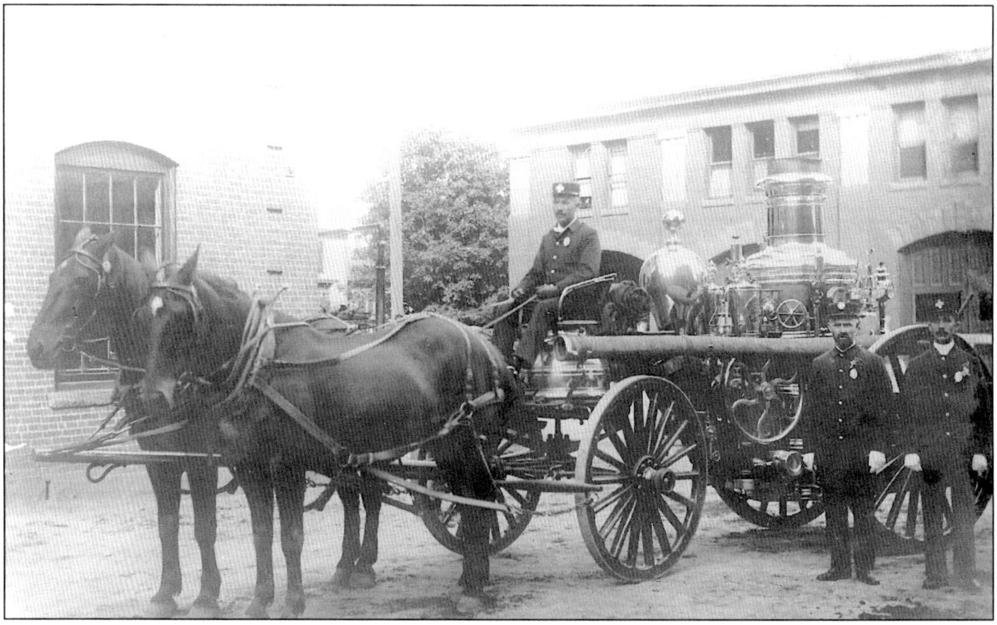

The crew of Leominster's Engine #1 pose with the 1870 "Aurora" steamer pump engine after the Annual Firemen's Muster on Labor Day in 1906. In the driver's seat is Albert R. Wood, who drove for the department for 42 years. Standing, from left to right, are Fredson N. Gray and Fred H. Barker. "Fanny" and "Prince," the horse team in the picture, were one of five teams stabled at the Central Fire Station.

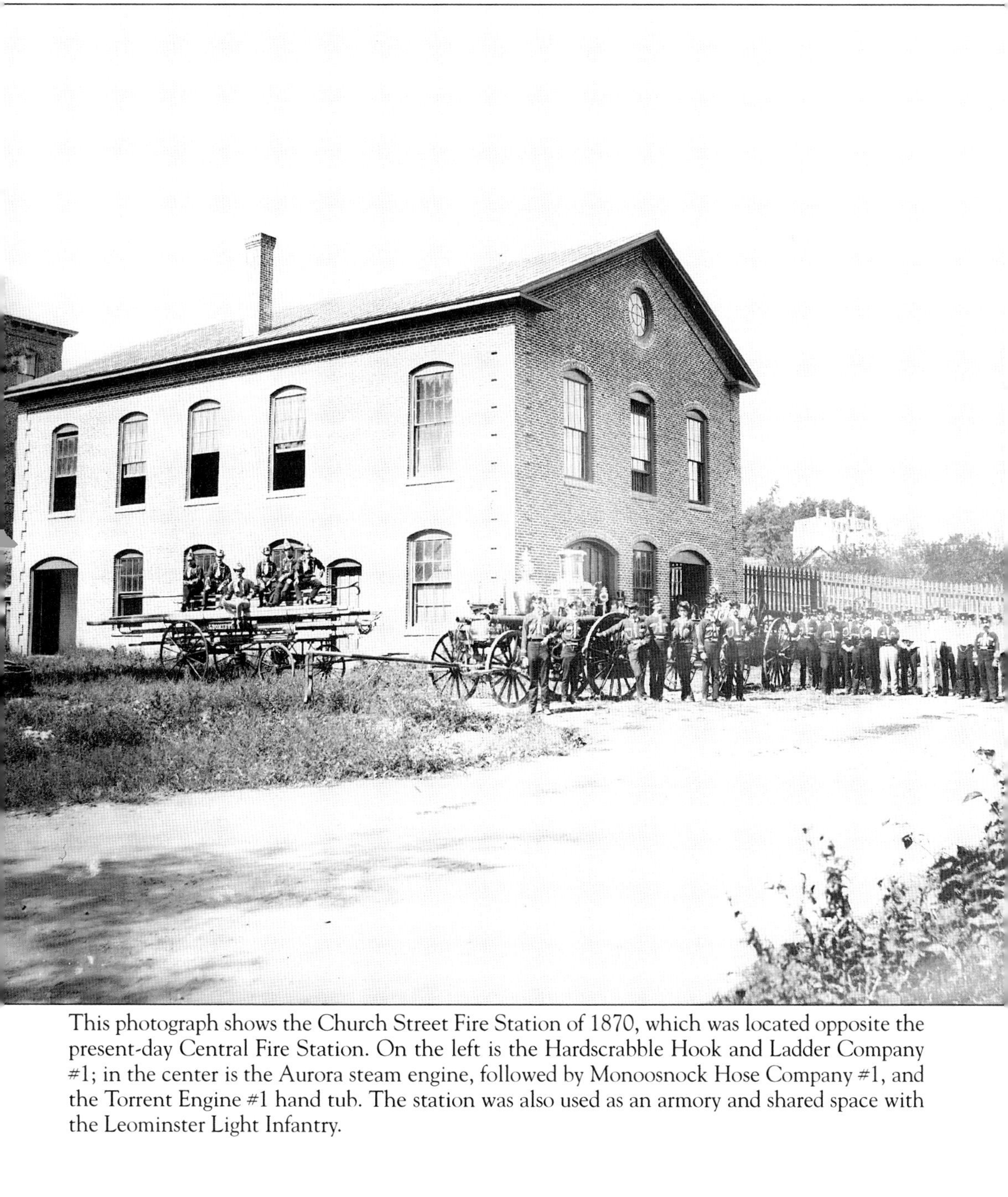

This photograph shows the Church Street Fire Station of 1870, which was located opposite the present-day Central Fire Station. On the left is the Hardscrabble Hook and Ladder Company #1; in the center is the Aurora steam engine, followed by Monoosnock Hose Company #1, and the Torrent Engine #1 hand tub. The station was also used as an armory and shared space with the Leominster Light Infantry.

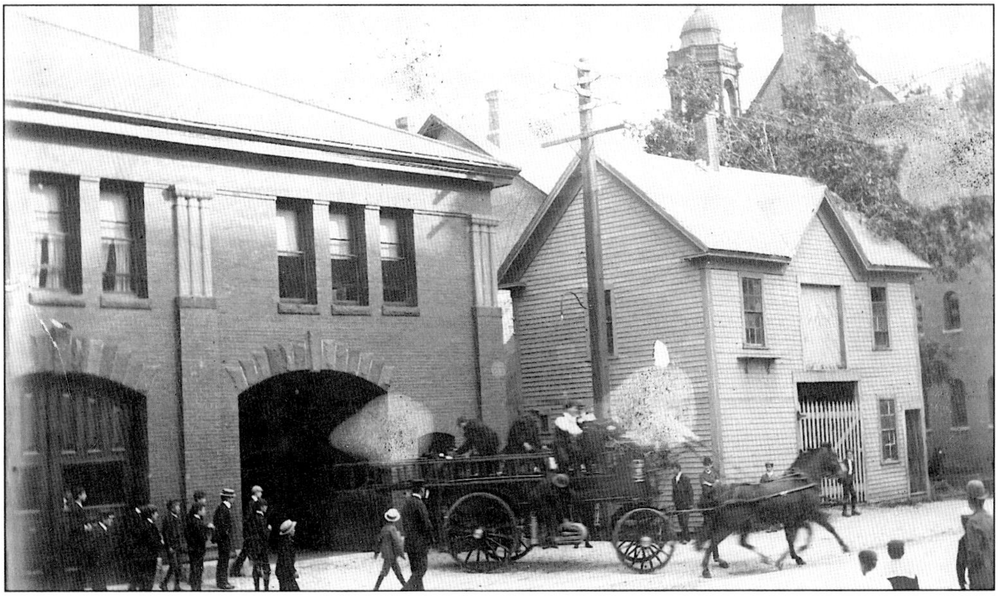

In this 1903 photograph, Edmund Davis captured the Hose #1 company racing to the fire purely by accident: he was on Church Street set up to take a photograph of another building. Hose #1 was known as the "Jumbo Truck." Leominster's Central Fire Station opened in 1898 and is still in use today; the horse barn to the right, however, is not.

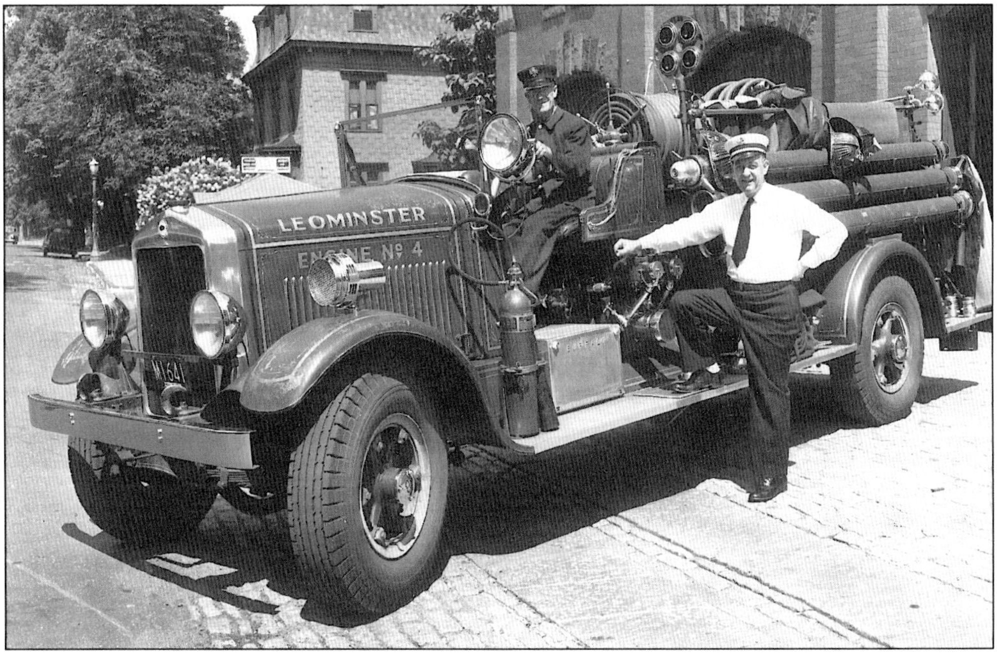

Leominster's "Buffalo" Engine #4 was purchased in 1933. Shown here in this *c.* 1946 photograph are driver Nathaniel Lowe and Acting Lt. Clarence W. Bentley. Note the rooming house at 29 Church Street, next to Central Fire Station. It was torn down to make way for the new police station in 1959.

When these 1937 rates were in effect, bread was 8¢ a loaf, the daily newspaper was 2¢, and the Sunday edition cost 10¢s. It cost 3¢ to mail a letter, and a new car sold for less than $600!

DOCTOR'S FEE TABLE

LEOMINSTER, MASSACHUSETTS

Effective March, 1, 1937

Office Hours: 1:30 to 3:00 P. M. and 7:00 to 8:00 P. M.
Sundays and Holidays by Appointment Only

Minimum Charges

DAY HOUSE VISITS	(7:00 A. M. to 7:00 P. M.)	$3.00
EVENING HOUSE VISITS	(7:00 P. M. to 11:00 P. M.)	$4.00
NIGHT HOUSE VISITS	(11:00 P. M. to 7:00 A. M.)	$5.00
OFFICE VISITS AND TREATMENTS	. .	$2.00 up
URINALYSIS ONLY	. . . . . .	$1.00
CONSULTATIONS	. . . .	$5.00 up

OBSTETRIC FEES
Minimum Charges

ORDINARY DELIVERY	(with three visits after)	$25.00
TWINS DELIVERY	" " " "	$35.00
FORCEPS DELIVERY	" " " "	$35.00
VERSION DELIVERY	" " " "	$35.00

PRENATAL CARE . . . Extra at regular rates
ANAESTHETIST . . . Extra at regular rates

SURGICAL OPERATIONS AT ACCEPTED RATES

Signed . . .

S. J. BENOIT, M. D.	W. G. LEBRECHT, M. D.
M. H. CHRYSTAL, M. D.	J. V. McHUGH, M. D.
C. B. CRONIN, M. D.	H. R. NYE, M. D.
J. J. CURLEY, M. D.	M. S. PHILBRICK, M. D.
W. E. CURRIER, M. D.	R. S. RUBIN, M. D.
H. S. GLICK, M. D.	F. C. SHULTIS, M. D.
P. F. HILTON, M. D.	B. P. SWEENEY, M. D.
C. J. LASERTE, M. D.	A. A. WHEELER, M. D.

Per Order of Charles J. Laserte, M.D., President of the Leominster Hospital Staff and Chief of Medicine

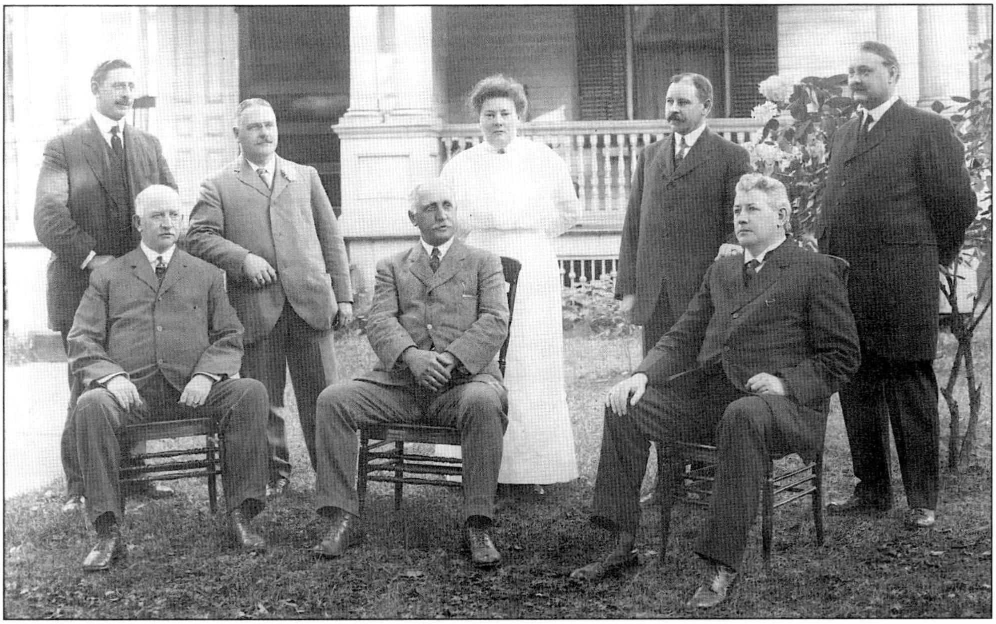

Pictured here is the medical staff in front of Leominster's first hospital at 11 Blossom Street in 1912. Seen here, from left to right, are as follows: (front row) Dr. Bigelow, Dr. Hall, and Dr. Cohan; (second row) Dr. Pierce, Dr. Wheeler, Matron A. Parker R.N. (Superintendent), Dr. Brigham, and Dr. Frechette.

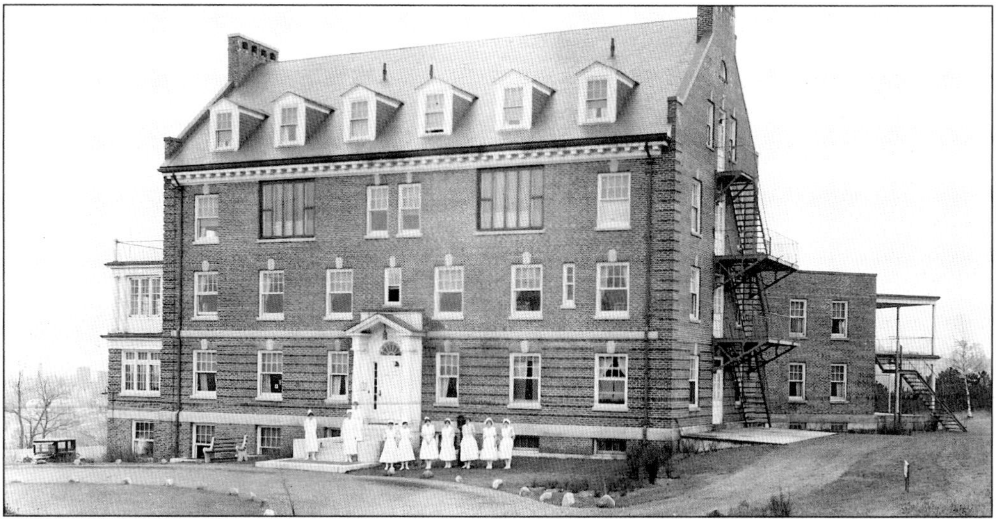

Leominster Hospital was completed in 1922; this picture was taken shortly after that. Funds were obtained through a public drive, with over 7,600 people contributing, and the generosity of Bernard Doyle. The first floor was administrative offices, the second floor had private and semi-private rooms, and the third floor housed the operating rooms.The two-story structure to the right rear is a V-shaped ell containing more patient wards on the first floor, and labor, delivery, nursery, and postpartum areas on the second floor.

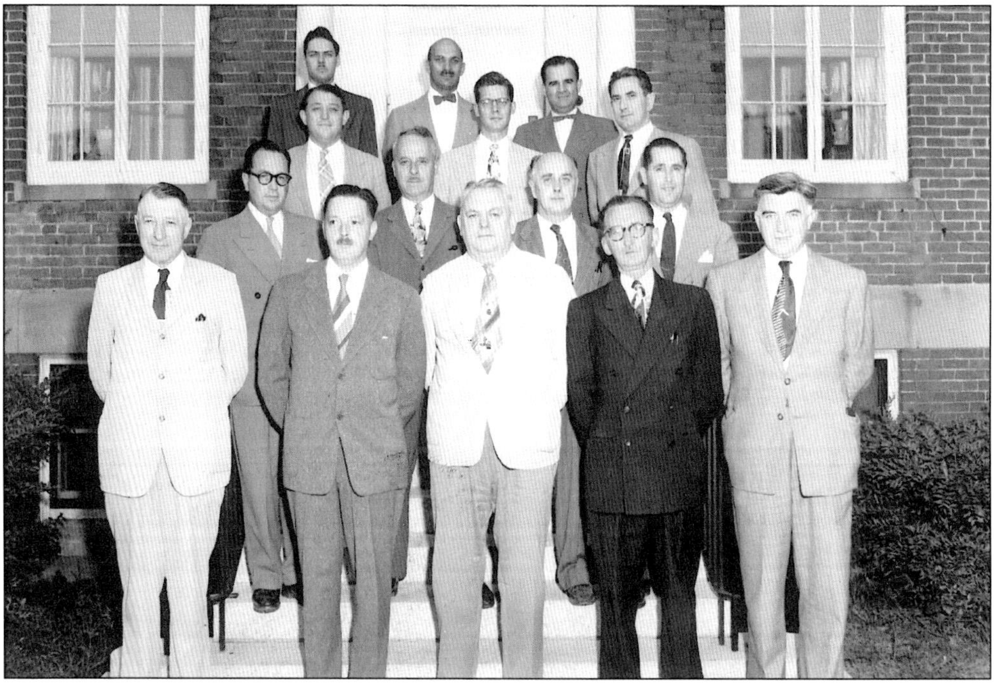

The Leominster Hospital staff in 1950 is pictured here, from left to right, as follows: (first row) Dr. Philip Hilton, Dr. James McHugh, Dr. William LeBrecht, Dr. Charles Cronin, and Dr. John Curley; (second row) Dr. Charles Wheeler, Dr. Erskine Pickwick, Dr. Albert Mainville, and Dr. Harry Glick; (third row) Dr. Alphonse Popoli, Dr. H.J. Sparling, and Dr. Jacob Parnes; (fourth row) Dr. Alvin Bixon, Dr. Robert Goldman, and Dr. Anthony Aloia.

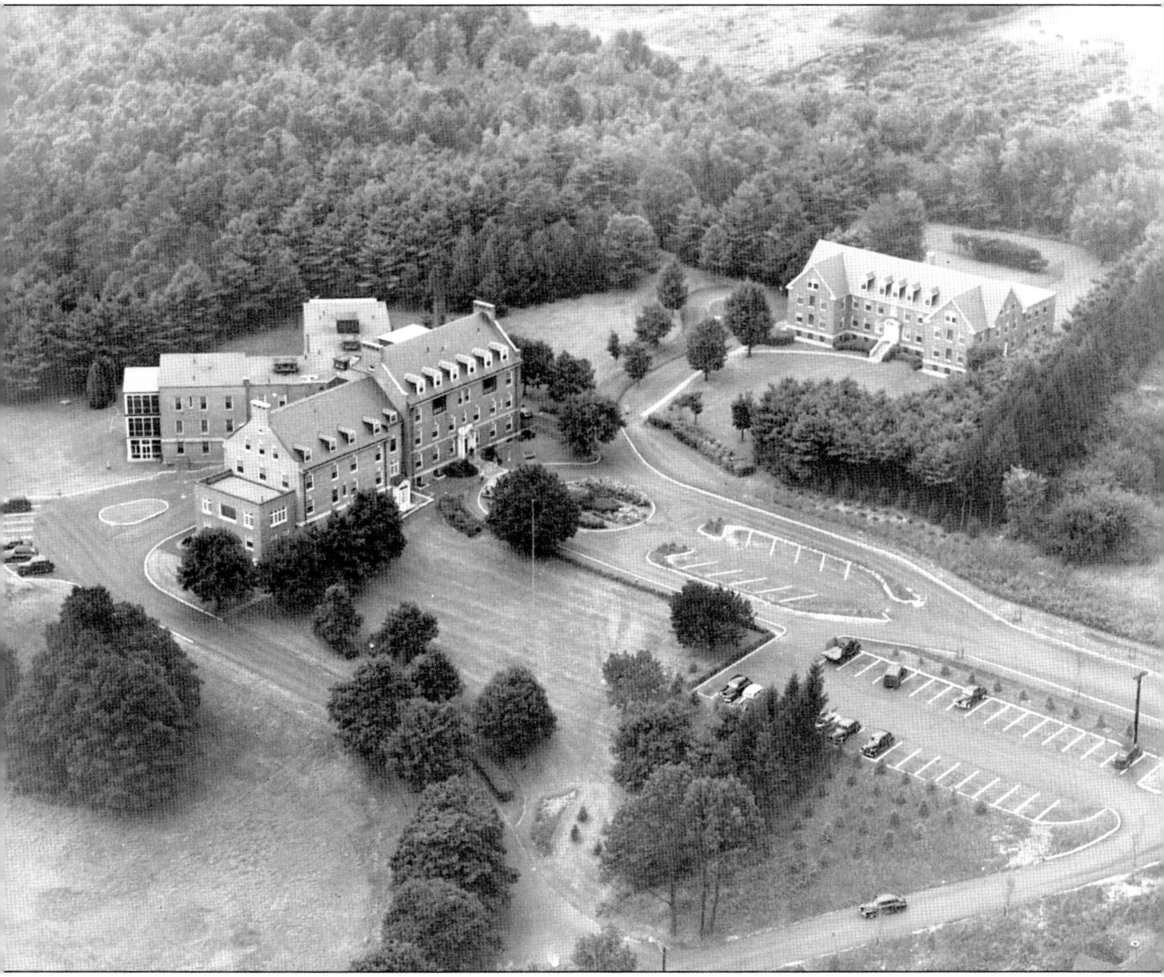

This aerial view of the Leominster Hospital and nurses' residence was taken in 1941. The building on the right is the School of Nursing and residence for the student nurses. The original 1922 hospital consisted of the 4-story front building with the V-shaped wings in the rear. A three-floor extension has been added on the left with a conference room and library at the extreme left. Shannah Macfadden was still the superintendent of nursing; she had started at the hospital on Blossom Street in 1920 and would retire in 1949.

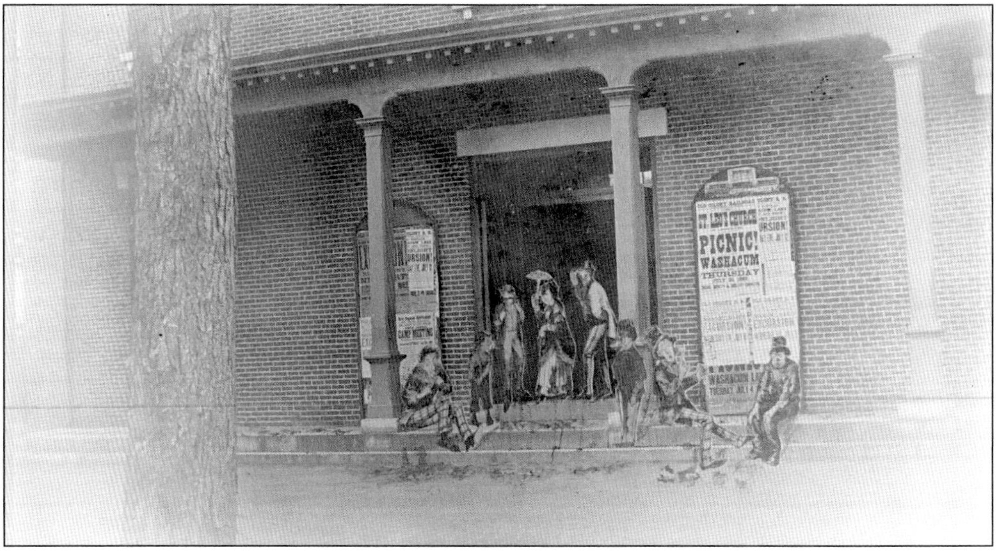

In this 1882 photograph, cardboard cutouts adorn the steps of Town Hall in an ingenious publicity stunt by the town librarian, Charles Bronson, who wanted to draw attention to the fact that Leominster needed an attractive and permanent home for the library. The cardboard figures of a respectable lady and innocent children are seen making their way past vagrants, drunkards, and thieves to use the library, which at that time shared space with the town offices and the jail.

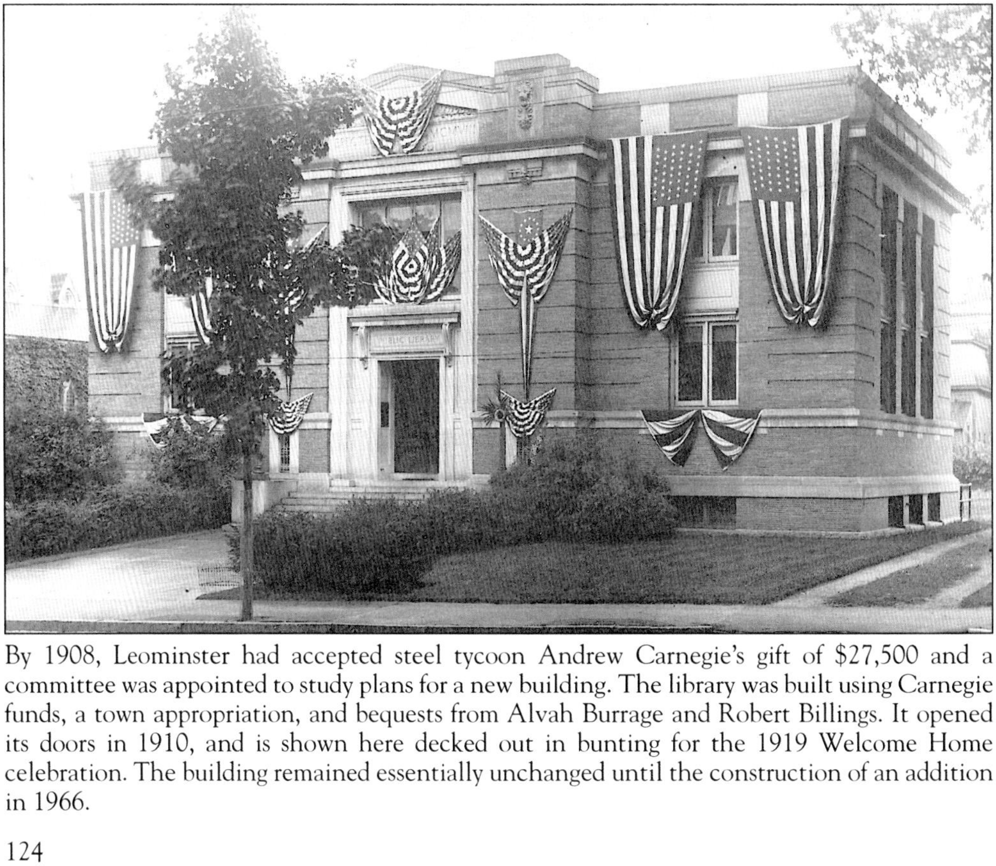

By 1908, Leominster had accepted steel tycoon Andrew Carnegie's gift of $27,500 and a committee was appointed to study plans for a new building. The library was built using Carnegie funds, a town appropriation, and bequests from Alvah Burrage and Robert Billings. It opened its doors in 1910, and is shown here decked out in bunting for the 1919 Welcome Home celebration. The building remained essentially unchanged until the construction of an addition in 1966.

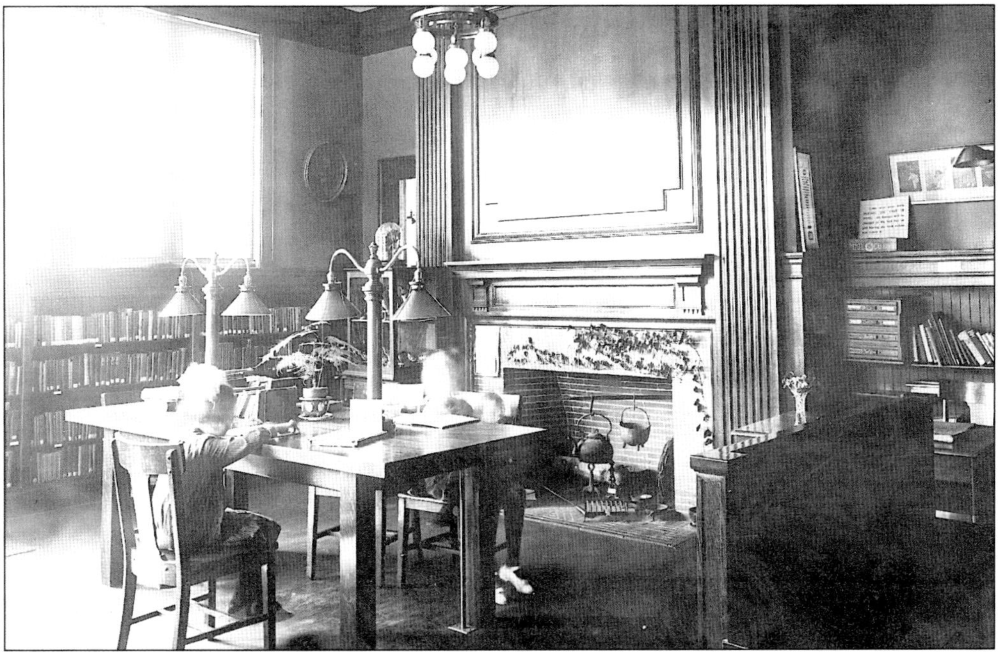

This picture of the children's reading room at the Leominster Library was taken shortly after the building opened in 1910. The fireplace is still visible today, behind the Children's Room circulation desk.

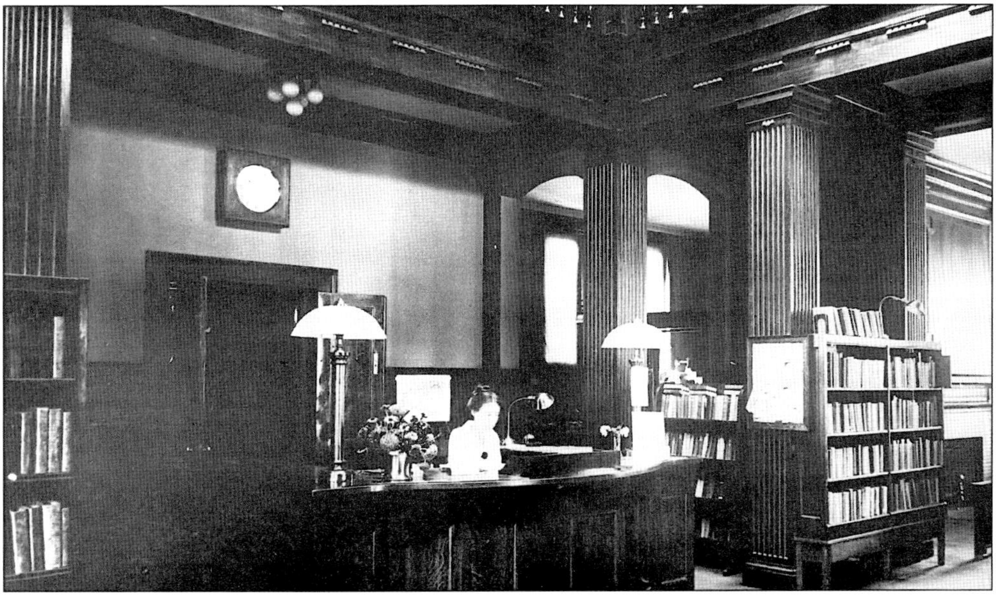

A library clerk sits at the circulation desk, c. 1915. Years later, a young Robert Cormier would become adept at sneaking around the horseshoe-shaped desk to become "lost" in the world of books in the adult stacks. The original woodwork of the Carnegie building, as well as the marble clock, still graces the library's Children's Room.

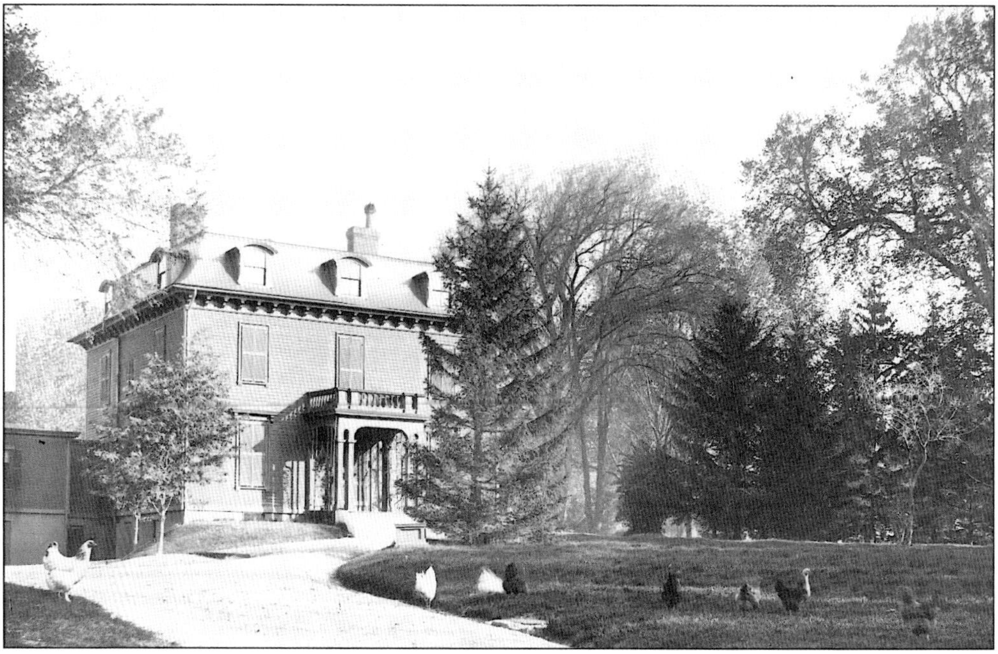

This property is located at 100 West Street and today is home to the Veteran's Center. The home, originally owned by D. Waldo Salisbury, was one of the oldest in the city. The pond beside the estate was an apple orchard at this time. Bernard Doyle purchased the property for the Leominster Girl Scouts in 1943. Note the chickens on the front lawn.

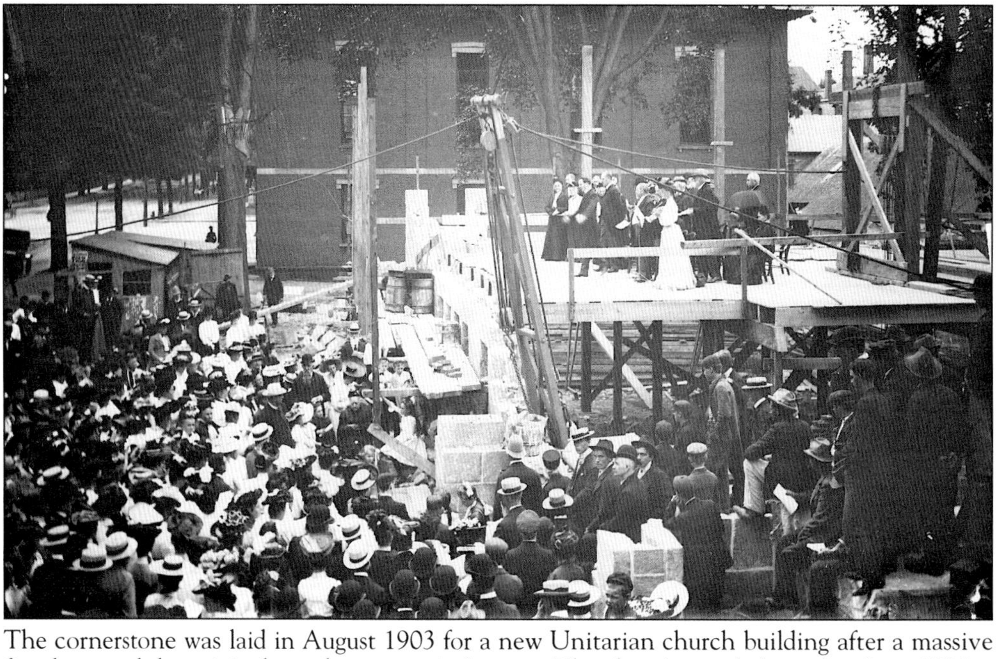

The cornerstone was laid in August 1903 for a new Unitarian church building after a massive fire destroyed the original wood structure in January. The church was dedicated in June 1904.

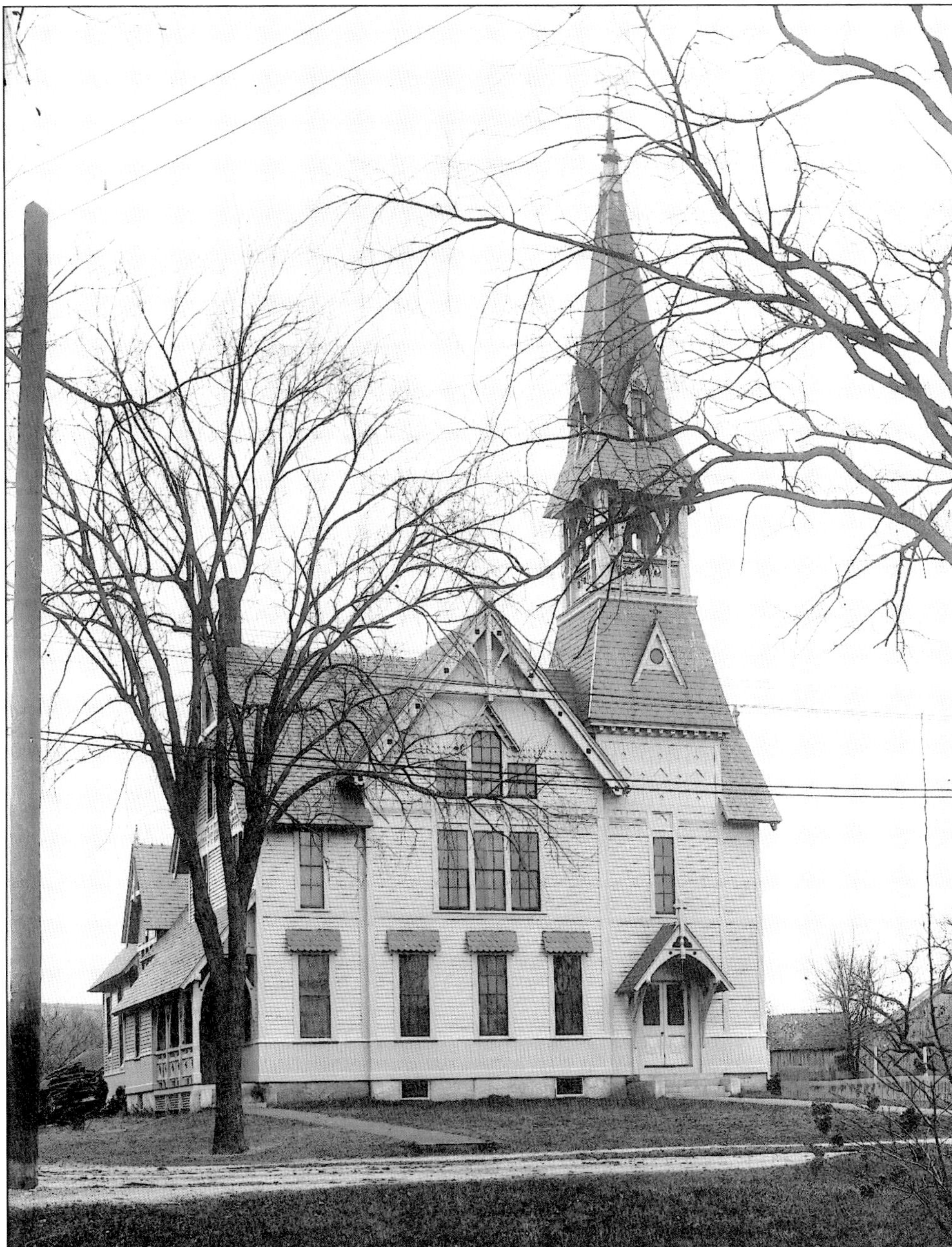

Residents of North Leominster met at the house of George Burrage in March 1874 to discuss building a church in "The Village." A council, which met at Kendall Hall in May to select officers of the "Congregational Society of North Leominster," was formed. For the next five years, church services were held in Kendall Hall. On April 7, 1880, the new church building was dedicated. The church cost $16,000; prominent donors for the building and furnishings were Augustus Whitman and Capt. Leonard Burrage.

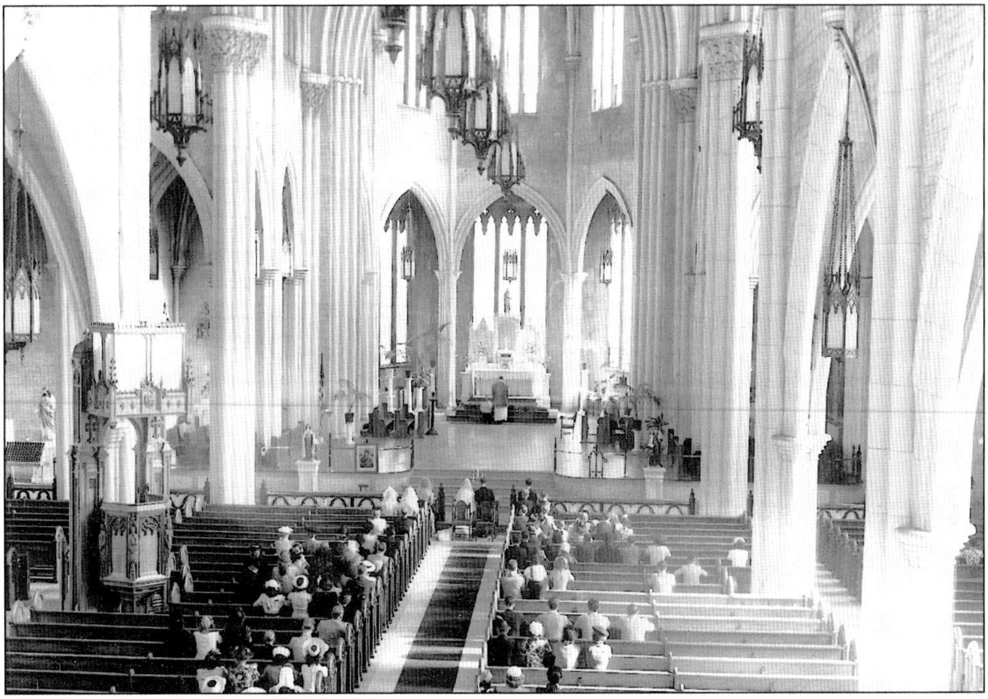

In 1889, a delegation went to the Bishop of Springfield requesting that he provide Leominster's French population with a parish staffed with French-speaking priests. St. Cecilia's first church was organized in 1900 on Third Street; shortly thereafter, land was purchased for the present cemetery. In 1931, construction of the present church was begun; it was dedicated in 1934. The beautiful church dominates the skyline as you approach the city; in 1998, the steeple was illuminated at night.

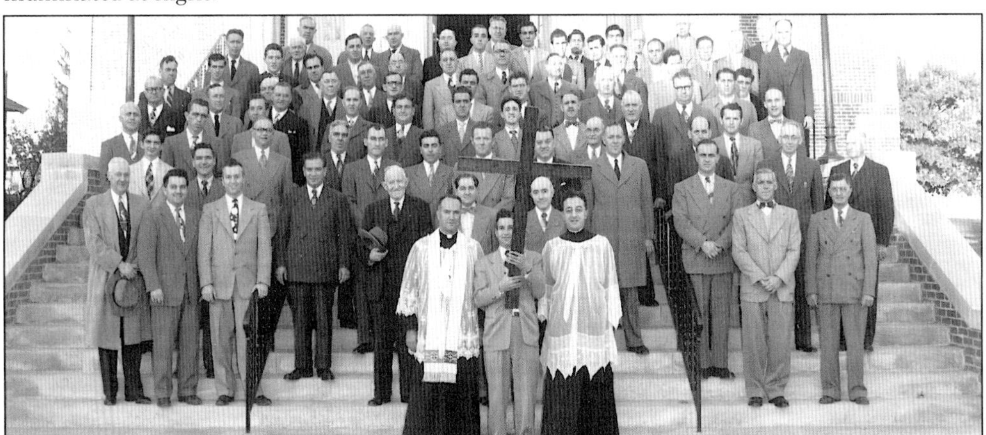

The Knights of Columbus hold a pilgrimage at St. Anna's Church on Lancaster Street. The church was originally established as a mission, but with an increasing Italian population it became obvious that a "church of their own" was both needed and wanted in this area of the city. In 1936, Lincoln Hall was purchased and necessary repairs were begun. A statue of St. Ann was purchased from Italy and placed on the front lawn; the first mass was celebrated in the church in March 1937. Renovations and additions several years ago changed the front of the church dramatically.